CLAUDIA
JONES

Beyond Containment

Claudia Jones: Beyond Containment Edited by Carole Boyce Davies
This edition first published in the UK by Ayebia Clarke Publishing Limited in 2011
Ayebia Clarke Publishing Limited
7 Syringa Walk
Banbury
Oxfordshire
OX16 1FR
UK
www.ayebia.co.uk

ISBN 978-0-9562401-6-3

Distributed outside Africa, Europe and the United Kingdom and exclusively in the USA by
Lynne Rienner Publishers, Inc.
1800 30th Street, Ste. 314
Boulder, CO 80301
USA
www.rienner.com

Distributed in Africa, Europe and the UK by TURNAROUND Publisher Services
at www.turnaround-uk.com

Co-published and distributed in Ghana with the Centre for Intellectual Renewal
56 Ringway Estate, Osu, Accra, Ghana
www.cir.com

British Library Cataloguing-in-Publication Data
Cover Design by Amanda Carroll at Millipedia, UK
Cover artwork Images: Museum of London, London Transport Museum and Carole Boyce Davies
Collection
Typeset by FiSH Books, Enfield, Middlesex, UK
Printed and bound in Great Britain by CPI Mackays – Chatham, ME5 8TD

Available from www.ayebia.co.uk or email info@ayebia.co.uk
Distributed in Africa, Europe, UK by TURNAROUND at www.turnaround-uk.com
Distributed in Southern African by Book Promotions (PTY) Cape Town, South Africa
For Enquiries: enquiries@bookpro.co.za or For Orders contact: orders@bookpro.co.za

The Publisher wishes to acknowledge the support of Arts Council SE Funding

CLAUDIA JONES

BEYOND CONTAINMENT

Autobiographical Reflections, Essays and Poems

Edited by Carole Boyce Davies

With an Afterword by Alrick X. Cambridge

ayebia

An Adinkra symbol meaning
Ntesie matemasie
A symbol of knowledge and wisdom

Ayebia Clarke Publishing Limited gratefully acknowledges Arts Council SE Funding

About the Editor

Carole Boyce Davies is an African Diaspora Studies Scholar, Professor of Africana Studies at Cornell University. She is author of *Left of Karl Marx: The Political Life of Black Communist Claudia Jones* (Duke University Press, 2008). An earlier work, *Black Women, Writing and Identity: Migrations of the Subject* (Routledge, 1994) is considered a theoretical base for many studies in the field of black feminist literary theory and the writing of migration. In addition to numerous scholarly articles, other published work include the following critical editions: *Ngambika: Studies of Women in African Literature* (African World Press, 1986); *Out of the Kumbla: Caribbean Women and Literature* (Africa World Press, 1990); and a two-volume collection of critical and creative writing entitled *Moving Beyond Boundaries* (New York University Press, 1995); *International Dimensions of Black Women's Writing* (volume 1), and *Black Women's Diasporas* (volume 2); *The African Diaspora: African Origins and New World Identities* (Indiana University Press, 1999) and *Decolonizing the Academy: African Diaspora Studies* (Africa World Press, 2003). She is general editor of *The Encyclopedia of the African Diaspora* (Oxford: ABC-CLIO, 2008) a 3-volume encyclopedia. Dr. Boyce Davies is currently writing a series of personal reflections called *Caribbean American Spaces: Between the Twilight Zone and the Underground Railroad*, dealing with the issue of transnational Caribbean/American black identity.

Praise for *Claudia Jones: Beyond Containment*

Carole Boyce Davies's brilliant book, *Left of Karl Marx*, did so much more than recover the life and legacy of Claudia Jones. She threw down the gauntlet, forcing us to rethink many of the fundamental assumptions and conceits of Marxism and to come to terms with Claudia Jones's radical critiques of racism, women's oppression and colonial rule. But Davies isn't done. In this stunning collection of Jones's essays, speeches, autobiographical reflections and poems, Davies not only underscores why Jones stands among the world's most important radical theorists and organizers of the 20th century, but she reveals the Trinidadian-born, transnational intellectual as artist and visionary.

> – Robin D. G. Kelly, Professor of American Studies and Ethnicity,
> University of Southern Carolina and author of *Freedom Dreams:
> The Back Radical Imagination.*

Claudia Jones: Beyond Containment lifts veils of ignorance and erasure that obscure a brilliant, 20th century human rights advocate. With this collection of Jones's writings, Carole Boyce Davies provides the 21st century with an important opportunity to revisit our collective histories and current struggles shaped by feminist, anti-racist, communist Claudia Jones, a Caribbean-born activist and intellectual who influenced international struggles of blacks, women and workers for social justice.

> – Joy James, Williams College, USA and author of
> *Shadowboxing: Representations of Black Feminist Politics.*

In *Claudia Jones: Beyond Containment*, Carole Boyce Davies has uncovered a super-excellent collection... commendable not only for their breadth-of-scope but largely also for their intellectual sharpness and acuity... while all based on past events these writings are so very directly relevant today, especially in the manner in which they assist our understanding of contemporary world politics with the

US and the Anglo-American bloc playing a leading role. Indeed, Jones's interventions are as deep and relevant as to provide a direct prognosis of contemporary US imperialism in the era of globalization. There can be absolutely no doubt that Jones was an activist and an ideologue, who used and tirelessly mobilized her identity as a member of the Young Communist League and other organizations to help in the fight to establish a new, more just, equitable and humanitarian social order.

– **Dr Kwadwo Osei-Nyame Jnr., Lecturer in African Studies,
School of Oriental & African Studies, (SOAS), University of London.**

Dedication

For the Caribbean family of Claudia Cumberbatch, her African American friends and co-activists, like Esther Cooper Jackson and her London friends, co-workers and family, such as Trevor Carter and Corinne Skinner-Carter, Donald Hinds, Alrick Cambridge and particularly Diane Langford and Claudia Manchanda, Abhimanyu Manchanda's daughter, named after Claudia, who wanted this collection published.

Acknowledgments

Diane Langford and Claudia Manchanda for making the now Claudia Jones Memorial collection available to me for the purpose of advancing knowledge of Claudia Cumberbatch Jones which included the publication of her writings. Corinne Skinner Carter is recognized for her generosity and for always insisting on recognizing the personal, familial and social Claudia; Alrick (Ricky) Cambridge for his assistance and clarity about her influence; Ranjana Ash for originals and copies of documents in her possession.

The Schomburg Research Library and Cultural Centre, New York Public Library, is acknowledged for permission to use photographs in their collection. Special thanks to Anthony Toussaint and Nydia Swaby. Redux Pictures representing *The New York Times* for permission to use identified photographs and the kind assistance of Rosemary Morrow. Eric Acree, Director of the Library and Sharon Powers, reference librarian at Cornell University's Africana Studies and Research Centre are acknowledged for tracking down documents at short notice. Finally, my Publisher Nana Ayebia Clarke MBE is acknowledged for her faith in and excitement about this project and her love for making the ideas of black contributors to world knowledge available to a larger community of readers.

The following essays were reprinted with permission from the journal *Political Affairs*:

"On the Right to Self-Determination for the Negro People in the Black Belt" (1946); "An End to the Neglect of the Problems of Negro Women" (1949); "International Women's Day and the Struggle for Peace" (1950); "For the Unity of Women in the Cause of Peace" (1951); "American Imperialism and the British West Indies" (1958).

Permission granted by *Freedomways* courtesy of Esther Cooper Jackson copyright holder to publish "The Caribbean Community in Britain".

Contents

An elegant Claudia Jones in New York City
(George Alexanderson, New York Times, 1951, Redux)

Chronology

1915	Born February 21, 1915, Belmont, Port-of-Spain, Trinidad, to Charles Bertrand Cumberbatch and Sybil (Minnie Magdalene) Cumberbatch, née Logan.
1924	Arrives February 9 on SS Voltaire in New York City with sisters Lindsay, Irene, Sylvia and aunt Alice Glasgow.
1930–1935	Attends Wadleigh High School. Active in Junior NAACP; Studied drama at Urban League; performs in Harlem and Brooklyn.
1933	Mother (37 years old) dies of spinal meningitis, two years before Jones graduates from Junior High School.
1934	Committed to Sea View Sanatorium for almost a year after having been diagnosed with tuberculosis.
1935	Graduates from High School. Works in laundry, factory, millinery and sales.
1935–6	Involved in Scottsboro Boys organizing. Writes "Claudia's Comments" for a black newspaper; becomes editor of a youth paper, organ of the Federated Youth Clubs of Harlem. Attends Harlem rallies.
1936	Joins Communist Party (February) and Young Communist League; assigned to Youth Movement.
1937	Becomes Associate Editor, *Weekly Review* and Secretary of the Executive Committee of Young Communist League in Harlem. Employed in the business department of the *Daily Worker*. Attends six-month training school of Communist Party.
1938	Becomes New York State Chair and National Council Member of Young Communist League. Attends National Council of Negro Youth, Southern Negro Congress, National Negro Congress. Visits American Congress. Files preliminary papers for US citizenship.
1940	Marries Abraham Scholnick.

1941	Becomes Educational Director of Young Communist League.
1942	Aggressive surveillance by FBI begins.
1943	Becomes Editor-in-Chief, *Weekly Review*.
1943–5	Becomes editor of *Spotlight*, American Youth for Democracy.
1945–6	Becomes Editor, Negro Affairs, *Daily Worker*; Elected full member National Committee, CPUSA at its annual convention.
1947	Divorced in Mexico (February 27). Becomes Secretary, Women's Commission, Communist Party USA.
1948	Arrested for the first time (January 19); imprisoned on Ellis Island under 1918 Immigration Act. Released on $1000 bail (January 20). Threatened with deportation to Trinidad (January 26). Speaks at May Day Rally in Los Angeles. Assigned by Party to work with working class and black party women for peace and equality. Tours forty-three US states, including the west coast, reorganizing state-level women's commissions, recruiting new party members and organizing mass rallies. Deportation hearing begins but is postponed because people will not testify against her.
1950	Deportation hearing resumes (February 16). Appointed alternate member of the National Committee, Communist Party USA. Gives speech in March ("International Women's Day and the Struggle for Peace"), which is later cited as "overt act" in her subsequent arrest. Arrested for second time (October 23) and held at Ellis Island under McCarran Act. Detained at New York City Women's Prison (November 17). Released on bail (December 21). Deportation order served.
1951	Speaks in Harlem while on bail. Arrested for third time (June 29) under Smith Act, along with sixteen other communists (including Elizabeth Gurley Flynn). Released on $20,000 bail (July 23, 1951). Deportation hearing continues.
1952–3	Serves on National Peace Commission at end of Korean War.
1953	Convicted under Smith Act (January 21). Sentenced to one year and a day and $200 fine. Suffers heart failure and is hospitalized for twenty-one days at the end of her trial. December, hospitalized again. Diagnosed with hypertensive cardiovascular disease.
1954	Becomes Editor of *Negro Affairs Quarterly*.

1955	Imprisoned in Women's Penitentiary, Alderson, West Virginia (January 11). Released October 23 after numerous petitions for health reasons. Sentence commuted for "good behaviour." Stays with her father. Hospitalized at Mt. Sinai Hospital, following heart attack identified as exacerbated by conditions of imprisonment. Deportation ordered (December 5). Leaves for London on the *Queen Elizabeth* (December 9). December 22, Arrives in London, welcomed by friends and Communist Party members, including earlier communist deportees from the United States.
1956	Hospitalized in London for three months.
1956–1957	Becomes affiliated with Caribbean members of Communist Party of Great Britain (CPGB); joins West Indian Forum and Committee on Racism and International Affairs. Works in various organizations in London, including the Caribbean Labour Congress (London Branch); reportedly helps with the editing of final issue of Labour Congress's organ, *Caribbean News*.
1957	Co-founds West Indian Workers and Students' Association. Becomes active in a variety of ways against racism, immigration restrictions and oppression of Caribbean community in London; and apartheid South Africa.
1958	Founds *West Indian Gazette* (later, *West Indian Gazette and Afro-Asian Caribbean News*) in London.
1958–64	Edits *West Indian Gazette and Afro-Asian Caribbean News*; active in political organizing of Caribbean, Pan African and Third World Communities in London.
1959	First London Caribbean Carnival, St. Pancras Hall, London (January 30).
1961	Afro-Asian Caribbean Conference, organized in part by *West Indian Gazette*, leads to formation of Committee of Afro-Asian and Caribbean Organizations.
1962	Visits Soviet Union as a guest of editors of *Soviet Women*. Visits school and studies developments in health care. Is hospitalized while in Soviet Union. Tours Leningrad, Moscow and Sevastopol. Returned to London (November 21).

1963	Visits Soviet Union again as a representative of Trinidad and Tobago to attend World Congress of Women. August, organizes with Committee of Afro-Asian and Caribbean Organizations a "Parallel March" on Washington to US Embassy.
1964	Works with African National Congress to organize hunger strike against apartheid, to boycott South Africa and for the freedom of political prisoners such as Nelson Mandela. Participates in protests outside South African embassy in London. Speaks at rally with novelist George Lamming and others (April 12). Meets Martin Luther King Jr. in London on his way to Oslo to collect Nobel Peace Prize. Writes editorial about King's visit in *West Indian Gazette* and *Afro-Asian Caribbean News* (it is her last editorial and is published posthumously). Gives speech in Japan as a delegate to 10th World Conference against Hydrogen and Atom Bombs. Serves as Vice-Chair of the Conference Drafting Committee; proposes resolution in support of liberation struggles in the Third World. Travels to China as a guest of China Peace Committee. Meets Chairman Mao, along with a Latin American delegation. Interviews Soong Ching Ling, wife of Sun Yat-Sen.
1964	Dies of heart failure in London, circa December 25, 1964.
1965	Funeral draws recognitions from governments around the world, diplomatic representations and media coverage. January 9, Cremated at Golders Green Crematorium, London. Memorial meeting held in Peking by Committee of British and American Friends of Claudia Jones (February 21). Interment of Jones's ashes in plot to left of grave of Karl Marx, Highgate Cemetery, London (February 27) following public meeting at St. Pancras Town Hall, Euston Road, WCI.
1984	Headstone erected; inscription reads: *"Claudia Vera Jones, Born Trinidad 1915, Died London 25.12.64, Valiant Fighter against racism and imperialism who dedicated her life to the progress of socialism and the liberation of her own black people."*
1985	Buzz Johnson publishes *"I Think of My Mother." Notes on the Life and Times of Claudia Jones.* London, Karia Press.
1988	Jennifer Tyson and the Camden Black Sisters publish book titled *Claudia Jones, 1915-1964: A Woman of Our Times.*

1993	Claudia Jones Organisation, Stoke Newington Road, London organizes "Wreath-Laying Ceremony, 20 February, 1993, marking first 11 years of organisation's community service.
1996	Claudia Jones Symposium at the Institute of Commonwealth Studies, London. Proceedings edited by Marika Sherwood, Donald Hinds and Colin Prescod, published as *Claudia Jones. A Life in Exile*, (London: Lawrence and Wishart, 1999).
1999	Schomburg Centre for Research in Black Culture. Symposium on Claudia Jones.
2000	Claudia Jones Memorial Collection deposited and established at Schomburg Centre for Research In Black Culture, Harlem, New York.
2008	Carole Boyce Davies publishes *Left of Karl Marx. The Political Life of Black Communist Claudia Jones*, 2008 (Duke University Press).
2008	Two plaques placed in her honour in Portobello Road and at Carnival Village, Powis Square, London, July, 2008.
2008	Royal Mail Stamp honouring Claudia Jones among six notable women, for Civil Rights activism, October 2008.

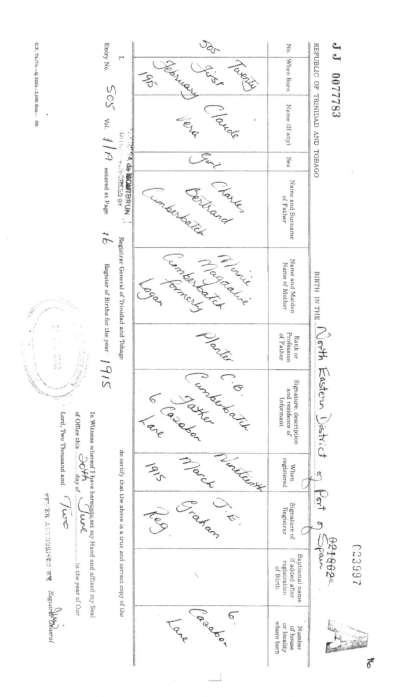

Birth Certificate of Claude Vera Cumberbatch

Registry of Birth and Deaths, Port of Spain, Trinidad (Entry no. 505. 1915)

Acquired by Carole Boyce Davies, 2002.

Beyond Containment: Introduction

Carole Boyce Davies

There is a letter that Claudia Jones writes to Dr. Eric Williams from London[1] requesting help with obtaining her passport and suggesting that she had identified two particular levels of discrimination as operable: 1) being a Caribbean person; 2) being a Marxist. These two selected identities, we already know along with others – her working class black and female identities had been the causes for an ongoing personal history of difficulty. But they were also the places from which her activism was generated. To remove them, one would have had to ask the activist in her then to renounce or give up her politics as some did but what about place of origin, gender and race. Better to fight, Claudia would say, for a world where these oppressions do not have viability, as she claimed, with confidence, her identities as political positions. Claudia Jones therefore describes herself with all her identities. We see this clearly expressed when she assesses her political life up to the point of deportation:

> I was deported from the USA because as a Negro woman Communist of West Indian descent, I was a thorn in their side in my opposition to Jim Crow racist discrimination against 16 million Negro Americans in the United States, in my work for redress of these grievances, for unity of Negro and white workers, for women's rights and my general political activity urging the American people to help by their struggles to change the present foreign and domestic policy of the United States] (Claudia Jones, "I Was Deported...", 1956)

[margin note: Intellectuals becoming more "global"]

In other words, she qualifies her communist politics with her identities as a black woman from the Caribbean. The strength of Claudia Jones is that she did not see any contradiction as she embraced all her identities and political positions.

In the introduction to the 150th anniversary edition of the *Communist Manifesto*, Robin D. G. Kelley asserts that there needs to be a left re-assessment of Marxism. While defending the *Manifesto*, he sees it as a "brilliant but outdated pamphlet not attuned to race, gender, sexuality, or the environment (v)." Kelley's argument here is to locate Marxism as a "manifestation of its time and place; ...a discourse (and a product of) class struggle during the era of capitalism's emergence – a history firmly rooted in the very ground that produced racism, patriarchy, imperialism and colonialism, as well as the idea of modernity...(v–vi)." Thus he continues, that Marx and Engels "understood how women's and children's labour not only produced surplus value for capital but also reproduced male labour power in the domestic sphere, but they also took gender roles for granted"(vi). He would have to assert then, that while "generations of twentieth century feminists found a starting point for a radical analysis of patriarchy, gender ideologies and heterosexism," a large group of activists and revolutionaries, among them Claudia Jones (vii) had to "remake Marxism to address questions of women's oppression and sexuality"(vii).

Cedric Robinson's work in *Black Marxism* (1983) is important in this regard for it is here that he attempts to define the black radical intellectual tradition. But unfortunately, no women seem to appear here in this black radical tradition of black Marxism though Angela Davis is mentioned towards the end of the book. For McClendon, in his analytical delineation of the problematic of a "Black Marxism" in his "Marxism in Ebony Contra Black Marxism," one has to make a qualitative distinction between the 'Black' in Black Marxism as a racial descriptor, i.e. identifying the race of those identified as Marxists, from those who identify that 'Black' as a type of Marxism. McClendon identifies Robinson's project as the latter. Thus he clarifies, 'Blackness' as an ethical and positional orientation from which one views the world, or with which one practices a particular discipline. His position though is that "Marxism is neither Black nor White (African or European) rather, it is the process of dialectical and historical materialist (scientific) analysis and critique aimed at concrete conditions that may include the evaluation of social relations, practices and institutions that are established on racist grounds within the framework of the capitalist mode of production." (2008:3)

My earlier work *Left of Karl Marx. The Political Life of Black Communist Claudia Jones* (2008) identified the ways in which Claudia Jones, as an Afro-Caribbean activist/intellectual, re-defined Marxism-Leninism, to meet the needs of an analysis of the position of the black working class, but also more directly issues of race, gender and, finally, the re-definition of the Caribbean Diaspora in England as the end- products of a series of migrations. So Jones would not be definable or visible as a "Black Marxist" in the Robinson sense, but as she repeatedly insisted as a Marxist-Leninist who was also a black woman of Caribbean origin. Thus, she would be left out of all of those analyses of Marxism even that of Harold Cruse, critical of Caribbean and other largely male communist and other activists.[2] Indeed, as I argue in *Left of Karl Marx*, Marx located specifically in his historical time, was unable to account for issues of race, gender and various black identities manifested in the 20th century. Indeed, Marx himself spoke about the need for new generations to remake philosophy in their own contexts. Still Marx has been recognized for offering what is still the most substantial reading of the nature of capital, from primitive accumulation to the current modes of corporate global- ization, a theory of history as well on the nature of the world's movements through different modes of production and thereby provides tools for a reading and understanding of political economy and the issues of labour exploitation even as these have to be revised. But one of the many limitations of Marxism that had to be revised was the idea that women would be liberated after the working class was fully empowered. Claudia Jones, following Lenin on the Woman Question would instead suggest that black working class women had to be at the vanguard of these struggles and would therefore argue for a parallel gender, race and class advancement. The woman, race and class orientation question would become a central feature of the Communist Party USA during the time of Claudia Jones (1940s and 1950s) and in its subsequent articulations. And indeed Claudia identified the republishing of the ideas of the major communist thinkers on the woman question as a project that would be undertaken by the CPUSA Woman's commission while she was its secretary (See her "For Unity of Women in the Cause of Peace" in this collection).

Kelley's defense is perhaps worth invoking again, as he suggests that while early Marxists were well aware of "conquest, genocide, slavery and slavery's demise and various forms of coercive labour that escaped the slavery label..." they would assign these to "Primitive Accumulation." Thus in the final analysis, he has to conclude that: "We need to pay attention to the Marxist traditions that rose out of anti-imperialist and anti-colonial struggles of the 20th century" (1998:x).

The *Manifesto* identifies the issues of modernity arising as:

> The discovery of America, the rounding of the cape, opened up fresh ground for the rising bourgeoisie. The East-Indian and Chinese markets, the colonization of America, trade with the colonies, the increase in the means of exchange in commodities, generally gave to commerce, to navigation, to industry, an impulse never before known and thereby, to the revolutionary element, the tottering feudal society, a rapid development (13).

Thus Marx gestures to the development of world markets as capitalism kept creating: "The need for a constantly expanding market for its products...chases the bourgeoisie over the whole surface of the globe. It must nestle everywhere, settle everywhere, establish connections everywhere(17)." Economic or corp- orate globalization is what it would be called today.

The issue of imperialism and its effect on colonized peoples would be more directly addressed in the work of the Lenin component of Marxism-Leninism which Claudia would consistently invoke. The critique of these limitations of

Marxism have been mounted by generations of intellectuals and activists. Many would abandon Marxism for this reason even if they worked with the Popular Front – a coalition of left groups. Indeed Césaire's *Discourse on Colonialism* (1955) makes interesting arguments, in a similar vein to the manifesto, as it engages the nature of European colonialism and the "thingification" of the colonized as it reveals the colonizer within a discourse of vampirism of the "third world." Still, Césaire's letter as he left the Communist Party has been referenced as providing the intellectual logic for other movements outside of communism, demanding not that communism include black positions but that it be made instead to serve black empowerment.

The work of Oliver Cox and a range of intellectuals and activists, again including Jones, resonate. Kevin Gaines in his essay "Locating the Transnational in Postwar African American History," identifies St. Clair Drake, as expressed in his essay "The Black Diaspora in Pan-African Perspective," with a certain kind of "Left of Karl Marx" assertion. In the analysis of the black experience, Drake had maximized the usefulness of the process and the results for Liberation activity in these terms:

> The most useful model for such purposes is one that modifies traditional Marxist-Leninist analysis to include not only the political economy of capitalist-imperialist expansion (studies of the "base"), but also the effect of *dependency* upon Third World Peoples, political, cultural and psychological, as well as economic.(3)

The emphasis for me here is on the word "modify" for this is precisely what Claudia Jones tried to do, in her application of Marxist-Leninist theory. Drake even spends some time defending Marx on the question of race and summarizing some of the limits of Marxism for political economy, but also clarifying the usefulness of Lenin's critique of imperialism to subsequent "generations of Asian and African nationalist leaders – even anti-Communist ones ..."(3). And even a later scholar-activist like Walter Rodney would also suggest that Marxism had not to be transferred but translated to suit particular locational needs as say Amilcar Cabral would in the case of Guinea-Bissau (Gibbons, 1994).

Gaines points out that no doubt because of the brutal treatment which Jones received, rendering her a "tragic" figure in a way, she would have been a "cautionary example for Drake and those of his generation." But this is precisely the point that *Left of Karl Marx* makes, that a specific targeting of black radicalism had in many ways "deported the radical black subject" from consideration, not just the subject Claudia Jones herself but what she represented in terms of ideas and practice. My essay "Sisters Outside: Tracing the Black Radical Intellectual Tradition" (2009) speaks to this erasure and marginalization from a range of histories.

Claudia Jones, would herself own this idea of black radicalism in a pamphlet titled *"Ben Davis, Fighter for Freedom,"* which is included in this collection. It is a spirited defense of communist congressman Ben Davis, who was tried and also incarcerated for communist ideas, in the group of prosecuted Communist leaders before Claudia's. She asserts:

> Today, the very meaning of any serious leadership in the fight for Negro rights brings one into opposition with the foreign and domestic policies of government. Ask yourself: Can anyone support the great national liberation struggles of the peoples of Africa-without facing the accusation of being a "Communist?"... Whether in writings, speeches, or needed organization endeavors, *any Negro leader who pursues any necessary manifestation of leadership is labeled "subversive," "communistic."*
> Well. Let us ask ourselves:
>
> > Do not our people have a *right* to *have* radicals?
> > Yes – a *right!*
> > Do not our people have the *right to seek some radical solutions* to their highly oppressed status?
> > And have a *right to be radicals?*
> > It would surely *seem* they have.
>
> Then, there are those who tell us that to be radical and black means three strikes against us, or to be black and red is even worse… The very core of all Negro history is radicalism against conformity to chattel slavery, radicalism against the betrayal of the demands of Reconstruction, radicalism in relation to non-acceptance of the status quo."

Indeed all activists and scholars who did any activism on behalf of black communities at that time, according to Gerald Horne in *Black Liberation/Red Scare. Ben Davis and the Communist Party* (1994) were considered communist; intellectual work and activist work of all black people was assigned to communism. The FBI became the machinery used to document and target black entertainers, poets like Langston Hughes, dancers like Pearl Primus, singers like Paul Robeson and activists of all kind. This would be continued in the deadly assault on black leadership in the 1960s and organizations like the Black Panther Party and a range of activists and intellectuals who were not communist.[3]

Angela Davis in an interview in *Abolition and Democracy. Beyond Empire, Prisons and Torture* (2005) sees a link "between the internationalism of Karl Marx's era and the new globalisms we are seeking to build today…" The commodity that Marx identified in *Capital*, "penetrated every aspect of people's lives all over the world in ways that have no historical precedent" (25). Thus she makes links with the global assembly line that has already been well documented. She also identifies an affinity with the Pan-Africanism of Du Bois which made links with people in Africa, Asia and Latin America.

Claudia Jones would make many of these linkages in the 1950s in her work on the *West Indian Gazette and Afro-Asian Caribbean News*. She had earlier in her journalism for the *Daily Worker* (1940s and early 1950s) spent a great deal of her time identifying the "half the world" logic in terms of accounting for women's lives globally located in struggle, black women in particular. In the *West Indian Gazette and Afro-Asian Caribbean News*, she was able to give space and voice to the articulation of political movements across the African and Latin American world.

Gaines makes the point that her location in the US during that pivotal post-war period provided her with the political context and space to become a leading Afro-Caribbean/American activist-intellectual. And, additionally, her internationalist orientation meant linking transnational economics with imperialism. Gaines's work also provides a bit more information on the Sojourners for Truth and Justice like Dorothy Hunton, wife of Alpaheus Hunton and particularly Shirley Graham Du Bois, wife of W.E.B. Du Bois who exercised "diaspora citizenship"[4] by relocating to Ghana residentially in the wake of combined Jim Crow and Cold War repression. Mary Helen Washington reports as well that when the Sojourners "gathered at a Washington church, two spaces were left empty, one for Communist leader Claudia Jones, who had been imprisoned under the Smith Act, and one for Rosa Ingram, confined in a Georgian jail for killing a white man who tried to rape her."[5] And recent work on Hubert Harrison reveals a range of active communist women who functioned in relation to Harrison. Jeffrey B. Perry's *Hubert Harrison. The Voice of Harlem Radicalism, 1883–1918* (2009) identifies for example Williana Jones Burroughs as a teacher, union activist and communist and Grace Campbell of Caribbean and African American descent as well as "British Guiana-born office worker and communist, Hermie Dumont Huiswoud. (2)" Joyce Moore Turner's *Caribbean Crusaders and the Harlem Renaissance*, has pretty good detail on Grace Campbell (1882–1943) who had moved to New York from Washington DC in 1905 and is identified as from Georgia originally, the daughter of a Jamaican father and an African American mother (77). Campbell is often identified as the sole woman member in the leadership of the African Blood Brotherhood (77) with an "unwavering dedication to the socialist cause (78)." The essays by Claudia Jones included in this collection also identify several other women active in the Communist Party at the time.

In further considering Claudia Jones as a Caribbean activist, it is worth identifying Harrison, another influential figure who was also erased from a variety of histories. Indeed, Harrison is one of those who captured the "left of Karl Marx" logic as did a number of radical intellectuals who saw Socialism as not being able to deliver fully because of the inability of its theorists and activists to deal with race. Some major black socialists and communists would leave the Party for this reason, finding it therefore not radical enough for the kind of work that needed to be done to liberate black communities. Hubert Harrison is definitely one of these figures – clearly an active socialist involved in Party work in the Socialist Party which would become later on the Communist Party USA by the time of Claudia Jones. Harrison is identified as well as being credited with gender consciousness and is on record as speaking on behalf of women's rights on several occasions.

An important connection between Claudia Jones and Hubert Harrison, though they would never have met, comes through the fact that both of them worked with Elizabeth Gurley Flynn. Harrison is identified as, speaking on the same platform with Gurley Flynn on May 19, 1913 during the Silk Strike in Patterson, New Jersey. A photograph of Harrison in the company of Elizabeth Gurley Flynn appears and description of their joint activities in union organizing around this strike is available (Perry, 203–204). Elizabeth Gurley Flynn and Claudia Jones would later work together on the Women's Commission and would actually be incarcerated in Alderson, West Virginia together. In this way, Gurley Flynn provides a necessary link between a Claudia Jones and a Hubert Harrison, who died in 1918. Knowing and working with both of these Afro-Caribbean intellectual-activists over the span of her very dynamic life gives us an interesting connection between these generations of Caribbean intellectual-activists.

Thus, when Claudia Jones, entered the Communist Party, there were already very active examples of black communist women and men who had visible identities that she could emulate and positions she could advance. In this context, Claudia Jones was not a lone, singular figure, or unusual as she was initially made out to be. What marks her instead is that she became both an **organizer** and a leading **theoretician**. Additionally, the Caribbean community was well represented in the early days of the Communist Party in the person of Richard Moore. Otto Huiswood and Cyril Briggs would along with Grace Campbell be founding members of the radical African Blood Brotherhood. Grace Campbell, in particular, who so far has also been only marginally recognized, was among a group that according to Solomon navigated Socialist and Communist Party structures.[6]

Kate Weigand also reports that in Communist Party schools, courses on black women became part of the curricula with "teachers such as Lorraine Hansberry, Claudia Jones, Charlotte Bass, Eleanor Flexner, Yvonne Gregory and Doxey Wilkerson [who] offered lectures and courses that explored topics such as 'Negro Women in the Struggle for Peace and Democracy' and 'Negro Women in Political Life' (110)." While this type of education which was not normally provided in university curricula of the time (predating the formalizing of Black Women's Studies) was clearly a CP project, the fact that this initiative was spearheaded by black party women like Claudia Jones with parallel ongoing activities to recruit black women members, would be significant elements of black communist women's organizing and educating strategies.

The question of gender would be seen as being opened for Communist Party thinking by Marx and Engels who would raise the issue of gender preliminarily but locate it firmly in the "abolition of the bourgeois family" and its relations. It is not until Lenin on "The Woman Question," particularly his discussion with Clara Zetkin, that we get a full reasoned discussion of the issue and relevance of gender though still located in its time. The argument would run that bourgeois family/bourgeois marriage functions on the logic of the exploitation of women and children. Women become "instruments of production" to be exploited in common and naturally. But, feminists ongoing repudiation, engagement and critique of Marxism are well documented, requiring all sorts of qualifiers to make it work – red feminism, Marxist-feminism – and so on.

Thus a variety of feminists have a range of positions around this issue of Marxism and feminism. Selma James, the founder of the International Wages for Housework campaign, in her pamphlet *Marx and Feminism* (1994) sees utility in Marxism but of course sees it as disputed territory. Her immediate assertion in terms of the gains of the Women's Movement post 1960s is the realization that "…we were subject to domestic slavery; that we were often financially dependent on men; that we didn't have equal pay; that we didn't control our bodies; that we were the victims of sexual exploitation of many kinds; and that we were much likely to be passive and much less likely to be effective compared to men – in a word, that we had colonized lives and personalities. (6)"

Still she finds Marx valuable in that he was able to articulate the issue of "labour power" (i.e., the social relationship) which he called *Capital*, then is that process which is called exploitation. For her, when one inserts the issue of women, this provided room for expansion, for housework which in her eyes is unwaged labour and while there is payment in the form of food, shelter, clothing, gifts, "we get no money in our own right for expending our labour power in producing other people's labour power (13)." Woman then attaches herself to a man's wage and becomes his dependent (14). Selma James asserts that the "dual rejection of "women's work" – exploitation in the home and exploitation out of it – was the starting point of the International Wages for Housework Campaign also called the Global women's Strike. She sees this issue as not being addressed by either Marxists or feminists – including Marxist feminists (23).

But there is also a substantial critique of Selma James's rather dated position (since many women work and women's salaries are far from equal to men) from London feminists. Writers in Ella Rule ed., *Marxism and the Emancipation of Women* (2000) devote an entire section to Selma James, arguing that her work naively and opportunistically returns women to a very dependent place: "The fulfillment of this demand would keep women as heretofore, backward, it would divide men and women and strengthen the bourgeoisie. The fulfillment of this demand would mean nothing less than the continued enslavement of women in the kitchen, nursery…(224)." They conclude that instead, the women's movement must "promote the understanding that for achieving the liberation of women, it is necessary to fight against capitalism, that it is necessary to build a women's movement which is part and parcel of the general working class struggle for the overthrow of capitalism (232)." Still, Rule, because her task is to re-inscribe Claudia Jones as singularly a communist, dismisses her other identities even going as far as to say that, "Because she was a communist, Claudia Jones could not be hurt by white racism" (See her "Claudia Jones, Communist" for this discussion).

But Jones, as her essays included in this collection reveal, would always return to the ways in which the crude Jim Crow racism had to be combated both inside and outside of the Communist Party and would consistently as well account for black women (therefore herself) in these contexts. And towards the end of her life, her work on behalf of the Caribbean community was what defined her. Her last essay, included in this collection, was on this subject.

Of course the specifics of black women's location in society and the fact that black women have always worked as people like Sojourner Truth and others had already articulated without any of the rewards, has provided a whole field of analyses of intersectionalities via black feminist studies. Angela Y. Davis's early work on black women in the community of slaves began some of this discussion, filled by a variety of other scholars who provided some of these historical analyses. And the more recent Angela Davis interview published in *Abolition and Democracy. Beyond Empire, Prisons, and Torture* (2005) which I mentioned earlier makes interesting links with prison, torture and related dehumanization already in existence, seeing these as she does rooted in part in the culture of torture perfected during New World enslavement as on the European working class.

Claudia Jones – Beyond Containment allows us to read the ideas of Claudia Jones in one place. Containment was the logic of cold war politics which meant to contain communism period by politically containing the USSR and any related communist relationships internationally but also significantly by containing and actually destroying communist leadership domestically and thereby any such movement in the United States. This was precisely the lot of Claudia Jones, an active theorist on the intersections of race, class and gender workings within the Communist Party USA's organizational structures, caught within the containment framework. But for Claudia Jones, these autobiographical writings, poetry and longer essays revealed she consistently moved beyond all forms of containment – gender, race, national origin, place – and was definitely a transatlantic activist, a black radical intellectual from the Caribbean who revolutionized Marxism-Leninism particularly because she addressed in her time those issues that Marx and Lenin left unarticulated. But perhaps more importantly she was solidly a Black World activist who saw the condition of black people as worthy of redress and set out to contribute her skills to this task. The logic of "Beyond Containment" is that in the end it is impossible to forever contain ideas, particularly if they have value for a community's liberation. Somebody will remember; somebody will document; somebody will recognize their value if they spoke with honesty and history is always the best judge.

In order to provide the reader with a full range of Claudia Jones' ideas and modes of expression, we have included her poetry, much of it written from prison which identifies the nature of her thinking through life as a political prisoner. But there are also poems written from Russia and China and reflective poems about friendship, activism and aging. We have also included her unpublished autobiographical writing, which set the personal tone and gives us an intimate sense of who she was in her moments of quietude. Many who knew Claudia personally and professionally indicate that she was working on an autobiography. So far, this has not surfaced. In the mean time, we are providing her own self-identifications that further clarify how the woman, Claudia Jones, saw herself. The essays provide the intellectual examination of a range of topics that have to do with black women, working class and black liberation in general but also on the Caribbean community, which was developing in London. There is quite a bit of journalism: editorials, book reviews, essays and commentaries available in the various media in which she wrote, but these await subsequent publication and are too numerous to be included here.

Claudia Vera Cumberbatch was born in Belmont, Port-of-Spain, Trinidad in 1915 (as the copy of her birth certificate included here indicates) and migrated with her siblings to join her parents in Harlem, New York City in 1924. She attended high schools in New York and joined the Communist Party, USA at the age of eighteen. Claudia Jones was then part of that first wave of Caribbean Migration – entering the US at the age of eight in the middle of what would be the Harlem Renaissance and coming of age in the depression era of the 1930s. I learned recently that Claudia Jones and her family went to meet, welcome and assist with the adjustment of Rosa Guy, who would later become a writer and her family when they migrated to and arrived in New York.[7] A victim of Jim Crow racism, she saw her lot as instantly tied in with that of the other struggling black people.

Irma Watkins-Owens and Winston James's work provide some of the historical and sociological contexts for this period. For example there were 40,000 immigrants between 1900 and 1930, settled in Harlem with the years 1911–1924 being the heaviest period. Until 1924, Caribbeans were able to enter the US unrestricted until the 1924 Immigration Act, which instituted quotas and placed Caribbean colonies under these quotas. Only 14 per cent were agricultural workers, many were urban dwellers or the educated elite who began as Marcus Garvey and his followers did, to interact socially and politically with African Americans. The secondary migrants, for example, the Panama Canal workers were male. But there were also black women who worked as laundry workers, hotel workers and prostitutes in the Panama Canal Zone. Some were wives as well. Many were single and young students like Claude McKay. Amy Ashwood Garvey co-founder of the UNIA joined Marcus Garvey in 1918. Many arrived with a sound primary and secondary British style education. There were also entrepreneurs. But above all they experienced racism and ethnic oppression collectively. Activists like Hubert Harrison and later Marcus Garvey who were street corner speakers were also defined as rabble-rousers. Several Caribbeans were also in the Communist Party; so activist Caribbean women included Grace Campbell, Claudia Jones and Amy Ashwood Garvey.

Deported from the US during the McCarthy period, Claudia Jones was meant to be erased. Making her way to London, though, doubly and then triply diasporized as Stuart Hall[8] would put it, Claudia Jones arrived in London just after the first massive influx of Caribbeans into London identified by the Windrush (1948) and therefore was able to have a role in shaping the nature of black community in London by creating tangible institutions. In London, she found ways to re-shape her politics in ways which re-defined her Marxist politics to account more fully for black women, people of colour and African-Caribbean and Asian migrants to Europe and so impacted that society that her burial left of Karl Marx is a fitting statement on the nature of her politics as on her life.

In a formulation like that of Harold Cruse that "Communists were West Indian men" as we have already established, the particular subjectivity of a Claudia Jones is rendered non-existent. By contrast, for the US government, it became too problematic a subjectivity. The speech for which she was arrested was published as the essay "International Women's Day and the Struggle for Peace," (1950) (included in this collection). Jones for her part was well aware of this complication that her gendered identity posed and says as much to interviewers whenever she was questioned. The interview with George Bowrin which I cited at the beginning of this essay and is also included in this collection is a good place to understand these combinations. And ironically it is her subjectivity as a "British Subject" of Afro-Caribbean origin, identified in her passport, which renders her more visible in the UK context. Still, for Jones internationalism in the US had already provided her with the tools to read the US and British varieties of imperialism as well as its immigration policies. She does this well in her essay on "The Caribbean Community in London" which is included in this collection, perhaps her last major essay, written for *Freedomways*. An earlier essay on "American Imperialism and the British West Indies" is also included in this collection.

It is important to say in closing that the case against Jones and her co-defendants, the thirteen communists prosecuted and punished for having communist ideas, was remedied in a subsequent case Yates vs. the United States (1957 – 354 US 298) which argued that having political views was not the same as acting on them. Whereas the Smith Act had made it illegal to have Communist ideas and prosecuted and punished communists on this basis, "the Court held that for the Smith Act to be violated, people must be encouraged to do something, rather than merely to believe in something. The Court drew a distinction between a statement of an idea and the advocacy that a certain action be taken." But by then, though Jones could have returned and have her case overturned, many of her colleagues had been so embattled and had moved on to other lives or indeed had had their lives significantly destroyed by the state. In my view, Jones was by then so heavily involved in the London community that a return to the US would not have been any more interesting to her. She had other vistas that she wanted to engage – China, Japan, Russia – and definitely her own developing Afro-Caribbean community in London

Claudia Jones – Beyond Containment offers to the new reader of her work the thinking of one of the most formidable presences who lived and activated between the 1930s and 1960s and preceded subsequent figures like Angela Y. Davis in the US with whom there is a definite intellectual and activist bridge. For the more informed readers and scholars, here is provided the textual material that can advance subsequent studies of this period, of activist women, of leftist women, of black left feminism, of Black life in the United Kingdom and of how one navigates a variety of political positions.

Claudia Jones was a smart, politically-wise, brilliant, transnational feminist, Pan-Africanist theorist and cultural activist who brought together in her speeches and writings the politics that some now see as a necessary way of intersecting a variety of political fields and positions. Known as the founder of the first London carnival and the editor of the first black newspaper in England, Claudia Jones's activism bridged the US and the UK with the Black World politics of decolonization, which ushered in contemporary community empowerment.

For the first time, in one place, *Claudia Jones – Beyond Containment* brings together her essays, poetry, autobiographical and longer writings, expanding our knowledge of several fields thus providing a new generation with the clarity of the ideas of a black woman activist-intellectual of her period who would have a major impact on subsequent political movements. For a fuller understanding of Caribbean, African American and the larger African Diaspora discourses, *Claudia Jones – Beyond Containment* is essential reading.

I
Autobiographical Reflections

Introduction

People who knew Claudia Jones are surprised that there is no full-length autobiography available as she was avidly working on one. She always kept a journal throughout her life and would read from it from time to time. This is perhaps heartening for future researchers who should imagine that this would be a major discovery once it is found. But for readers today, its absence leaves us without any full life story of one of the 20th century's most significant contributors to the analysis and amelioration of the lives of countless people across the African Diaspora. Those who knew Claudia well believe that what is now the Claudia Jones Memorial collection (which had been in the possession of her London partner Abhimanyu Manchanda and later his wife Diane Langford, after his passing) is only a small portion of her fuller collection. Some suggest that the various intelligence interests (CPGB, KGB, FBI, MI5) would have had an interest in securing sensitive documents, had rifled through her belongings after her untimely passing. Others think that there is more material in the possession of other comrades and colleagues in London. Ricky Cambridge who was her last assistant indicated that there were many more volumes and files in her library and that the few boxes of material that remained is but a much-reduced version of what was available (as we viewed two boxes of material which we saw at the house of Diane Langford in Hempstead, London in 1996). Still, the boxes with the material spilling over of its sides created the visible image for the title of this book: *Beyond Containment*.

The autobiographical material available and included in this section consists of her deliberately titled "Autobiographical History" written for Comrade Foster of the Communist Party, USA, as she was about to leave the United States in December, 1955. It details her childhood, her arrival in the US, her joining the Communist Party USA's Young Communist League and her justifications for her political choices. She indicates as pivotal the Scottsboro Boys' Trial (1931–1937) in which nine young African American boys in Alabama were tried repeatedly in various combinations and convicted and sentenced to death, threatened with lynching and accused of the gang rape of two white women which proved to be false in the end. The case became for CPUSA at the time a lead issue and it generated a great deal of activism against Southern racism.[9] Claudia, for her part, saw CPUSA activists as having the best explanations of the dire conditions of black people and its internationalism as a way of understanding this worldwide issue dialectically. In this regard another event would provide a second impetus. Benito Mussolini, the Italian dictator had invaded Abyssinia (or Ethiopia the African country situated on the horn of Africa) in October 1935, in an attempt to colonize this country). Haile Selassie the then Emperor of Ethiopia's response to this invasion and his resistance to colonization would catapult Ethiopia iconically into black consciousness worldwide.

Claudia also identifies her migration, schooling, poverty under US racism, numerous petty jobs and eventual training as a journalist trial, various arrests and incarceration and deportation as critical sequences in her personal history. She also provides good detail about the experiences of the Caribbean community in New York during the Depression of the 1930s. Her various illnesses and their medications are also detailed. Interestingly, she identifies her marriage and divorce as footnotes.

This then is her own best autobiographical summary of her life and would have provided the skeleton for any subsequent autobiographical narrative; so it is perhaps the most important piece of autobiographical material available and in her own handwriting. But since it covers only the United States period, up to her deportation, for a longer narrative there would have been much more to write about her migration to London, her arrival and activism, the loves of her life and her various journeys afterwards to Russia, Japan and China. In a way though, autobiographical elements permeate all her other works: her poetry, her long essay in defense of Ben Davis her letter to John Gates for example (cited in *Left of Karl Marx*) which describes incarceration in Ellis Island.

Perhaps it is her statement before the court, one of the recognized official places where one can intervene against being silenced publicly, which best summarizes the combination of her skill at theoretical argument with personal self-assertion. This speech has been titled in various ways (See for example Veronica Gregg's titling of it as "The Thinking Process… Defies Jailing" or Buzz Johnson's titling of it as "Speech to the Court" or *The West Indian Gazette*'s republication of it as "The Limits of Tyranny is Proscribed by the Measure of Our Resistance to It"). We have titled it here with the critical portion of her words which challenge the construction of black women as silenced and unthinking i.e. not intellectuals with agency –i.e. thinking, writing, speaking human beings. It offers her own defense of her ideas as it challenges the court's inability to fully represent the values which it allegedly holds. It challenges as well the situation of being tried for one's ideas, which runs counter to US claims of being a just society. In the end she would be vindicated as this kind of willful prosecution of communist ideas during the Red Scare, carried out under the leadership of Senator Joseph McCarthy during the late 1940s and through the 1950s, was overturned by Yates vs. the United States (1957). In this speech, which is included in this section, Claudia mounts a spirited defense of herself and her comrades as she asserts the right to her own political orientation. Along the way she challenges internal US racism and its international versions in its policies against Third World peoples. She challenges the evidence, the trumped up witnesses which made a mockery of the judicial system itself and remained firm in the end that history would absolve her.

A third autobiographical piece done in interview form upon her arrival in London identifies the various reasons why she was deported and clarifies for her audience the nature of US racism of that time and its oppression of those who would challenge it. This interview was conducted by George Bowrin, from Trinidad and Tobago, from the very active Oilfield Workers Trade Union, who was studying in London at the time and became a loyal personal friend. Here she further clarifies her earlier explanation for joining the Communist Party indicating that she had "learned through study and participation in the Communist movement that the Communist Party, based on its political science, the science of Marxism-Leninism, that these conditions were man-made and therefore could be changed by mankind..." But more significantly she identifies as a "West Indian" fully in this interview, indicating by these means a claiming of her identification with the developing UK definition of Afro-Caribbean identity. Bowrin's line of questioning and his firm Caribbean identity can be taken as in part setting up these responses. He stays with questions about the Caribbean community in the US which Claudia explains as very active in anti-racist movements in the US. These questions are significant as Bowrin himself, was also involved in union activity and in struggles against colonialism and for self-government in Trinidad. Interestingly for its time, (1956), he also raises a question about women's political role in the West Indies, which she also answers affirmatively.

These autobiographical reflections then provide a window into the thinker who was Claudia Jones and explore her personal background as well as her political orientation. While some may want more intimate personal information, alas she herself does not provide any of that kind of material and, as indicated above, mentions her marriage and divorce in handwritten footnotes to a typed document. A further plan to re-marry upon arrival in England "within the next few months" suggest a relationship of some consequence but no details are provided. Various letters in her personal papers provide some of these nuances; these include private and business letters to Manchanda, letters to and from Ben Davis, postcards from friends, references to a variety of colleagues and photographs which capture her in more relaxed moments. These too are autobiographical but not in the extended narrative sense.

Finally there is the last available reflective piece "Tonight I Tried to Imagine..." which attempts to project into the future, but also to pose questions to herself about her own tendencies. It is perhaps the most self-reflexive of the autobiographical pieces but also the most cryptic. Even as she interrogates her own feelings, she confesses a certain evasion: "I have admitted nothing; but sought to analyze all this for self-understanding; I find I have deluded myself – conscious though I ever am that delusion is unrealistic, can never replace togetherness or evoke happiness – nor sympathetic friendship or understanding."

Claudia, in her speech to the court, quoted at the start of this section, indicates that: "If, out of this struggle, history assess that I and my co-defendants have made some small contribution, I shall consider my role small indeed." Clearly, we can agree that through her entire life work and the honours she has received in recent years, history has vindicated Claudia Jones.

"... [Black] women can think and speak and write!"

Statement Before Being Sentenced to One Year and a Day Imprisonment by Judge Edward J. Dimock after a nine months trial of 13 Communist leaders at Foley Square, New York, 1953[10]

Your Honour, there are a few things I wish to say. For if what I say here serves even one whit to further dedicate growing millions of Americans to fight for peace and to repel the fascist drive on free speech and thought in our country, I shall consider my rising to speak worthwhile indeed.

Quite candidly, your Honour, I say these things not with any idea that what I say will influence your sentence of me. For, even with all the power your Honour holds, how can you decide to mete out justice for the only act to which I proudly plead guilty, and one, moreover, which by your own prior rulings constitutes no crime – that of holding Communist ideas; of being a member and officer of the Communist Party of the United States?

Will you measure, for example, as worthy of one year's sentence, my passionate adherence to the idea of fighting for full unequivocal equality for my people, the Negro people, which as a Communist I believe can only be achieved allied to the cause of the working class?

A year for another vital Communist belief, that the bestial Korean War is an unjust war? Or my belief that peaceful coexistence of nations can be achieved and peace won if struggled for?

Another year for my belief that only under socialism will exploitation of man by man be finally abolished and the great human and industrial resources of the nation be harnessed for the well-being of the people?

Still another year's sentence for my belief that the denial of the exercise of free speech and thought to Communists only precedes, as history confirms, the denial of the exercise of these rights to all Americans?

– 6 –

Trial of Eslee [handwritten]

Et cetera, Honourable Judge?

Of course your Honour might choose still another path for sentence.

You will no doubt choose as the basis for sentence the concocted lies which flowed so smoothly from the well-paid tongues of stool pigeons and informers who paraded before you here and gave so-called evidence which the Court has asserted was "amply justified".

"Amply justified", your Honour? What has been amply justified? The lies of degenerate witnesses like Younglove who can only be compared to Van Der Lubbe, of the famous Reichstag Trial? The despicable forced admission of the Negroes witness Cummings who laughed at the thought of his $10,000 Judas gold jingling in his pocket when he said he would turn informer on his own mother for a mess of the prosecutor's pottage?

The ill-practiced and unspeakable droning of the other Negro informer Rosser, who blurted out his well-memorized script, and even, on your Honour's prodding, would drift off into half-intelligible intonations, "I don't' know what you are talking about", to name but a few examples!

"Amply justified!" Indeed! This "evidence!"

There was no official stamp powerful enough, your Honour, to dignify the obscenity of this trial of ideas. Hence, for me to accept the verdict of guilty would only mean that I considered myself less than worthy of the dignity of truth, which I cherish as a Communist and as a human being and also unsuitable [margin: *cherish as a human being* ®] to the utter contempt with which I hold such sordid performances.

That is why I find now, as throughout this trial of the ideas of Marxism-Leninism, that it is we, the defendants, who are morally free and conversely it is the prosecutors and the Court itself that stands naked before the Bill of Rights and the Constitution and the people of our country.

It is this, your Honour, that explains the not-so-strange reason that you yourself observed that we feel no guilt. For true though it is that the prosecutor has its framed-up verdict on a framed-up indictment and trial, it is not we Communist defendants who tremble at this final stage of these trial court proceedings, but the very prosecutors of our ideas.

Truly, the prosecution's victory sits shakily. For our ideas were confirmed in the course of this trial itself.

It was the world-renowned Karl Marx, founder of the Marxist-Leninist science, [margin: *Communion as science*] for which application to American and world historical conditions we were so fearfully convicted, who long ago predicted that *"The time would come when the powers* [margin: *Haymarket Trial*] *that be would no longer live by the very laws they themselves have fashioned."*

In the libraries and great institutions of learning and yes, your Honour, particularly in the homes of Negro and white workers, will not such reading —which will not stop with this or any other Smith Act trial -— will not men, women and youth think and ponder that such a time is here?

The thinking process, as your Honour well knows, is a process that defies jailing. When it is all boiled down what shows is not the strength of the policies and practices of our prosecutors – which are akin to police-state practices – but their desperate fear of the people. Nothing shows this more, your Honour, than our exposure of the biased jury drawn from a system which virtually excludes Negros, Puerto Rican and manual workers. This virtual exclusion exists not because of lack of qualifications or even financial hardship, but because of deliberate discrimination based on consciously cultivated white supremacist ruling class prejudice which sullies our boasted Western culture.

This conscious white supremacist prejudice, which Mr. Perry so well pointed out, was shown in the gingerly handling by the prosecutors and ofttimes, the Court of the Achilles heel of this alleged "force and violence" charge against us in relation to the Negro question.

Introduce a title page to show Claudia Jones wrote an article during the indictment period, but you dare not read even a line of it, even to a biased jury, on which sat a lone Negro juror, there by mere accident, since he was an alternate well through most of the trial. You dare not, gentlemen of the prosecution, assert that Negro women can think and speak and write!

Moreover, you dare not read it because the article not only refutes the assertion that the ruling class will ever grant equality to 15,000,000 Negro Americans, but shows that what we are granted is unrequited force and violence not only in the unpunished barbaric crime of lynching, but in eating, in everyday existence, in living, in the armed forces, in jails, in the denial of land, in recreation – yes, even in the nation's cemeteries.

The prosecution also cancelled out the overt act which accompanied the original indictment of the defendant Jones entitled "Women in the Struggle for Peace and Security." And why, your Honour? It cannot be read, your Honour – it urges American mothers, Negro women and white, to emulate the peace struggles of their anti-fascist sisters in Latin America, in the new European democracies, in the Soviet Union, in Asia and Africa to end the bestial Korean war, to stop "operation killer," to bring our boys home, to reject the militarist threat to embroil us in a war with China, so that their children should not suffer the fate of the Korean babies murdered by napalm bombs of B-29s, or the fate of Hiroshima.

Is all this not further proof that what we were also tried for was our opposition to racist ideas, so integral a part of the desperate drive by the men of Wall Street to war and fascism?

One thought pervaded me throughout this trial and pervades me still, and it is this: In the nine and one-half months of this trial, millions of children have been born. I speak only of those who live. Will the future of those children, including those of our defendants and even your Honour's grandchildren, be made more secure by the jailing of 13 men and women Communists whose crimes are not criminal acts but advocacy of ideas? Is this

– 8 –

not a <u>tyrannical</u> violation of the American ⟨dream⟩ of "life, liberty and the pursuit of happiness"?

It was in an American junior high school where I first learned of the ⟨great⟩ traditions of |popular liberty| of American history, for which I then received the Theodore Roosevelt Award for good citizenship. — *Irony*

That I have learned to <u>interpret</u> that history and to work to <u>influence</u> its change for the |betterment| of the <u>people</u> with the indispensable weapon of Marxist-Leninist ideas, that is the |real crime| against me. *Cultural critic*

Of all other charges I am <u>innocent</u>.

It was here on this <u>soil</u> (and not as Mr. Lane would depict to this Court, as a young child of eight years of age waving revolutionary slogans), that I had ⟨early⟩ <u>experienced experiences which are shared by millions of native-born Negroes</u> – the <u>bitter indignity</u> and <u>humiliation</u> of ⟨second-class citizenship⟩ the special status which makes a mockery of our Government's prated claims of a "free America" in a "free world" for 15 million Negro Americans.

It was out of my <u>Jim Crow experiences</u> as a young Negro woman, experiences likewise born of <u>working-class poverty</u> that led me in my search of ⟨why⟩ these things had to be that led me to join the Young Communist League and to choose at the age of <u>18</u> the philosophy of my life, the <u>science of Marxism-Leninism</u> – that philosophy that not only <u>rejects racist ideas</u>, but is the <u>antithesis</u> of them.

In this courtroom there has often flashed before me the dozens of <u>meetings</u> of <u>Negro and white workers</u> in the <u>great auto plants</u> at the Rouge, of New England <u>textile</u> workers, of <u>students</u> and of <u>women</u> active in the peace struggle which I have addressed on behalf of my Party. Just as now, there flashes in my mind's eye those young Negro women I have seen at the Women's House of Detention, almost children, of whom, but for my early discovery of Marxism-Leninism, I might have had to say now, "There might I have been." *Defailing*

⟨For what crimes?⟩ <u>Petty crimes born of poverty</u>, of the ghetto, of Jim Crow *the* living, the <u>crime of being born black on American soil</u>, of resisting treatment, *effect of* rebellion against which un-channelled, became lawless against the very Jim Crow *the incarceration* society that perpetrates their lawlessness. *of people*

One need only be a Negro in America to know that <u>for the crime of being a</u> *for ideas* <u>Negro we are daily convicted by a Government</u> which <u>denies</u> us elementary *as crime –* democratic rights, the right to vote, to hold office, to hold judgeships, to serve *people* *description* on juries, rights forcibly denied in the South and also in the North. And I want to concur with Mr. Perry's proposal to Mr. Lane that he recommend to the Department of Justice that they show more zeal, since they have not ever prosecuted a single anti-Semite or a Klu Kluxer in these United States with its ⟨well⟩ total of <u>5,000 lynched Negro men, women and Children</u> since the <u>1860s</u>.

I am aware that these things are not to the liking of the prosecution or even of this Court, but that cannot be helped, for one of the historical truths of all history is that the oppressed <u>never revere their oppressors</u>.

Now I come to a close. The probation official who interrogated me was a Negro official. Your Honour undoubtedly has his reports before you. One of the questions that he asked me was did I ever believe in any religion. I told him then that this was a personal, private matter and was guaranteed under the First Amendment of the Constitution. I wonder now, your Honour, if he somehow falsely reckoned, as many officials falsely reckon, that a change of belief or conviction in one's mature life is like putting on a new dress or a new hat? I could have quoted Scripture to him, the Scripture applied by a leading Negro religious figure in tribute and in observation of the Smith Act jailing of one of the outstanding sons of the Negro people, Ben Davis, now incarcerated in the Jim Crow Federal Penitentiary of Terre Haute, Indiana. The Scripture runs: *"Smite down the shepherd and the sheep will be scattered!"*

And this, Honourable Judge, is exactly what is the purpose of all Smith Act trials, this one in particular. I share the faith of Elizabeth Gurley Flynn and Pettis Perry and all my co-defendants that America's working people, Negro and white, will surely rise, not like sheep, but with vigilance towards their liberty, to assure that peace will win and that the decadent Smith Act, which contravenes the Bill of Rights, will be swept from the scene of history.

It was the great Frederick Douglass, who had a price on his head, who said, *"Without struggle, there is no progress."* And echoing his words was the answer of the great abolitionist poet, James Russell Lowell: *"The limits of tyranny is proscribed by the measure of our resistance to it".* (Locke)

If, out of this struggle, history assesses that I and my co-defendants have made some small contribution, I shall consider my role small indeed. The glorious exploits of anti-fascist heroes and heroines, honoured today in all lands for their contribution to social progress, will, just like the role of our prosecutors, also be measured by the people of the United States in that coming day.

I have concluded, your Honour.

"Autobiographical History"

December 6, 1955

To Comrade Foster:

Dear Comrade Foster: The following is the autobiographical (personal, political, medical) history that I promised to forward to you.

Personal: As a child of eight, I came to the United States from Port-of-Spain, Trinidad, British West Indies. My mother and father had come to this country two years earlier, in 1922, when their economic status (which were middle-class (land owners)— on my mother's side and hotel owners on my father's side) had been worsened as a result of the (drop in the cocoa trade) on the world market, from the West Indies which had impoverished the West Indies and the entire Caribbean. Like thousands of the West Indian immigrants, they hoped to find their (fortunes) in America where "gold was to be found on the streets" and they dreamed of rearing their children in a "free America."

This dream was soon disabused. Together with my three sisters, our family suffered not only the impoverished lot of working-class native families and its multi-national populace, but early learned the special scourge of indignity stemming from Jim Crow national oppression. *communist language*

My formal academic education on American soil began when I entered public school – entering 4A. I have early recollections of being (hurt) by youngsters of my own age who mouthed anti-West Indian propaganda against me and my sisters. But by the time I reached Junior High school, I had formed friendships and become integrated in the student body and was nominated in Harriet Beecher Stowe Junior High for the highest office in the (school) and was subsequently elected Mayor. (The form of student administration of this particular junior high was patterned after the then – established pattern of the NY City administration). One incident I recall with some (pride) today; namely that running with me then, as President of the Board of Aldermen was a young Chinese girl. Numerous teachers tried to pressure me to (refuse) her as a running mate, on the grounds that she was Chinese and that had the situation been reversed, this would not happen in the China of that day. I refused to be drawn in or to accede to any such narrow concept – choosing instead to have her as my (running mate) (To use the phrase I exercised 'my peremptory challenge!') We were elected by an overwhelming majority of the students, proving the teachers wrong and showing the (internationalist approach) of the student body. *Parents any influence?*

I began to wonder (why) there was wealth and poverty; (why) there was discrim-ination and segregation; why there was a contradiction between the (ideas) contained in the Constitution and the Bill of Rights, which contravened its precepts of the pursuit for all of "life, liberty and happiness." *Political biography?*

My mother had died two years earlier of (spinal meningitis) suddenly at her machine in a garment shop. The conditions of non-union organization, of that day, of speed-up, plus the lot of working women, who are mothers and undoubtedly the weight of immigration to a new land where conditions were (far) from as promised or anticipated contributed to her early death at the age of 37. My (father) who together with her had come earlier to America was left to rear four young girls, the oldest of whom was 14. I am the second child of my parents. This was during the days of the Great Depression. Because of my (pride) I didn't ask friendly teachers *(more personal note)*

– 11 –

to help provide me with a graduation outfit, at which I was to <u>receive high honours</u>, including the Theodore Roosevelt Award for <u>Good Citizenship</u> and officiate as Mayor of the school, choosing instead to stay away sending them some lame excuse while I bawled my eyes out in <u>humiliation</u> and <u>self-pity</u>.

I was later to learn that this lot was not just an individual matter, but that millions of working-class people and Negro people <u>suffered this lot under capitalism</u> – if not identical, in one degree or another.

Following my graduation from Junior high school I entered Wadleigh High school. Here I was <u>confronted with Jim Crow</u> in the classrooms and in the <u>social</u> life of the school. White kids would borrow notes from me in school and then on leaving the school would <u>turn their faces the other way under pressure</u> of the Jim Crow society. Teachers with audacity would hold Negro students after school, asking if we wanted to make an extra dollar by doing <u>domestic work</u> for them or as they not-so-quaintly put it, whether I wished to "wear a pretty white apron" at their own social affairs. Or they would select poems in dialect and ask Negro kids to read these <u>pointedly</u>. While I even then had, as do other Negro youth, a <u>searing indignation</u> for these things, <u>I didn't know that they were part of a conscious plan designed to perpetuate the national oppression of the Negro people</u> in the US of which these <u>incidents were reflections of the badge of inferiority perpetrated on the Negro people</u> in the North, with the more hideous features of lynching, poll taxes, crop lien laws and economic strangulation devolving on the Negro people in the heartland of their oppression in the black belt of the South.

My <u>formal academic education</u>, in a bourgeois sense, ended with my <u>graduation</u> from Wadleigh High School. One year before my graduation however, in the midst of the great depression where I was one of the so-called "lost generation" of American youth, I contracted <u>tuberculosis</u> of the lung. My family's <u>economic condition had worsened</u> as had <u>millions</u> of American families, native and foreign born and second generation etc. My <u>Dad</u> who was an <u>editor of an American-West Indian newspaper lost his job</u> and also later when he became a <u>furrier</u> and had to guarantee our support became a <u>superintendent</u> of an apartment in Harlem where I lived all my life in the US. In the room where I slept, it was later discovered that an <u>open sewerage</u> flowed and undoubtedly it was this <u>dampness</u> that contributed to my contraction of TB. I was sent to Sea View <u>Sanatorium</u> from <u>Harlem Hospital</u> at the age of <u>17</u>, where, with pnemothorax treatment for my condition, I fully <u>recovered</u> since fortunately my sputum was never positive. I was there for one full year. There too, I had an opportunity to <u>read</u> avidly, to <u>think deeply</u> about the social ideas instilled in me by my mother and father. My mother had <u>left the Catholic Church</u>, in which faith we were baptized from early childhood choosing to become a <u>Bible</u> student, since her alert mind rejected early the hierarchal teachings of Catholicism. My father's social ideas instilled in us were that of a pride and consciousness of our people, of our <u>relation to Africa</u>, from which my

[margin notes: Personal & political; Racism conscious plan; Black hospital; shadow characters; ideas he learnt pero per for; Communism political thinking; Pan-Africanism? Diaspora?]

antecedents sprang, to our interrelationship to Caribbean independence the dream of San Simeon, great Caribbean patriot, to the new recognition of the struggle for Negro equality in the US linked indissolubly as I later learned with the freedom and equality in the American trade unions and working-class as the future class of society. One incident, I remember while in Sea View – namely when I gave a blood transfusion voluntarily (since I was her blood type), to a young Italian woman patient. This created quite a stir in the hospital on the question of "black blood" and "white blood". Many of the white patients looked for days to see if the young Italian woman, who was eternally grateful (to the point of my embarrassment!) to me would turn "black". One of the first hospital speeches I ever heard was from a young Jewish doctor who in the midst of this scientific ignorance stood in the middle of the ward and gave a lecture to the interracial patients asserting the inviolability of blood types as the antithesis of any false teaching on "race". *1940s → even then race was a lie*

Upon recovery, I completed the last term of High School at Wadleigh. Upon graduation, I went to work in a factory, since college was out for me and I had to help support myself and contribute to the family larder. *↳money? Application?*

My first job was in a laundry, where I observed, under the incredible (to me then) conditions of overwork (speed-up) etc., in the heat of summer, young Negro women fainting regularly because of the unbearable conditions. I didn't want to become like them, so I went to work in a factory. But being unskilled, my job was setting nail heads – with a toothpick, a small jar of paste and placing these in the nail head setting. Boredom and ennui set in and I quit this job. Besides the pay was about $14 a week. Next, I got a job in a Harlem millinery store and lingerie shop as a salesgirl. This continued for quite a while about two years or so.

These were the years of the Ethiopian war and the invasion of Mongolia. During this period (1935-36) I worked on a Negro Nationalist newspaper, where I wrote a column (circulation about 4-5000 copies) and had a weekly column called "Claudia's Comments." My job consisted there also of writing précis of the main editorial comments on Ethiopia from general commercial press, Negro rights, trade union press etc. To my amazement, on attending one of their meetings (of the nationalists) I saw my boss reading my précis to the applause and response of thousands of community people in Harlem, men and women. When the next day, he would come in and tell me what a "Big Negro" he was I would challenge his facts. What he did was to read books on Ethiopia all day and fuse his accumulated knowledge with my précis, which were listened to by thousands of people in the mass rallies held by nationalists in Harlem. I spent a lot of time coming from work listening also to the street corner meeting of the various political parties and movements in Harlem. This was the days of the famed Scottsboro Boys Frame up. I was, like millions of Negro people, white progressives and people stirred by this heinous frame up. I was impressed by the

Harlem as colour · *famed frame.*

Communist speakers who explained the reasons for this brutal crime against young Negro boys; and who related the Scottsboro case to the struggle of the Ethiopian people against fascism and Mussolini's invasion. Friends of mine, who were Communist, although I didn't know it then, seeing my interest began to have frequent discussions with me. I joined the Party in February 1936 and was assigned to work in the YCL shortly after. My first assignment was secretary of the YCL executive committee in Harlem and it was about this time, I got a job in the Business Dept of the DW. This job coincided with my application for a $150 a week job in the field of dramatics with the Federal Theatre Project under WPA. I took the job at *The Worker* for $12-15 a week instead.

During my teens I was active in numerous social clubs on the community in Junior NAACP, in tennis clubs and also studied dramatics at the Urban League. I performed in this capacity with a troupe in many churches in the Harlem community and in Brooklyn.

The National Negro Congress first organizing conference had been held in Chicago. It was when I met James Ashford, outstanding Young Communist Leader who died at the age of 27, that I was oriented to work in the youth movements, in the YCL.

During the next ten years from 1936-1946-7 I was active in the YCL and the youth movement. Served as organizer of the YCL in Harlem for a year. In 1937, I was sent on a 6 month National Training School of the CP. On my return, I was elected to National Council YCL and became associate editor of the *Weekly Review*. I was active in the work of the great American Congress, the organization of the National Council of Negro Youth, the Southern Negro Congress (where I attended many conferences in Alabama, Atlanta, Richmond VA) and also in the National Negro Congress.

Later I became editor of the *Weekly Review*, 1938–40. During 1943–45, I became editor of *Spotlight* national publication of American Youth for Democracy. This publication, many of whose articles were entered into the Congressional Record and for whom admirals and Senators wrote inspired the victory in the anti-fascist war among youth and was widely read by GI subscribers throughout the war fronts.

Worked from 1945–46 as editor of Negro Affairs *Daily Worker*.

Elected full member of the National Committee 1945 Convention CP.

Assigned on "graduation" from youth movement to be Executive Secretary, National Negro Commission CPUSA (1945-46).

Arrested January 28, 1948 under ancient statute or warrant for deportation to my native Trinidad, BWI. Sent to Ellis Island. Bailed out overnight $1,000.

Arrested June 29, 1951 with 17 working-class Communist leaders, including Elizabeth Gurley Flynn under the infamous Smith Act for writing an article which described the forward movement of Negro and white women in opposition to the fascist bent world domination US foreign policy. Bail $20,000.

Rearrested under Walter McCarran Law, October 1951.

[handwritten margin notes: "seerd the people out first" · "Could've worked for the gov't" · "well" · "reach like resume" · "Communion to Democracy"]

Held with 18 working-class and Communist leaders on Ellis Island in special "Walter-McCarran" wing for 18 days until bail was won $5,000.

From 1947–52 – active in national women's movements and united front movements such as Congress of American Women; National Council of Negro *(wells)* Women; toured nation –43 states – in connection with main Party assignment of work among women, organizing Party Conferences of work among women, helping to implement this arm of our National Committee's work among the masses of women, particularly working class and Negro Women in struggle against the Korean war, for peaceful coexistence between nations, for peace; national dignity, full equality for women and the equal rights of women. This was the basis of my " overt act", an article I wrote, printed in *Political Affairs* which urged American women, Negro and white, to unite lest their children like those in Korea suffer the fate of Hiroshima's atomic destruction.] *Not afraid of rhetorical language*

From 52–53 – worked on National Peace Commission of CP giving leadership activity to peace centres, to peace struggle namely around Korean war for the programme registered at Geneva for peaceful coexistence among nations, international friendship in a world of peace.

July 4, 1953, at the end of trial of 17, suffered heart failure diagnosed as hypertensive cardio-vascular disease. Hospitalized at Mt Sinai for 21 days. Took 5 months leave of absence Placed on digitalis and drugs for control of hypertension. Hospitalized again for coronary heart disease in December 1953. Two months leave. Returned to work again served as editor of Negro Affairs Quarterly and special fields of work among Negro people, participated as member of NAC, throughout this period.

January 11, 1955 entered prison serving a year and a day sentence at the Federal reformatory for Women at Alderson, W. VA. Got 72 days off, serving 9 months and 18 days for so called "good behaviour". Won first Prize, Blue Ribbon on August State Fair of W.A. for women... skills learned there. Was to be summarily deported straight to the Caribbean from prison on October 23 day of release of this year... but for protests here and abroad and intervention of British authorities. Brought suit for first time in challenge to the Walter McCarran Act *resume of* which declares it a "crime" to be a non-citizen even or permanent resident alien *guerilla* but was forced to withdraw my suit due to my health status which is precarious *fighter;* and must be guarded. *jumped from jail or ...*

December 9 – scheduled to leave the US after residing here for 32 years in the United States.

I think this sort of summarizes it. I should add (happily), due to digitalize poisoning while imprisoned I was taken off digitalis August 3, 1955 and have not had to use other than occasionally nitroglycerine for the heart pain – which I have used now for 2 months and only used on two occasions during the last year when imprisoned. Now on drugs (supercil) for control of hypertension. If you summarize the medical status you should know that at the time of my imprisonment admitted by a court appointed physician – contrary to the attitude of the first women prison physicians I was diagnosed as suffering from essential hypertension, cardiac disease and coronary arteriosclerosis – with my background of arrested tuberculosis – the exact diagnosis of my personal physician.

I wrote this quite fully in the full knowledge, Dear Comrade Foster that your extracts would contain only what you consider pertinent, but I gave it as fully as I can to facilitate that end.

Best personal regards
to you and Comrade Esther
Comradely yours,

Claudia Jones.

P.S. I was married to Abraham Scholnick in September 1940 in NYC. I was divorced February 27, 1947. My plans are to remarry in England within the next few months.

P.P.S. At the age of 23 I applied and received my certificate for first papers for American citizenship – but this was denied me by the US Government since I was politically active from the age of 18.

"I Was Deported Because..."[11]

An Interview with Claudia Jones by George Bowrin

Why were you deported from the United States Miss Jones?

I was a victim of the McCarthyite hysteria against independent political ideas in the USA – a hysteria which penalizes anyone who holds ideas contrary to the official pro-war, pro-reactionary, pro-fascist line of the white ruling class of that country.

I was deported from the USA because as a Negro woman Communist of West Indian descent, I was a thorn in their side in my opposition to Jim Crow racist discrimination against 16 million Negro Americans in the United States, in my work for redress of these grievances, for unity of Negro and white workers, for women's rights and my general political activity urging the American people to help by their struggles to change the present foreign and domestic policy of the United States.

Peace fighter

I was deported and refused an opportunity to complete my American citizenship because I fought for peace against the huge arms budget which funds should be directed to improving the social needs of the people. I was deported because I urged prosecution of the lynchers rather than the prosecution of the Communists and other democratic Americans who oppose the lynchers and big financiers and war mongers, the real advocates of force and violence in the USA.

Racist Bias

obviously, yes → under-hand question

Is there any special significance to the fact that you are a West Indian and as such were deported from the United States?

Q: Did any w. Indian contribute to deportation

Yes, I definitely think so. The very law under which I was deported, the reactionary Walter-McCarran Law widely known for its special racist bias towards West Indians and peoples of Asian descent. This law, which came into being as a result of the whole reactionary drive against progressive ideas in the United States, encourages immigration of fascist scum from Europe but restricts West Indian immigration, once in their thousands annually to the United States, to 100 persons per year, from *all* the Caribbean islands. This works special hardship among West Indians who have family ties and who are permanent residents and citizens of the USA.

You are a communist, are you not Miss Jones? Would you tell us what led you to become a communist?

penalty sometimes

Gladly. From an early age, like most native Negro Americans and with the additional penalty of being foreign born and a Negro in the United States, I experienced the indignity of second-class citizenship in the US. My parents emigrated from the West Indies in 1924 in the hope of finding greater economic opportunity and freedom to rear their children. But what we found instead in the US was not only economic poverty for the working-class, but the special brand of American racism – Jim Crow.

No Escape

Different from others; some claimed that communism were racist themselves

In the USA, no matter what the social class status, no Negro escapes the scourge of Jim Crow. I learned that those who fought most consistently for the interest of the workers, for their trade union organization and social needs were the Communists. My daily experiences as a Negro youth in the USA led me to search out political forces that were doing something about these things; political forces who not only fought on a day-to-day basis to alleviate these conditions but who had a perspective as to a radical solution of these conditions. I learned through study and participation in the Communist movement that the Communist Party, based on its political science, the science of Marxism-Leninism, that these conditions were man-made and therefore could be changed by mankind through understanding of their origin and to eliminate these practices and conditions.

Dangerous Ideas

So that it is as a result of these struggles that you were indicted, convicted and jailed in the United States?

Yes. For these struggles, I was indicted, convicted and served a year and a day sentence despite a heart condition and related illnesses, under the infamous Smith Act – a reactionary statute under which progressive fighters are convicted and jailed not for committing any overt act, but merely for their ideas.

Did you ever meet West Indians in the US? Could you tell us something about their conditions?

Yes. There are over 100,000 West Indians in New York City alone. The West Indian community in the States plays an active political, economic and social role in the life of the nation and particularly lends its strength to advancing the struggles of the Negro people in the USA for full equality and freedom. Numerous West Indians are among the most active trade unionists in industry.

Then there are numerous West Indian professionals associated with various political and social welfare organizations in the community. As a whole West Indians in the USA constantly express concern and support for the liberation of struggles of the people in the West Indies, for freedom from colonial exploitation and slavery, for dignity and self-government.

Would you say something about your view of the role of women in the West Indies?

I have been quite impressed with the activities of the women of the West Indies and their growing participation in the liberation movement as well as the international movement for peace, security and the rights of children. There is no question but that West Indian women represent an indispensable ally in the fight for colonial freedom, because women are triply exploited in the colonies, as women, as mothers and as colonials, subjected to indignities and great suffering because of the status of their countries.

Participation of increasing numbers of West Indian women side by side with their men in the struggle for national independence and self-governing will grow because women above all, want a better life, (dignity and equality) and a better world in which their children will live.

ties women + children together

Is there anything else you would like to add?

Yes, I would like to thank West Indians in the Caribbean, in Britain and America, as well as all other democratic and progressive forces who interceded on my behalf while jailed for my ideas in an American prison.

"Tonight I Tried to Imagine What Life Would be Like In the Future"[12]

Not a feminist   *Too 'committed to a cause'?*

Tonight I tried to imagine what life would be like in the future – personal that is. For on the broad highway of Tomorrow, despite craggy hills and unforeseen gullies, I am certain that mankind will take the high road to a socialist future.

My certitude for this broad future has never matched my certitude for my personal fortunes. I have not been endowed either with the ability to apply that certitude or indeed to experience its harbingers. Perhaps dialectically this is why: my very certitude and commitment has overshadowed in the eyes of some of my personal interest in people. To those with whom I share this broad vision this seeming weakness has been resented or more kindly, if not resented – rejected. Whereas this characteristic has impinged on personal relationships, it has nevertheless served as a liberating force making and shaping the being that I have become. I, in turn, have rejected any tendency to reduce this result, even perhaps to stifle its evocation. *nothing in way of work?*

No time for personal in political work?

Evocation is a mutual emotion. To evoke a response of togetherness – in all things (maturity tells me this is probably impossible in a single relationship) and remembering human limitations – there must be togetherness. Togetherness also is not an abstraction; its inner laws and contradictions must be studied *Bonds of connection*

Yet another characteristic may be strength of character and a tendency to fight weakness, not to openly sympathize with it. Is it because a lurking fear exists that capitulation to manifested weakness in others (even when not self-imposed) may in turn impinge on what I regard as essentially impermissible? *shield against personal struggle*

In the strongest I have witnessed impermissible weaknesses. I do not exclude

– 19 –

myself but I have never been able to condone personal weaknesses and therein, perhaps is another antagonistic contradiction. Fundamentally regarding the impermissibility of personal weakness, not entirely lacking in my own share of these, I seek to counter my own (and others) with a harshness that is also impermissible in close human relationships.

For most of my adult years this has been the essence of my approach; the *raison d'etre* of my function. I find I have been praised for a single-mindedness of purpose– and this is true enough; only my sincerest friends have observed the one-sidedness of my existence something (again the characteristic rears its head) I have hardly allowed myself to admit far less to fully examine!

Perhaps a third reason (happily I do not publicly avow or practice this characteristic) at root has been a 'protective' one – a general personal injury. Those who truly know me know this – and I have often known even as I strike back, the verbal flows from which I flee are nourished in an identical soil.

Fearing the perpetuation of this one-sidedness in personal relation, I persist in it, fearing the disappointment of non-togetherness. Knowing that evocation of a different approach means change, on my part, I have no certitude that change will strengthen togetherness. But this certitude is related not only to faith in the future – which is not blind but scientific; one needs to apply the same scientific inquiry to all phenomena. And if one resists that inquiry, can it be because no one knows that the application of that very science will reveal an uneven development; or that one fears to admit failure, or even that one's own limitations will stand naked and bare? Is it that in so examining the very characteristic will be proven a migratory patterning the repeated violation of it? Or even that it will be found that one is no *bargain?*

Penchant that I have for introspective discussion, I seem to have wound up where I began I bore no one but myself. I have admitted nothing; but sought to analyze all this for self-understanding; I find I have deluded myself – conscious though I ever am that delusion is unrealistic, can never replace togetherness or evoke happiness – nor sympathetic friendship or understanding.

And as I become too aware of this state to even try to change – – I realize I not only have become lethargic in these matters (a state not to be emulated!) but positively without *nerve*. All weavers know of tangled skeins. The bad thought then become "threads to deceive." Sometimes they can be untangled and sometimes they serve as webs. How I believe in the Loom of Language! – and in the Family of Man!

June 18, 1964.

– 20 –

II
Essays

Race And Black Human Rights

"I was deported from the USA because… [of] my opposition to Jim Crow racist discrimination against 16 million Negro Americans in the United States"

[Editor's Note: We have tried to remain faithful to the layout, stylistic and linguistic elements of these essays, making minor adjustments only when necessary. This explains the variation sometimes between the use of italics and indentation for quotes. These are as they appeared in the originals.]

Introduction

In this section are essays by Claudia Jones which deal with race, black human rights and black self-determination in the United States. The above caption from her autobiographical statement captures the particular orientation of this section. As a matter of protocol, we have retained Claudia Jones's use of the word "Negro." As this was the language of her time, one hastens to inform that such language is time-specific and in her own case she capitalizes the word in much the same way that the word "Black" was/is capitalized as a descriptor when "African" is not used. We did not think it appropriate and faithful to her turn of phrase and text to change all the numerous references of "Negro" to "Black," though in my own titling I have done so.

Of particular note is that these essays were written beginning in the early 1940s when Claudia Jones was in her early twenties. The first essay is dated 1940, four years after she joined the Young Communist League in 1936; so she would have been twenty-five years old. This by itself is significant as we see already at such a young age, the development of sophisticated ideas as far as analyzing the black condition is concerned. At that time, the Communist Party USA, as she indicates, was one of the few avenues for organizing against the poverty and racism, which combined, had reduced black people in the United States to positions of continuing servitude whether as sharecroppers in the south or as northern wage workers in factories. Claudia Jones, as we see already from her autobiography, had experienced precisely these conditions personally through low-paying and difficult jobs available for black women when she entered the job market and from her family's own impoverishment.

So she was not afraid to use her experience to aid an argument for black empowerment.

The essays in this section on race and black human rights are "Jim Crow in Uniform" (1940); "New Problems of the Negro Youth Movement" (1940); "Lift Every Voice – for Victory" (1942) and "On the Right to Self-Determination for the Negro People in the Black Belt" (1946).

"Lift Every Voice – For Victory" was published as a pamphlet which has a photograph of a young armed Joe Louis on the cover and another photograph of him with army "buddies at Camp Dix" on the frontispiece. The descriptor at the back of the pamphlet describes her as follows: "Claudia Jones, the author of this pamphlet, is a young Negro woman leader of the Young Communist League, Editor of the popular anti-fascist youth magazine, *The Weekly Review.*" The significance of using Joe Louis, who was the champion boxer of that time is justified in the essay and would have been a clever rhetorical move which would have drawn in black readership.

These four essays together provide with us a great deal of material on the arguments that were taking place in the black community in the United States in the 1940s. The particular challenges that black people faced as they began to organize after the depression and the kind of thinking from the black left which challenge at times blind integrationist tendencies without self-determination. The essays also clarify as well subsequent debates internal to the black community, as between for example Martin Luther King and Malcolm X around the issue of self-determination. In the 1960s, self-determination was a Nation of Islam position. The more integrationist positions of the NAACP and the Southern Christian Leadership Conference out of which Martin Luther King came would in the end be the option which was followed to lead to Civil Rights.

The first essay, "Jim Crow in Uniform" provides us with important background information on the critique of a segregated military up through the 1940s and 1950s prior to the ascendency of a Colin Powell, which accompanied a fuller post-Civil Rights black participation in the US armed services, to being the first and still the only black man to become Chairman of the Joints Chiefs of Staff of the US military (1989-1993) and later on US Secretary of State (2001-2005). Powell would address this issue of discrimination in a different way by his own rise through the ranks of the US military in the post 1960s period, joining the military in 1958. But in the 1940s this is an important essay as it critiques the tendency in American political leadership to fight abroad for democracy while maintaining at home and in one of its essential structures (the military) a pattern of rank inequality. Structurally, the essay begins and ends with the heroic contributions of a representative soldier but continues to counter American racism by revealing its operation in the language of racism, the crimes of lynching, the structures of separation, the nature of the political parties and the international links between struggles against racism at home and against colonialism abroad.

– 24 –

It also references some of the ongoing protests at the time by black communities against for example "Birth of a Nation" and provides a good history of the earlier and contemporary contexts in which these take place. It also references the Scottsboro Boys and Angelo Herndon cases and addresses lynching as an ongoing reality of the time and therefore continues some of the work of Ida B. Wells on lynching. It is therefore an excellent summary of racism in the military in the era of the two world wars (World War I 1914–1918 and World War II 1939-1945). It provides important history of the period as it describes what was happening to black soldiers when they returned from WWI and still faced racism in the US and the continuing segregated facilities even while these soldiers gave their best to the country. It also highlights her knowledge of the Mussolini invasion and its implications, the role of Toussaint L'Ouverture in Haiti and makes the point that wars for national liberation are justified, i.e., that one has to have a critical analysis of warfare. There is clearly in the essay's end some of the promotional aspects of CPUSA recruitment and an idealism about the Soviet Union, but the relating of these larger international issues to domestic US racial problems in the 1940s makes it an important piece of history.

A second essay, "New Problems of the Negro Youth Movement," gives us a nice summary of the kinds of issues that were confronting black youth at the time (again during the 1940s) and ways in which the youth, like Claudia Jones, were able to manifest their activism. She describes the National Negro Congress (1936) and the move towards unity of black youth movement, a rising militancy which would not be realized until the rise of the Student Nonviolent Coordinating Committee (SNCC) led by people like Stokely Carmichael (Kwame Ture), (like Claudia also born in Trinidad) in the 1960s. The youth issues then as identified by Claudia in the 1940s would be against war, for peace, citizenship, the right to vote, an end to lynching and above all for a unified youth movement of black and white youth.

In the third essay, "Lift Every Voice – for Victory" Claudia Jones has been accused of shifting to a pro-war position, which she had rejected earlier. As one reads the essay though, it is clear that she saw a fight against Hitler and fascism *Closing* as a fight against similar white supremacist movements and tendencies in the *our reading* United States. She uses Joe Louis' historic victory over Max Schmeling in 1938 *much?* and the fact that he had enlisted in the war as the launching point for her argument as to why one had to support the war: i.e., an anti-Nazi position was co-terminus with an anti-racism position in the United States. She speaks of the Double V slogan of the time, which black interests promoted at the time as being a Victory at home and a Victory abroad but suggests that in the end they will combine into a single victory. This piece which carried the support for the anti-Hitler war effort and again calls for equality in the military as represented by Joe Louis' service is evocative in that it uses the "Lift Every Voice" titling of the song created by James Weldon Johnson which has become the Black National

Anthem. Claudia indicates that the victory against Hitler extends to a victory over Mussolini and Hirohito.

Finally, one of the most historic essays is her "On the Right to Self-Determination for the Negro People in the Black Belt," which I think should be essential reading for anyone serious about studying the Black condition internationally. It had been preceded by a "Pre–Convention Discussion Article" (1945), which contained some of the same arguments and would serve as a sketch of the ideas developed in this larger article. This is a good article for understanding the internal colonialism argument that was put forward at the time, that black people in the United States were an oppressed nation. As such it is a black nation argument coming from a black left intellectual activist. She uses the accepted international law arguments of what was a nation (though it is identified here as a Marxist-Leninist argument) – in terms of language, geography, culture, with their own black bourgeoisie and economic life and existing in the southern states of the United States which constituted a 'black belt' but living under oppression by white racist capitalists: "as the question of a nation oppressed by American imperialism, in the ultimate sense as India is oppressed by British imperialism and Indonesia by Dutch imperialism." This was therefore an internally oppressed nation of black people in this line of thinking. Her position also reveals an internal debate against revisionism which was taking place in the Communist Party USA at the time. But it also challenged the logic of integration without self-determination as a mistake.

These four Claudia Jones essays on race and black human rights provide us with important information on the 1940s, in particular the activism which would prepare the way for the Civil Rights Movement in the United States in the 1950s and 1960s.

Jim Crow in Uniform (1940)[13]

Jesse Clipper, Negro Hero, 1895–1917

In the heart of the 5th Ward, centre of the segregated Negro residential section in Buffalo, New York, a monument stands erected to the memory of Jesse Clipper, a Negro hero who died in battle in the First World War of 1914–18.

Jesse Clipper is so honoured because of his bravery and his valour. Young Jesse Clipper died believing that he had done his share "to make the world safe for democracy." He must have died happily too, at the thought that he and his buddies had given their lives "in this war to end all wars" – that the armistice which was signed would be a permanent one. But this belief was a shocking illusion.

Twenty-three years ago, in 1917, three years after President Wilson proclaimed the neutrality of the United States and had implored the citizens to "refrain from taking sides," America, at Wilson's advice, took sides and Jesse Clipper enlisted.

Jesse Clipper died in battle. He had no chance to weigh the aftermath of the war. How could he know, for example, two years later, when it was all over, that the war dead of America together with the rest of the world numbered some 12 million? How could he know that the war had given birth to some 25,000 new millionaires? How could he read the same press, which now blatantly confessed that many of the atrocity stories concerning the Belgians weren't true, after all?

No, Jesse Clipper could never know, not even if he could come to life again; he would probably die again of disillusionment. He would see at a glance, that the very things he fought for and was promised – freedom, equality, opportunity, were still denied his people. He would see the tragedy of Natchez, Mississippi – in which over 240 Negroes died – the pyres of charred bodies which is symbolic of the half-slave, half-free Jim Crow oppression which Negroes in America still suffer from, economically, politically and socially.

But the thing that would perhaps alarm Jesse most would be the realization that the Second World War was in progress. That reaction did "break faith" with those who sleep in Flanders Field. That already, the youth of three continents; Europe, Africa and Asia, were in trenches again. That the threat to American liberty and freedom was becoming more real every day, by the studied build-up in the press of America of prejudices, hatred against countries, all under the similar guise to preserve democracy."

He would hear the laughter of the Wall Street clique, while they manoeuvred in Congress making loans and selling arms to belligerents, already cashing in on the blood money of the war. He would see the formation of a "national unity" among men who only a few months ago were bitter enemies on both domestic and foreign policies. A "unity" designed to take us into war.

Whose War Is It?

The newspapers are saying in our time, some of the things they said in Jesse Clipper's time. They are saying that this war, between two of the major imperialist powers in the world, Great Britain and Germany, is a war "to preserve democracy." They say that it is a "holy crusade" which will decide whether freedom and democracy will forever prevail, or whether force and violence will rule the world.

The newspapers ask you and me to believe this. But how can we believe this, when we are aware of the fact that democracy has been a farce to some 500,000,000 enslaved colonials under the domination of English rule? Can this war give the kind of real democracy which previous centuries did not give? We're sorry if we cannot believe this, just because the newspapers say so. No, the colonial peoples, black and white, cannot support this war.

For it is a war that is imperialist in nature, which means that both England and Germany are out to get more territory, out to gain more influence in international affairs, are out to have a showdown as to who can exploit and enslave more peoples, small nations as well.

Colonial Folk Against the War

British imperialist "democracy" in action, besides, has in each previous war made things *worse*, not better for the colonial peoples. While pretending to be fighting for the rights of small nations and for democracy, the British ruling class denies to its colonies the most elementary democratic rights. That is why the progressive forces in the West Indies take the stand as indicated in the editorial columns of the *Barbados Observer*:

> "We colonial workers have not forgotten the last World War, when all kinds of promises were made to us... Therefore we are determined never again to allow ourselves to be used as cannon fodder by *either camp* in the war." (My emphasis – C.J.)

Some apologists for British imperialism argue that under British rule, Negro colonials have fared better as compared with their status under German rule and for this reason, beginning with the premise that either side must win in the end, it is better for Negroes to support British imperialism in this conflict. Mr. W.A. Domingo, British export-import Negro merchant, openly supports this proposition.

This argument is fraught with danger for two reasons. First, it is a vicious acceptance of the status of Negroes as inferior, who *must be ruled*, regardless. Secondly and perhaps more important, it is a statement designed to lull the actions of Negroes, who want peace, not war and to offset their attempts to raise their voices and act to halt the war, now.

Besides, it is also a false premise, when it is assumed that either side must win. For the ever-present desire for liberty on the part of Negro colonials will never be achieved through a change of masters, both of whom are interested not in the freedom, but in the further enslavement of them. Only through organization, education and struggle against reaction, against war-profits, against reaction's drive on civil liberties, under the guise of war emergencies, can this new threat to the ultimate freedom of the colonial peoples be met. Only the abolition of imperialism, of the whole system of the war makers will guarantee peace and security for the peoples.

Who knows that yet Ethiopia may not rise again soon in revolt against both Anglo-French imperialism and Italo-German imperialism, showing the path to all

– 28 –

colonial peoples of Africa to freedom and liberation from imperialism as a whole? This is the real choice!

Lindbergh – Spouse of the Morgan Fortune

Sometimes the reactionaries themselves let the cat out of the bag as to the true situation.

Take the speech made by Colonel Charles A. Lindbergh, the lawful spouse of the fortune of Morgan, decorated by and friend of Field Marshal Goering of Germany, for instance.

The speech is entitled simply "Aviation, Geography and Race," delivered over a national network and re-printed in the *Readers Digest* of 1939. He says:

> "... Western nations are again at war, a war likely to be more prostrating than any in the past, a war in which the White race is bound to lose and the others bound to gain, a war which may easily lead our civilization through more Dark Ages if it survives at all."

Lindbergh then goes on to warn that his "civilization" is menaced by "the infiltration of inferior blood."

It is clear that Mr. Lindbergh feels that the war is a white man's war – or more correctly – a war for white supremacy. That it is a war, which, unless his Western nations win, will mean world domination by darker peoples, which will then be a civilization equivalent to the Dark Ages. Obviously, civilization as he sees it does not include the black man.

What contribution can "inferior blood" make? Ask George Washington Carver, Negro scientist and inventor of 100 or more uses of the peanut, for instance. Ask Marian Anderson, outstanding Negro contralto. Ask Paul Robeson. Ask Joe Louis, who tore down the myth of "Aryan" supremacy. Ask all the millions of heavily-pigmented people throughout the world, whose sweat and blood have been given for centuries to build up empires, profits and wealth.

They have even contributed their "inferior blood" time and again in defense of democracy because they believed the cause was theirs, also. Ask the dead who fought with Crispus Attacks [sic] (Attucks) in Concord, for American independence. Or the Negro soldiers who died on the battlefields with Jackson in New Orleans. Or the War of 1812. Ask a few Negro Civil War veterans who fought with Sherman. Ask the Negro dead who lie in Flanders Field.

The False Theory of a White Man's War

Prof. Rayford Logan of Howard University and Elmer Carter of *Opportunity* are bearers of a theory of ill-repute, the theory of the "white man's war." The fact remains that Negroes comprise a good bit of the cannon fodder for Europe's war makers.

In our own communities, since the war, the bubble of the false theory of a "white man's war" quickly explodes amidst the rising cost of living, the corresponding lowering of income, as a result of the Roosevelt war and hunger budget. The Negro population is delivered not only as cannon fodder but the acute brunt of the war crisis is first felt by them. The falsification of actual fact as shown here is for one main purpose: to weaken the domestic front of Negro and white unity, to lull the Negro population against fighting the imperialist war and to slander the white working population who want and have no part in this war. The theory must be fought against, for it is both anti-Negro and anti-working class.

The Administration Gives a War-Deal to the People

That the New Deal has become a war-deal, is an ever-conscious growing fact on the minds of everybody. The few concessions of appointments of Negroes to hitherto-unheld Federal, state and city posts, the integration of Negroes into the Federal programme, in theatres, labour and social service, have been forsaken by Roosevelt.

Only 200,000 Negro workers are not left on the WPA rolls as a result of the Woodrum amendments and the Roosevelt war and hunger budget.

If the United States intends to keep out of war, why the huge armaments programme as against social betterment for the people of America? And what kind of security can the people have, when even the temporary security of WPA, NYA, PWA is taken away from them? The President's message offers neither peace nor security to the people of America!

The demagogic slogan of "national unity" means that Roosevelt, has been promoted to full leadership of the rulers of America and they are nationally united against the people, to make more profits, by starvation, by clamping down on the civil rights of the people, on the basis of war.

The Anti-Lynching Bill –
Touchstone of American Democracy

In urging unity of the nation behind his budget message, the President ended on the note that now is the time for everyone to come together, forget past quarrels and so establish once and for all that democracy as a system still remains unchallenged as the best way of life yet devised by man.

For whom? might be the query of the Negro. How can he forget past quarrels when in the heart of the nation's capital, prejudice against the Negro abounds?

Only recently, at the premiere opening of "Abe Lincoln in Illinois," Negro citizens in Washington picketed the theatre because Negroes are not allowed to mingle with whites in the unwritten laws of American democracy.

High in the annals of achievements of American progress of 1939 is the passage of the Anti-Lynching Bill in the House of Representatives for the first time. But reaction in the person of Representative Rankin of Mississippi recorded the typical yearly slander when he shouted in the House:

"You are trying to placate a few *nigger* communists who are infesting the gallery."

"Nigger Communists…" And in this slander, the Tory Representative Rankin paid unwilling tribute to the Negro Communists who have, together with white Communists, fought for the passage of the Anti-Lynching Bill, fought against distortions of the role of Negroes in American history, fought against every manifestation of prejudice where the Negro was concerned.

Representative Rankin rants, with the Bilbos, Ellenders, Cotton Ed Smith, because his idea of democracy is being challenged by progress.

As it was challenged by Angelo Herndon, Negro Communist, who led the fight for Negro and white unemployed workers in the heart of the deep South, in Georgia.

As it was challenged and brought to a new high by Ben Davis, young Communist editor of the *Daily Worker*, who, in the Senate caucus hearings upset the dignity of the "Democratic reactionaries" and "Republican Hypocrites" by exposing the truth.

The President has never once raised his voice in support of the Anti-Lynching Bill. It is still the touchstone of American democracy and it will require even greater mass support if it is to become law. Current reactionary lies to the effect that lynchings no longer take place, therefore there is no need for an Anti-Lynching bill, must also be answered. In the year 1939, 20 "silent-lynchings," the new technique of reaction, minus the mob, took place. Since 1940 already five lynchings have occurred. This – in the face of the reactionaries' lie that this is a "lynchless year." That is why the voice of progress must be raised ever louder and clearer to Pass the Anti-Lynching Bill!

The 1940 Elections — really? how?

Negroes constitute a balance of power in most of the major cities of the nation. Already there is being recorded in the press bids for their support by both the Democratic and Republican parties – twin parties of reaction. These old traditional major parties have today less of a division on real issues and political currents in American life, than in any former period of their existence. On a domestic scale both the Republican and Democratic parties fully agree to scrap all labour and social legislation as much as possible, to militarize labour, to drastically curb civil liberties, to lower the standard of living of all the people.

– 31 –

They are both agreed on dubbing peace lovers and fighters for democracy – "fifth columnists," because they both want to bring about America's entry in the present war. The real fifth columnists can be most easily recognized, because it is they who most openly sow the seeds of race prejudice, the seeds of Negro-baiting, or if they don't do it openly, they are in secret agreement with those who do. The leadership of both parties contains the real fifth columnists.

But Negroes cannot agree to such a programme, for the Negro people want peace, want to keep America out of war. The Negro people want jobs, economic security, civil liberties, passage of social legislation, such as the Anti-Lynching Bill.

No, the answer is not in a return to support of either of these parties. The answer lies in independent political action of the people in 1940, aligned with labour, as expressed recently by Earl Browder, when he called for a People's Platform for Jobs, Peace, Civil Liberties.

Such independent action will make the people's answer clear against the war and hunger budget of the Roosevelt Administration, against the policies of the Republicans who in effect give support to his policies.

Such independent action can be a powerful force for support of progressive congressional candidates regardless of their party labels.

This, coupled with day to day actions against America's entry into war, for peace, for social legislation, for an advanced standard of living, against step by step involvement policies of the Roosevelt Administration can be the means for making 1940 be symbolic of the people's will for peace and prosperity.

The only party which fights of the interests of all the people is the Communist Party. The only party which truly fights for the interest of the Negroes is the Communist Party. Vote Communist! Vote for Browder and Ford, its standard-bearers! For jobs, peace and civil liberties! Vote Communist!

Historical Comparisons of Two Presidents

In 1917, too, the people of America had to make a choice on how best to keep America out of war.

Then, as now, Wall Street's profit-making men, under the guise of free trade, were pouring money and supplies into "little Belgium." Loans were followed with human security.

The recent historical analogy is "Little Finland." Remember the headlines. For months the typewriter generals in Helsinki issued thousands of dollars' worth of ink, paper and type, in an effort to create the impression that here was a moral cause to be rightfully defended. Roosevelt and Hoover urged its defense with loans, with arms, with a huge "Relief" campaign.

Today there is peace in Finland. Today, the same press, which threw you off your balance, candidly admits its lies. Why the lies? Why the fakery?

It was because the newspapers spoke the aims of the imperialists whom Roosevelt leads, who would drag America into war. There is peace in Finland because of the peace policy of the Soviet Union, which aims to defend its own borders, which aims to limit the sphere of World War, and establish peace. There is peace because the Finnish generals have become convinced that they were being used as pawns of the Allies against Germany.

Herbert Hoover, Chief Egg in the Scramble of Finnish Relief

The truth about the Finnish-Soviet conflict is most clearly understood when we look at the person who raised the most noise about it. Remember Hoover of "apple a day" fame? Well, Herbert Hoover was the chief egg in the scramble of Finnish relief. Hoover, who couldn't help the millions of Americans, Negro and white, who starved while he was President, headed the committee which raised loans and contributions for the "relief" of the Finns. What of the millions of Americans who are in need of relief today, Mr. Hoover?

But Hoover was well interested in this cause. Hoover, together with Roosevelt and the imperialists of America and England, was responsible for egging Finland on to perform aggressive acts on the Finnish border, which resulted in the death of Red Army patrols there.

Yes, Hoover hopes to add to his fame, his humanitarian efforts for the rich of Finland. But since we're talking of fame, let us not forget to give Hoover his due. He has one outstanding action to his credit, not often told.

Hoover may have sent your grandmother, or my aunt on a segregated freighter which was really a cattle boat to France. You remember the Gold Star mothers, who were Negroes, went over in a cattle boat provided by Hoover, to see the graves of their dead sons.

Wasn't This a War for Democracy?

Thousands of sons of Negro mothers were also led to believe that joining the Army, fighting for Uncle Sam, would help to win them freedom. For after all, wasn't this a war for democracy?

It was no wonder then, that in 1917, when an NAACP editorial called for support of Negro Americans in the newly declared war, that Negro America, as in the past, "closed ranks" in support of American democracy.

Stories of Jim Crow treatment of Negro men in arms seep through even the most conservative journals. No matter what their qualifications, Negroes were given the most disagreeable jobs. Negro professionals were taken out of their ratings and given jobs as labourers, while white doctors were assigned to Negro troops.

Jim Crow in Uniform

Did you know that Negro soldiers in uniform were stoned, jeered and mobbed on the streets? The 8th Illinois, on the way to Texas, suffered such treatment. When the 92nd Division, at Camp Funston, Texas, refused to recognize the Jim Crow line at local theatres, the notorious Bulletin 35 was issued by the white commanding officer which read, "*Don't go where your presence is not desired. White men made the Division and they can break it just as easily if it becomes a troublemaker.*"

It is a historical fact that in Houston, Texas, where the 24th Infantry was stationed, members of the provost guard had to endure the humiliation of going about their duties unarmed. Local white policemen disregarded their authority constantly. The famed "Houston Affair," which resulted in the killing of 18 persons, is another example of Jim Crow in uniform. Court martial proceedings, which followed this incident, without War Department review, resulted in the hanging of 13 (not even granted the usual military death by shooting), 41 got life, 4 short terms and 5 were acquitted.

The nation-wide protests which followed this and other "troublemaker" actions, forced the Wilson Administration to pass a statute which declared that soldiers were not to be executed without War Department review. But this was not the only verdict resulting from Houston. The people also gave one.

Significantly, many white soldiers from the north protested such treatment of their brother soldiers.

Anti-War Sentiment Among Negroes

But these protests only climaxed the great anti-war sentiments and agitation for Negro rights which punctuated the response of the Negro people to broken promises from the start of the war.

Most of the historical books written about the Negroes' participation in the First World War give the impression that nowhere was there any anti-war sentiment expressed among the Negroes. This omission is designed to keep the false halo of complacency about the Negroes, wishfully expressed by reactionary historians.

Before America's entry into war, for instance, in 1915, great protest developed around the premiere of "Birth of a Nation." Even the reactionaries argued – for their own purposes, it is true – that this play developed antagonisms between whites and Negroes. Already then, preparations for America's entry into war were on the way. Today, "Gone with the Wind" typifies the same, though subtler, slander of the Negro people and is designed to whip up the war spirit of hysteria and race prejudice.

One of the most significant protests, recorded in the Negro Year Book of 1918–1919, was a parade of some 5,000 Negroes along Fifth Avenue in New York, held on July 28, 1917, in demonstration of the indignities which Negroes suffered in this war "to make the world safe for democracy." The parade bore such banners, with slogans: "Make America Safe for Democracy"; "Taxation Without Representation Is Tyranny"; "America Has Lynched Without Trial 2,876 Negroes in 31 Years and Not a Single Murderer Has Suffered"; "Put the Spirit of Christ in the Making and Execution of the Laws."

Further evidence of anti-war sentiment among the Negro people is unwittingly brought out in a letter written to George Cacel, chairman of the Committee on Public Information in Washington, by Trumbull White, of the Investors' Public Service in New York, informing him that:

> "...The big Negro colony in Harlem is badly infected with a series of rumors arousing great distress and disquiet... The rumors are of various kinds... One is that the Negro regiments are being terribly abused by their white officers. Another is that the Negro regiments are being discriminated against in the distribution of troops where the danger and suffering will be the greatest...Another is that already more than 200 Negro soldiers with eyes gouged out and arms cut off, after having been captured by Germans and then turned loose by them to wander back to the American lines have been sent home to this country and are now in the Columbia Base Hospital, No. 1 in the Bronx..."* (*The American Negro in the War, by Emmett J. Scott).

He concludes his letter by making two recommendations. One, that a permit be arranged for a Negro preacher, doctor and an "intelligent" Negro woman from Harlem be sent to the hospital for complete inspection. And the others that preferably, Irvin Cobb, lecture in Harlem on the subject of Negro troops in France since "Cobb has the Southern affection for the Negro and could do the thing right."

It is obvious that things were not right either at home or in France and the Negroes were answering back with protest and signs of discontent.

Other outstanding examples of anti-war sentiment would include the work of William Monroe Trotter, progressive Negro editor of the Boston Guardian who, during the war, fought in his columns against America's participation in the war and the treatment of Negroes. Among the outstanding present-day leaders who protested against the injustices was James W. Ford, now an outstanding leader of the Communist Party, its present candidate for Vice-President of the United States, then with the 8th Brigade of the 92nd Division in France, in 1918. And foremost against the imperialist war was, Earl Browder, now general secretary of the Communist Party of the United States and its candidate for President, who went to Leavenworth prison because he spoke against the war.

Commissioning of Officers and "High Blood Pressure" Removal

Have you ever heard of Col. Charles E. Young, highest ranking Negro West Point graduate? But, even though it was before our time, you probably didn't hear of him, because he was suddenly retired, supposedly because of "high blood pressure" when American entered the last World War.

He was returned to active service soon after. You know, that after once having been retired, you need not necessarily be considered for promotion.

It is to be wondered if all the "high blood pressure" wasn't that of certain super-patriotic gentlemen, which rose at the thought of a Negro officer being promoted to a high position in *their* army over the heads of many white officers. Equality is at a premium *even* for black men in most armies.

Most of the 1,200 Negro officers who were commissioned during the war were in Jim Crow regiments. It was the pressure of the Negro and white progressives against the quartering of troops in the South which led to the establishment of the first Negro officers' training camp at Ft. Des Moines, Iowa, from which 275 Negro officers were commissioned.

Such was the treatment accorded Negro men in arms at home in this "war for democracy." What could they expect fighting for American democracy abroad?

Men of Colour Abroad

Negro troops in France numbered a small percentage of the AEF, but they furnished 75 per cent of the AEF's labour supply. Given the stevedore jobs, in the main, they were used to doing road building, loading and unloading ships, and cars, building depots, re-burying the dead, and detonating scattered explosives.

The Negro troops who fought, however, were outstanding. The 8th Illinois (part of 92nd Division), officered by Negroes, received more citations and Croix de Guerres than any other regiment in France.

"Secret Information" and Slander Against Negroes in France

Carter G. Woodson, in his book, *Negroes In the World War* exposes certain "Secret Information Concerning Black American Troops," August 7, 1918, issued in a document by American reactionaries in France. He writes:

> "...The Negroes were branded as a menace of degeneracy which could be escaped only by an impassable gulf established between the two races."
>
> "This was an urgent need because of the tendency of the blacks to commit the loathsome crime of assault, as they said Negroes had already been doing in France.

The French was therefore cautioned not to treat the Negroes with familiarity and indulgence, which are matters of grievous concern to Americans and an affront to their national policy. The Americans, it continued, were afraid that the blacks might thereby be inspired with undesirable aspirations. It was carefully explained that although the black man is a citizen of the United States, he is regarded by whites as an inferior with whom relations of business and service are only possible; and that the black is noted for his want of intelligence, lack of discretion, and lack of civic and professional conscience. The French army was then advised to prevent intimacy between the French officers and black officers, not to eat with them nor shake hands nor seek to talk or meet with them outside the requirements of military service.

"They were asked also not to commend too highly the black American troops in the presence of white Americans... The French were urged also to restrain the native cantonment of population from spoiling the Negroes, as white Americans become greatly incensed at any deep expression of intimacy between white women and black men."

The Returned Negro Soldier

The Noble Sissles, the John Henrys, all the Negroes who returned came back to learn that the percentage of lynchings had increased during the war years. Total 96: 38 in 1917, 58 in 1918! Five were Negro women! When five Negro soldiers were lynched in uniform, the last remnant of belief faded for hundreds of returned Negro soldiers and their families.

The post-war crisis, causing race riots, because reaction played Negro against white, native against foreign-born, lynched the returned Negro soldier economically.

To his great surprise, after fighting "for democracy abroad" the returned Negro soldier found it still had to be fought for at home. Democracy had to be won for Negroes too. Bitter, yet undaunted, he began to learn that it could only be won with the help of other workers. Negro and white workers began to organize while rebuilding wastes of the war here at home.

Just and Unjust Wars

Today, with the Second Imperialist War raging in Europe and Asia, Negro youth face almost a similar situation as that preceding America's entry into the last World War.

However, unlike Jesse Clipper, we have a chance to contrast the experiences of Negroes during the First World War and also in wars since then.

All wars, for example, are not fought for a false democracy, as was the First World War for empire, or the present war between Germany and England. Didn't we support Ethiopia? It was because they were genuinely fighting for democracy, for their independence, against the intervention and brutal aggression of Fascist Italy. At that time, the governments of France and England and the United States did nothing to stop Mussolini's brutal aggression.

Another such genuinely democratic war was the war of the Spanish people against the fascist Franco and his cronies, Hitler and Mussolini.

That is why the returned Negro and white youth speak only with pride of their service across in Spain. Ask such men as Walter Garland, who rose to the rank of lieutenant in that army. Ask the brave young Ethiopian fighter who fought in Spain "to get the murderer, Mussolini, in his lair." Ask Sterling Rochester, Negro machine-gunner and hero.

Today in China, Chinese people for over two and one-half years have been heroically fighting a genuine war for democracy, against Japanese imperialism, backed by 80 per cent of American products.

These are wars of national liberation. These wars are modern versions of the type of wars that Toussaint L'Ouverture fought for the independence of the black thousands in Haiti.

Enemies of Peace

There are many enemies of peace. There are those who cry peace and simultaneously stir up racial hatred and intolerance. There are those who cry "civil liberties for all" and proceed to deny to Communists and others, their civil rights. Where was Dies in the case of Angelo Herndon? Or the Scottsboro boys? He has been a Congressman for some twenty-two years, now.

We can record many instances of the rise of anti-Negro violence, to a higher pitch today. Only recently from South Carolina came reports of several vicious attacks on Negro citizens exercising their constitutional right to vote.

Yes the KKK rides Again with "Gone with the Wind" in the Saddle.

But anti-Negro violence is limited not alone to the South. For over two years, John Williams, 23-year-old Brooklyn Negro youth, was confined to prison on a trumped-up charge of rape, despite the fact that the decision was twice set aside by the Appellate Division of the Supreme Court.

The jury, which did not have a single Negro on it, found John Williams guilty and he was sentenced to 7 ½ to 15 years.

At the second trial the presiding judge was the anti-Negro, anti-labour Justice Peter J. Brancato. In passing sentence, the judge declared: *"I would give him 20 years if I could. Remember she is a white woman."*

On June 17, as a result of the mass fight against this northern "Scottsboro Case," John Williams was released.

This is a major victory for civil liberties of Negroes and for that matter, for all progressives today, in the face of reaction's drive to war, led by the Roosevelt Administration.

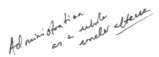
Administration as a whole effect

That is why the reactionary District Attorney O'Dwyer of Brooklyn met the delegation of the Communist Party and Young Communist League, who brought 10,000 signatures to him, demanding the release of Williams, with the words:

> **"Millions of American boys will shed their blood before this war is over and there will be plenty of 'black boys' too."**

Out? or in?

It is clear that the fight for civil liberties is inherently connected with the fight to keep America out of the imperialist war.

Just imagine what such action would mean on a national scale against the war. Remember reaction wants a divided people in order to drive more quickly to war!

Fight the War Every Inch of the Way!

We don't want to wait until the war is upon us. This was the mistake that the youth made in 1914. Whether it is a question of the high cost of living, whether it is a question of sale of arms and planes, whether it is a question of loans to the belligerents, to foreign registry, or attempts of British propagandists, on "visits" to America who are trying to sell us their cause, whether it is the apologists who speak for British imperialism while invoking the good name of the colonial people, whether it is the newspapers who would feed us a blind pro-Ally allegiance, we must fight the war-makers every inch of the way!

The young dead that lie in Flanders Field are telling us everyday, "Don't Raise Another Generation of Poppy Sellers!" "Fight the War Every Inch of the Way." Young Jesse Clipper is telling us "Keep alive to get a job, to marry, to raise a family!" "Keep alive to demand passage of the American Youth Act, which would bring permanent federal aid to youth!" "Keep alive to free the four Scottsboro boys!" "Keep alive by fighting the war profiteers!" "Keep alive to get the Anti-Lynching and Geyer Poll Tax Repeal Bills passed!"

Young People Against the War

As a matter of fact young people are already doing some of these things. All the major youth organizations have gone on record against the war as an imperialist war. The American Youth Congress, the American Student Union, The United Student Peace Committee and the Southern Negro Youth Congress have taken such a stand in their resolutions.

These anti-war resolutions of the youth and of the Negro people are but reflections of the broad anti-war sentiments among the whole American people.

In Harlem, South Side of Chicago, and other communities, young Negro people have been active in declaring that they want no part of the European war. They have specifically pointed to the need for conducting a fight for civil rights, for jobs, democracy and peace. This is the only war that they are interested in, as was so ably demonstrated in the historical Third National Negro Congress when they rejected the path of the former progressive, A. Phillip Randolph to choose support of reaction by supporting the Roosevelt Administration, by supporting anti-Soviet schemes, by preaching segregation for the Negro *and chose instead* the path toward working with labour, through Labour's Non-Partisan League, who has now agreed to make passage of the Anti-Lynching Bill the first job of labour!

What You Can Do   *Ida B. Wells*
facts

You can help spread the truth as to what kind of a war is being fought today. You can help to educate young people to the fact that the Roosevelt Administration and the Republican Parties, twin parties of reaction are dragging America to war. You can help keep America out of war.

You will find that you are not alone in doing this, for right in your own community, you will find an organization, willing and ready to help you achieve this.

This organization is the Young Communist League, an organization of and for American young people, who look forward to a better future. There is no future in Flanders Field. All youth, regardless of race, creed, or colour, belong to and are equals in this organization.

The Young Communist League fights for the interests of the toiling youth and the working class. It fights against imperialist war. It fights against the discrimination of Negro youth. It fights for the economic betterment of Negro youth for jobs and security.

The League opposes all measures aimed at the militarization of the youth. It opposes the militarization of the CCC camps, the extension of the ROTC, especially on a compulsory basis: the proposed increase in the Army and National Guard, the M-Day plan. Its guiding slogan is:

> "Not a Man, Not a Cent, Not a Gun for Imperialist War Preparations!"

We believe that our ideals can best be achieved by socialism, by establishing a new social order in which the working people will own and control all the vast natural resources and means of production and use them for the benefit of all the people, instead of the few.

The Soviet Union – Home of Free Peoples

Look here, fellows and girls, this system called capitalism, with all of its talk of free enterprise is free, all right but for the bankers and Wall Street, for the German bankers, for the Bank of England, for the French bankers. Can you dream what it would mean to have the worry of a job eliminated? What if it was law that your security, your job, was guaranteed? Then you could finish high school, college. Then you could marry, raise a family, get that coat, that radio, that library you always wanted. This is what the youth of the Soviet Union have because they live in a socialist society. That is why the bankers want to take it away from them.

All roads are open to youth of the Soviet Union.

There is no national or racial oppression in the Soviet Union and in the USSR people of all nationalities, all colours, live as free and equal peoples.

All young people are guaranteed free education in the USSR to the age of 18. Equal opportunity exists for all.

For millions of us darker peoples, for oppressed peoples throughout the world, the Soviet Union stands as a beacon of light, hope and truth!

While the majority of the people in America today are not for socialism, they are willing to work in common with those who similarly desire such things as jobs, security, democracy and peace. That is why we Young Communists stand together with the majority of American youth – Negro and white, who desire above all *PEACE*, so that they can pursue the American dream of "life, liberty and the pursuit of happiness."

Negro America remembers the false promises of the last war. They are saying The Yanks Are Not Coming.

The dream we mentioned earlier, can become a reality. In the course of the struggle for these things, we will learn that these can only be achieved and kept in a more permanent society – Socialism.

We support no dreams of war abroad. We go to the wars at home. For jobs and civil liberties! For democracy and freedom!

Jesse Clipper, Negro hero, died believing he was doing his share to make the world safe for democracy. If Jesse Clipper were alive today, he would again fight for democracy. He would do it, however, not by following the loans of Wall Street to another Flanders Field, but by fighting for jobs, for relief, for better housing, better healthy conditions – security for the people. We must make the world safe for democracy by making democracy safe for America. This is Jesse Clipper's dream now. We, the living, take our stand today on the side of *Life and Peace*.

a lot of thinking for Clipper

New Problems of the Negro Youth Movement (1940)

Significant new developments are today <u>apparent</u> in the <u>Negro youth movement</u> as a result of the outbreak of the second imperialist war. Fresh problems have arisen, not only for the <u>achievement</u> of a greater Negro youth movement, but also raising <u>serious dangers</u> which threaten it.

To begin with, the conditions of the Negro people and their youth have become <u>greatly aggravated</u> since the outbreak of the war. While the attacks on the democratic rights and civil liberties of the American people are being severely felt by them, the <u>attacks on the doubly oppressed Negro masses</u> have <u>increased</u>. The howling mob of lynchers have given way to the <u>silent</u> new technique of lynching, resulting for instance in 20 <u>silent lynchings</u> in Mississippi, alone, and already four known lynch deaths have been cited by the International Labour Defense since 1940.

This technique is put in effect while the pen-pushers of reaction <u>blandly</u> maintain that the crime of lynching is non-existent, that the past year has been a "lynchless" year. A more subtle from of anti-Negro violence is typified in the Selznick four million dollar movie, "<u>Gone With the Wind</u>," which depicts Negroes as "<u>lazy, good-for-nothings</u>" who were sorry slavery was eliminated and which, moreover, is an attempt to whip up war hysteria and race prejudice.

Direct quote from last essay

The Ku Klux Klan rides again in the South as well as the North. Witness the case of youthful <u>John Williams</u>, Negro, who was kept imprisoned on a false charge of "rape" after having twice been declared not guilty by the State Supreme Court. Side by side with this picture of anti-Negro violence, is the tragedy of <u>Natchez, Mississippi,</u> in which over 240 Negro youth were killed. Natchez stands as a reminder to all Americans that Negroes in America are still economically, politically and socially "disfranchised."

The desertion of the New Deal by Roosevelt hit the Negro people and Negro youth with particular impact. There is not a single Negro community in which the war and hunger budget of Roosevelt has not left disaster in its train, with its cuts in relief and WPA.

The Liberation Movement

There is a growing militancy evidenced among the Negro people and the Negro youth symbolized particularly in the <u>Third National Negro Congress</u> which in the forefront of the struggle for Negro rights, took a stand against the imperialist war, against the war and hunger budget and called upon the Negro people to rally for jobs and civil liberties, for democracy and for keeping America out of war, in conjunction with organized labour through a working agreement with Labour's Non-Partisan League.

As against these progressive developments, which are but a reflection of the strong deep-seated anti-war sentiments among the Negro people as a whole, there is evidenced the attempts of reaction by the so-called leaders of the Negro people such as Walter White and Roy Wilkins of the NAACP, who live by the hands of the former liberal bourgeoisie, to win the Negro people and youth for the support of American imperialism. There are others like W.A. Domingo, who attempt to rally, consciously or not, the support of the Negro people under the false banner of the "lesser evil" theory with its variations of "fighting for democracy" under the banner of British imperialism. Comrade Winston in the first issue of *Clarity* dealt with some of these trends and arguments. It is my purpose to deal not with these, but with the present aspects of the Negro youth movement in relation to these changes.

Since 1936, with the inauguration of the first National Negro Congress, the movement for unity of the Negro people has been given impetus and developed in the main around community issues such as jobs, civil liberties, democracy and peace. The growth of the NNC was largely responsible for the development of community councils and federations of Negro youth in every major Negro community in the nation and most outstanding for the initiation of that growing movement of southern youth, the Southern Negro Youth Congress.

The American Youth Congress centre of all organized youth movements in the United States, too, has been responsible for the growing participation of Negro youth organizations in the larger issues of the nation, as was seen in the participation of over 200 Negro youth in the recent Youth Institute of Washington, DC.

But the new high in the Negro liberation movement was evidenced in its developing alliance with labour. It is seen in the direction of the struggle against the main enemies of the people as a whole, in the development for the first time of an articulate, anti-imperialist, anti-war front of the Negro people's organizations. It is seen in the rejection of the path that A. Phillip Randolph, former president of the National Negro Congress, would have had the Congress take, in which he urged them to "cast down their buckets where they are," in which he urged support of imperialism, in an attempt to win the Negro delegates at the Congress for anti-Soviet statements in his address.

Toward Negro Youth Unity

This new high in the Negro liberation movement has its counterpart in the new trend, which is developing in the Negro youth movement, *towards a movement for national unification of Negro youth organizations in a national Negro youth movement.* All fighters for Negro youth rights and Negro liberation will welcome such a step which was initiated by a Committee of 100 which was set up at the Youth Institute meeting in the District of Columbia for that purpose. Unity of Negro youth is necessary first of all today, in order to defeat the threatening reaction, which is stimulated by the war situation. It is necessary in order to protect the threatened civil liberties, economic needs and democratic rights of Negro youth; it is necessary in order to organize the thousands of unorganized Negro youth; to serve as an important ally of the growing organized movement of youth, symbolized in the American Youth Congress which in turn can help serve as an important barrier against America's being dragged into participation in Europe's imperialist war. *This movement for national unification is the first new factor of importance with regard to the Negro youth movement.*

This new orientation was seen two years ago and was expressed in some circles when the growth of community activities and community conferences began to more and more become conferences not alone of "council" but of "action." It received an additional spurt when Negro and white unity around such issues as the rights of Negroes to play professional baseball in the big leagues developed. When on the campuses of Lincoln and Missouri State Universities, for the entrance of Lloyd Gaines to the School of Law, which resulted in reversing the decision by the US Supreme Court upholding the federal right of the petitioner, Lloyd Gaines, for legal education in the Missouri State University. This decision marked a new milestone in the struggle of the Negro for increased educational opportunities, which was won through initiative of the Negro youth on campus, together with Negro and white unity. Support for the national unity of Negro youth organizations developed further with the convening in the summer of 1938 of the World Youth Congress, which for the first time brought representatives of Negro youth together on a world scale and which made the American delegation of Negro youth more conscious as to their responsibilities to the colonial youth of the West Indies and other coloured youth of India and Africa, who look towards the Negro youth movement in America as their hope and support. Subsequent national gatherings through the facilities of the Youth Congress and regional gatherings of the Southern Negro Youth Congress furthered this orientation.

In the words of some of the members of the Committee of 100, "*Negro youth want a vehicle of national scope in which to express their aspirations, their needs, their hopes.*" In all of this participation around local, domestic and international issues, there is an ever-growing, rising militancy among the Negro youth of the nation. *Such is the second new factor in the Negro youth movement.*

This militancy is expressed in approval of such a step towards national unification it is expressed in the awakening interest and participation of Negro

— 44 —

youth at the National Negro Congress, where they numbered 31 per cent of the nearly 2,000 delegates. The majority of these organized Negro youth groups have expressed through their federations and councils that they are against the imperialist war. They want to keep America out of war and they are becoming more alert so as to be able to distinguish as to who are their friends and who are their enemies, regardless of whether these people were former progressives.

It was on the basis of such sentiment that the Youth Council of the National Negro Congress, a body of 25 Negro and white youth throughout the country, was set up at the Third National Negro Congress, in order to work for educating Negro youth in the ideals and principles of the National Negro Congress and to further assist the Committee of 100 youth in developing sentiment and interest for the convening of a national conference of Negro youth representatives, to launch a national Negro youth organization.

Community Action

But such a movement will only come about and will only be successful to the degree that increasing masses of Negro youth are involved in working for its achievement. It will only get that degree of success, if leading up to the establishment of such an organization, actions on a state, local and community scale are initiated around the burning issues of the youth in that particular community or locality. There is need for dramatizing the plight of Negro youth today, not alone in a general way but on specific issues. Negro youth throughout the country today feel that acute brunt of the war crisis, in the effects of the war and hunger budget of the Administration through the cuts in relief and WPA. Young Negro men and women living with their families, unable to get jobs, are denied the benefits of single maintenance on WPA or relief. Young women domestics under the usual exploitation of their jobs, find it increasingly hard to get along since it is thrown up to them by their employers that they can't do better since there is no more relief, anyway. Discrimination of Negro youth is on the increase in the communities today, especially because of the war situation and reaction is welding more solidly its divide-and-rule tactic. Negro youth are deeply interested in the cause of peace, in the cause of keeping America out of war. They are interested in doing something about the anti-lynching bill, in the passage of the Geyer Anti-Poll Tax Bill, they are interested in the coming 1940 elections.

It is around these and other such concrete issues, wherever they may exist, that the Negro youth movement will be able to weld unity and draw increasing numbers of unorganized Negro youth into its ranks. Action around these issues should not be limited to old forms of conferences alone, which remain important, but simultaneously, there must be devised new forms of dramatic mass action in the communities, that can serve together as a powerful educational lever for all who witness it.

Most important, if this development is to be realized, it will be necessary that the youth movement develop and re-convene job campaign committee activities, in an independent fashion. These will redirect its activities against the monopolies and public utilities, like the American Telephone and Telegraph Company, which takes millions of dollars from the Negro people yearly, but does not have jobs for Negro boys and girls. And activity and education must be developed simultaneously in the Negro youth movement around passage and support for the passage of the American Youth Act, which can be the instrument around which a realistic job struggle and campaign can be won. Special brochures on "What the Passage of the American Youth Act Will Mean to Negro Youth" can be the beginning of a broad educational campaign, which will find fruits in the Negro youth movement's activities.

A further new factor of importance with regard to new problems of the Negro youth movement and one also bred of the war situation, is the type of attention being given by many mouthpieces of capital to the problems of Negro people and the Negro youth movement. Some of them, sensing the growing deep anti-war sentiment of the people, attempt to lull it by presenting the plight of the Negro masses in our American democracy as if it were not so bad after all. The purpose of this manner of treatment is obvious. It is to prepare the ground for an easier organization of the Negro people's sentiments to "close ranks" again for American imperialism abroad. Others more wisely see the need for reaction paying some attention to the plight of the Negro youth, since they are aware of the growing progressive outlook of the Negro people in every sphere of their existence, in order to win them away from unity and progress with labour, and with the white working class.

An example of the latter is seen in the article, "The Story Behind Native Son," which appeared in the May 21st issue of *Look* Magazine, which, in a photograph study of Harlem's "244,000 Native Sons," says that the pictures *"disclose the essentials of Negro existence in any American City — whether it be New York City or South Chicago.* It is not pleasant, it continues – this story of how thousands of our fellow citizens live, under conditions which often produce vice and crime – but it is a story which every socially-minded American must contemplate.

The Pittsburgh *Catholic*, in its May 2nd edition, calls attention to *"the long neglect and worse, of which Americans in general have been guilty with respect to the problems of their coloured fellow citizens and brothers, has created a rare opening for Communists and it is not surprising that they have had considerable success in winning followers. Evidence of this success was apparent at the recent National Negro Congress and at the All-Southern Negro Youth Conference in New Orleans. A distinctly Communistic trend was observable at both gatherings. There should be no impatience or anger at this development. Rather there should be a fresh determination that the influence of Catholicism shall be more strongly exerted in the Negro's behalf. And this influence must take the basic forms of justice and charity."*

Certainly the dubbing of the National Negro Congress and the Southern

Negro Youth Congress's decisions as "communistic" are the attempts of the Catholic hierarchy to dissuade Negro Catholics from participating, but it is interesting to note that the developments of these movements have forced even the hierarchy to take note of the Negro's plight, more consciously. On such a development, on such statements, the Negro youth movements in the localities can for instance, query the local Catholic Church in Harlem which withdrew its support from the list of organizations supporting the drive for organized baseball in New York City. In such a manner will the Negro youth movement be able to bring into active participation the young Negro Catholics into the organized youth movement.

Catholic Youth Sentiment

Significant also, are the recent writings of a student from Xavier University, published in the *"As Youth Sees It"* column of the *Interracial Review*, a Catholic monthly in Harlem, which gives Catholic Negro student youth sentiment with regard to the European war.

The student writes:

> The general trend of thinking here at Xavier, as I don't doubt that it has been on most college campuses, has been expressive of a strong keep America out sentiment. True, few of us know or profess to know just how America can be kept out of war, for we are aware of the intricate economies involved in the formulation of foreign policy, but we are almost unanimous in voicing the opinion that under no conditions other than actual invasion, should America enter the present war.

Speaking further of the sympathies of certain Americans for an Allied victory, he writes:

> In discussing the attitude of most young Negroes with whom I have had conversations relative to the war, however, it is necessary to qualify this pro-Allied sentiment; for it does not grow out of an admiration of England, but rather out of a distrust of Germany.

The article goes on and expresses confusion with regard to the Soviet-German pact but ends with:

> But any inclination that we may have to sympathize with England finds difficulty in expressing itself when we begin to recall England's policies in India and her other colonial possessions. To be

sure many of us have difficulty in differentiating between Germany's present policies and England's consistent disregard of justice and principle in her treatment of her colonials of darker hue. When we remember that England actually took India, that her interests have been for the greatest part the enrichment and glory of the 'Empire' and that under the whip of the British military the people of India have been no less than the cringing slaves of unbelievable cruel commercialists, our pro-Ally ardor dampens considerably...

Such is the typical sentiment among large numbers of Negro youth outside the organized Negro youth movement, who as yet do not understand the similarity of all imperialists today, who do not know that the people's solution, is the third alternative, the only way out. In all of its activities, the Negro youth movement if it is to remain independent, if it is to be a progressive movement, must constantly educate the youth as to the false ideological arguments put forward by reaction today, to win Negro youth again to fight for a "false democracy." But more and more Negro youth are saying: We refuse to become cannon fodder for the Maginot and Westwall lines. The only line we are interested in smashing is the one here at home – the Mason-Dixon line.

New Features of Negro Youth Movement

Such was the sentiment expressed at the historic Fourth All-Southern Negro Youth Congress which branded the European war as an imperialist war, which pledged solidarity with the colonial youth of India, Africa and the West Indies, which in its programme for Southern Negroes urged all America *"To hear our voices, we of the Southland, we the dispossessed of the land . . . "* It went on record for the development of an even broader citizenship, right-to-vote campaign, in which passage of the anti-lynching and Geyer poll tax repeal bill are the kernel of the campaign. Such sentiments are to be found in the major Negro youth federations in the north, of which the Harlem Youth Congress, the Philadelphia Youth Council of the National Negro Congress and the recently formed Connecticut Youth Federation are the most outstanding.

The major new features of the Negro youth movement, all produced and developed by the war situation are therefore:

> *(a) A new trend towards the development of a movement for national unification of Negro youth organizations into a national Negro youth movement. (b) There is an ever-growing rising militancy among the Negro youth of the nation to fight for their needs: jobs, security and civil liberties. (c) The new attempts of reaction through giving attention to the problems of the Negro youth movement to therefore*

lull the fight against them and to dissuade the trend of Negro youth to progressive and labour leadership.

Not alone does big capital and reaction attempt to appeal to the Negro youth today, but if we are to really fight against false ideologies, which are attempting to pervade the Negro youth movement, we must point out the influence and attempts of Social-Democracy to poison the minds of Negro youth. Social-Democracy finds its expression among the Negro youth as it does in the ranks of the labour movement, in the form of petty-bourgeois nationalism today.

Imperialist war is chauvinism and coupled with the bourgeois attempts to divide the people on the basis of prejudices, which they themselves foster, we find the servants of the bourgeoisie spreading nationalism among the Negro youth today.

How does this express itself? Mainly through the leadership of the nation-alists who preach the ideology of separatism for the Negro people and their youth. When we consider the pro-Ally statements of such leaders as Roy Wilkins and Walter White together with their anti-Soviet incitements, it is clear that even if they are not organizationally connected with Social-Democracy, in effect they express and give voice to their ideas. It is seen in the manner in which they raise the question of discrimination and Jim Crowism of Negroes in the army, today, which in effect says: *"Give us a break"* and we will support the war. But this is not the issue at all – rather directing the attention of Negro youth to the real character of the war, which is imperialist, which they can help stop, by keeping America out of war, by fighting against reaction here at home, against discrimi-nation socially, economically, politically.

There is need to expose such arguments before the Negro youth today. There is need to make clear that there is no such thing as "healthy" nationalism for nationalism today serves reaction, which encourages the idea of separatism of people in order to more quickly exploit and drive them disunited to imperialist war. It is in the recognition of the fact that nationalism finds its social base among the petty-bourgeoisie, that we must *"explain, explain and again explain,"* in the words of Comrade Dimitroff, the true character of the imperialist war, the need for unity of Negro and white against the war, to these sections of the Negro people, if we would keep America out of war, if we would win the Negro youth for a firm anti-imperialist position.

Overcoming Weaknesses

These major new features dictate, however, the need for correcting many weaknesses, which are apparent in the Negro youth movement. For while the influences of the progressive developments in the field of labour, the youth movement of the American Youth Congress and the Negro adult liberation movement are felt among the Negro youth, the influence of reaction in the form of opportunism is apparent. It takes such form as was seen in the Illinois Youth Congress, in which former progressive leaders of this movement did their best to squelch discussion on the character of the war by the young Negro people of Illinois in conference. It is seen in the attempts of certain youth leaders to "go easy" on peace activities because it may jeopardize their present jobs; something which they anticipate in case America goes to war, despite the overwhelming anti-war sentiments of over 95 per cent of the American people. Such people must be exposed as misleaders of the youth, as careerists, who hope to grow prosperous as a result of the slaughter of the sons of Negro people.

To some extent this opportunism has been responsible for the second weakness of the Negro youth movement, which is the lack of consistent struggle on the part of local Negro youth federations and councils around the needs of the youth. The leadership of the Negro youth movement in addition is for the most part burdened with too many responsibilities, leaving little time for them to take time and thought in developing a real mass movement of Negro youth in the communities. There is need for more alertness on the part of Negro youth leaders to the sentiments and needs of the young Negroes in their communities, in taking hold of issues which, Negro youth will fight for, the main ones of which are jobs, civil liberties, security and peace. To the extent that these weaknesses are corrected, to that extent will the Negro youth accept the leadership of the Negro youth movement more fully. The Negro youth movement will have to begin concretely to struggle to win the demands of the Negro youth if they are to chalk up victories for them. It is true that many federations have made significant improvements in this regard, such as the Harlem Youth Congress, the Connecticut Federation of Youth and the Brooklyn Negro Youth Council of the American Youth Congress, but as yet the trend is still weak.

The Role of the YCL

The perspectives of the Negro youth movement are greater than they have ever been before. Negro young people are making their voices heard and are looking for leadership. Our Negro Young Communists, because of their understanding and loyalty to the Negro youth needs, have done much to make the YCL an accepted part of the broad movement of Negro youth. Our weaknesses take the main form in our failure to recruit the many progressive and active contacts who are already convinced of our position on the major issues today and who follow our leadership. A change is essential if we intend seriously to rally Negro youth for continued progressive action.

The coming 1940 elections, of major importance for all progressives of America, must bring the Negro youth movement into fuller activities than ever before. It will be the task of the Negro youth movement largely, to rally and win the Negro youth away from the leadership of the twin parties of reaction, for independent action, for a third party.

The establishment of a National Federation of Negro Youth will mean the development of an ideological unity of Negro youth against the war, for peace, for keeping America out of war. It will mean bringing into organized action the hundreds of thousands of unorganized Negro youth under progressive leadership. It will mean developing to a new high the cultural heritage of Negro youth. It will mean the heightening of Negro and white youth unity. White young people can give impetus and practical aid to the Negro youth movement by cooperation, by being informed on the new developments and by struggling for the needs of Negro youth. Negro young people must more and more participate in the unity movement of youth, symbolized in the American Youth Congress, to provide the broadest possible inclusion of the problems of Negro youth in the organized youth movement. Only through such a process will Negro and white unity become a real developing process that will prevent any attempts on the part of reaction for a divided youth movement.

These new developments of the Negro youth, with their advanced programmes for peace, citizenship, the right to vote, passage of the anti-lynching and Geyer poll tax repeal bills, for job security, puts them in line with the developing anti-imperialist, anti-war front.

Lift Every Voice – For Victory (1942)[14]

Remember June 22, 1938? The eyes and ears of the world were turned on a fighting ring in Yankee Stadium Joe Louis world heavyweight champion, dealt an opponent a knockout blow that was heard 'round the world.

For the opponent Louis kayoed was the Nazi hope, Max Schmeling.

The Nazis had called Joe Louis *"der sogennante weltmeister,"* – "the so-called champion."

In proud defiance of the Nazis' "Aryan" arrogance – the people everywhere, Negro and white, hoisted their own banners: – *"Hail Joe Louis, the People's Champion!"*

Joe was not alone in that fight...

Detroit, home town of Joe, proud of its world champion, cheered...

Harlem echoed the joy in the Stadium – indescribable joy that was marked in the flow of thousands to the streets...

And banners were everywhere:

"Take the Nazi Bum Back to Hitler!"
"Down with Hitler and Mussolini!"
"Joe Louis Wins, Hitler Weeps!"
"Who said "Aryan" Supremacy?"
"Alabama Produced Joe Louis, Free the Scottsboro Boys!"

Victory demonstrations in Pittsburgh... Cleveland... Philadelphia... Chicago... and elsewhere. Underlying the festivities was boundless anti-fascist solidarity of all the people. It symbolized the fight and the hatred of the peoples everywhere against fascism.

What Are You Fighting For, Joe?

"I'm fighting for my country," Joe Louis told reporters, who, on the occasion of the Louis Baer bout for Navy Relief, asked him why he was fighting "for nothing."

Joe's an army man now. He fights in a larger ring, a ring that covers the entire globe. And millions of people the world over are fighting with Joe in this battle. On Joe's side is Dorie Miller who, on May 11, was awarded the Navy Cross by President Roosevelt for conspicuous bravery at Pearl Harbour. On Joe's side is Lieutenant Bulkeley, holder of the Distinguished Service Cross, who sank a 5,000-ton Japanese ship on the west coast of Luzon Island.

The stakes in this fight overshadow by far the Louis-Schmeling bout of 1938. For the stakes are the freedom, progress and advancement of *all* humanity. We fight an enemy who is out to conquer the entire world, to destroy the freedom and independence of all nations and peoples, to enslave and as stated in *Mein Kampf*, to wipe out such peoples as the Negroes and Jews.

Joe Louis, native son of America, was born March 13, 1914, in a cabin on Buckalew Mountain in Alabama. At the age of 12, together with his parents, two brothers and three sisters, he came North. He had to leave school at the age of 14 to go to work. And many of the tasks known to young workers were Joe's tasks, delivering ice, selling papers and the like.

His fight for the championship was not easy. He had to fight against un-American sports writers who constantly sniped at him with tales that he was "slipping," that he "couldn't take it." Joe had a tough time of it, fighting both able challengers for his "crown" and also the barriers of discrimination that face any Negro youth.

Joe Louis is an American and proud of it. In spite of every handicap that still hinders him and other Negro Americans from giving their best efforts to the country's defense, Joe eagerly put on the uniform of the United States Army. Because it symbolizes, with the uniform of the British Tommy, the Red Army soldier, the Chinese guerilla, the Indian soldiers, the Ingorots and the Filipinos, everything that we are fighting for.

we're fighting for peace?

Joe's fighting for America – for all people. So that his people can get on a broader scale what he's battling to get: recognition, equality and fuller participation in the life of the nation as a whole.

Joe knows what he fights for. As he declared at the all-star show for Navy Relief: "I'm doing what any red-blooded American would.

Hitler Won't Fix It *Different Claudia?*

Joe Louis is a man of few words. But he said a mouthful when he declared: "There's a lot of things wrong with America but Hitler won't fix it." Joe is right. Even the thought of what Hitler fascism would mean to our beloved America proves that.

Our country's traditions of constitutional liberty and democratic rights would be lost. *no communism* There would be no labour unions, no people's organizations. And all youth would be taught the Nazi brute worship of force and "Aryan" superiority to replace everything that youth holds dear. Books would be burned, culture and science destroyed and perverted to work for fascism.

In the opinion of Hitler, Negroes are "latent brutes." This pictures vividly what the fate of Negro youth would be in the event of a Hitler victory. The policies of the Ku Klux Klan and the Black Legion would be the official policies of the government in Washington. No longer would the great voices of such outstanding Americans as Marian Anderson and Paul Robeson be heard. No longer would such great literary works as *Native Son* appear. Joe Louis would not be able to give the lie to "Aryan" supremacy. *just blots?*

Yes there are "things wrong with America." The existence of poll-tax laws, lynchings, and discriminatory practices are shameful blots on our democracy. But the opportunity to fight to abolish these things and to win victories by so doing is a part of our democracy today. The destruction of that democracy under Hitler would mean that our only law would be the "law" of the slavemaster; our only "rights" the rights of the slave.

Have Negro Americans reason to expect anything better as far as Hirohito is concerned?

Of course not! Japan is no more a champion of the darker peoples than Hitler is a champion of the world! Look at the record of Japan in Korea, Manchukuo and China! Moreover, Japan is a partner of the worst enemy of the Negro people – Hitler and of the bloody Italian fascist rapists of Ethiopia.

Hitler's pretense of being the champion of the "Aryans" has been drowned out in the blood of millions of Europeans of a dozen nations. And the Mikado's lie of being the "protector of darker races" is exposed by the barbarous war he wages against the darker peoples of the Far East. Both ends of the axis use the same method – to conceal the fact that both are the enemies of all decent people – white and coloured.

The only difference is like the difference between a snake's head and his tail. The Hitler end of the Axis is more poisonous and deadly. But if the serpent's head, Hitler, is crushed by the combined might of the great Red Army of the Soviet Union striking from the West, then the tail- end – Japan, can be taken care of relatively easily.

How ridiculous to call this a "white man's war," and how dangerous! This is our war. Joe's war. Your war and mine. It is a people's war to preserve the integrity and independence of our nation; to preserve the opportunity and the chance we have to fight for a better life; a war for freedom of all mankind so that men can once again think and breathe freely the whole world over.

Joe Louis – Symbol Of Patriotism Of All America

Joe's in there, doing his part, like so many thousands of Negro youth with their white buddies. Who will deny that Joe's contributions to Army and Navy relief helped to accomplish the gains made in beginning to break down discrimination in the Navy and the Army? Like Dorie Miller, Joe is the answer to our enemies within and without who claim that Negro Americans do not have an all-out stake in this war and aren't out to win it. They fight in the spirit of Crispus Attucks at Boston Commons, in the spirit of the thousands of Negro soldiers who fought at Gettysburg, in the spirit of the great Abraham Lincoln who at the demand of the people took the needed steps to unite the people and to win the war – the freeing of the slaves by the Emancipation Proclamation.

Yes, in the solid spirit of patriotism of Negro Americans. In the spirit of Frederick Douglass, who urged all-out support of the Negro people of that day to the war effort. Douglass urged all-out support by Negroes to the Civil War; urging coloured men to join the Union army and to fight for freedom and liberty. He declared the "logic of events" should convince all Negroes that their basic interests demanded their participation as fighters in the ranks of the Union Army.

Of the slave-holders' rebellion against the Union, Douglass stated: "A war undertaken for the permanent enslavement of coloured men and women, calls logically for coloured men and women to help suppress it."

If in the Civil War this was true, how much more true is it of this democratic war, when both Negro and white men and women are threatened with enslavement by fascism! No wonder then that Negro youth, as the Southern Negro Youth Congress at its recent Fifth Annual Conference, have pledged "full and unswerving loyalty and service" to the cause of the nation and its war effort.

"We Must Remove The Weight That Doth Beset Us"

In these words Paul Robeson, another great American and world-famous people's artist, in the midst of his concert programmes in a Kansas City auditorium, spoke out against lynching, poll taxes and all forces of discrimination, as injurious to the war effort.

Yes, we must remove the "weights" which hinder our war effort because they deprive the Negro people of full citizenship and participation in the war effort. Some of these hindrances are being removed as a result of the action by labour, government, progressive and people's organizations. To cite but a few examples: the hiring of Negro workers in aircraft and other war industries as a result of Executive Order 8802 and the President's Fair Employment Practices Committee.

The National Maritime Union, backed by the President, won the fight against the ship-holders, establishing the practice of mixed ship crews. Local 475, united Electrical, Radio and Machine Workers of America, CIO, only recently announced a policy, unanimously adopted by their executive board, that 10 per cent of all persons sent out for jobs from their hiring office will be Negroes.

The War Labour Board recently cited over twenty unions for their consistent work in securing jobs for Negro workers. These are the straws in the wind that show which way it is blowing. And it is a broad, sweet, democratic wind that is beginning to clear out of the way many of the barriers to fuller integration of the Negro people in our national life and in the war effort.

Joe Louis's hometown of Detroit symbolizes the great changes taking place. Joe used to work on the Ford assembly line. Now Detroit has become a great city of organized labour. Along the assembly lines working side-by-side are organized Negro and white workers, who produce the planes, guns and shells to defeat Hitler.

The shiny new planes that slide off some of the nation's belt lines in Douglas, Glenn Martin, Wright and other places to defeat Hitler are being built today with the hands of Negro and white youth. *Since experiments?*

For the first time in our history, Negro pilots, fly those planes. At the great air base in Tuskegee, Alabama, the Negro pilots are the pride of their people – of all America. These pilots tell you proudly of their service and of the fine planes they fly. They are lauded by their instructors as being as equally skilled and as capable as any pilots in the country.

In Detroit, Negro and white union workers together with the whole people are fighting to wipe out Klanism. Only recently, a Klan member, found to be holding a union card, was unanimously expelled from the union. It was this same union, the United Automobile Workers of America, that was instrumental in bringing about the victory at the Sojourner Truth Homes. Backed by the government, the Negro workers, supported by their white fellow Americans, defeated the Klan effort to exclude Negroes from this housing project built for them. Now they live in the Sojourner Truth Homes! Today the Ku Klux Klan is being investigated by the government. This and the investigation undertaken by the government of peonage, lynchings and poll-tax laws are more than timely. This is the way to defeat the enemies of the nation, who prefer to see a victory for Hitler than see full democracy extended for all people.

These are the signs of the time. And ever more vigorously the demand goes up from the Negro youth, from the ranks of labour, from among all patriotic people, that if America is to win the war, the doors must be opened even wider to Negro youth to enter into defense production, into the Army, Navy and Air Force on the basis of full equality. *This is something new.*

But more than that, the need to mobilize everything for the war, to produce, to fight, to win, requires that *new* gains be made.

Some among the Negro people say we need a "Double V" – a victory at home and abroad. The majority of Negro people who adopt this slogan do so because of the anti-Hitler and pro-democratic faith, which they hold. But are there really two "V's" here? We have already shown that *everything* depends upon defeating Hitler! There will be no "home front" or permanent gains at all without a victory over Hitler. Thus it can be seen that all victories won on the "home front" against discrimination today are inseparable from the struggle to defeat Hitler. Clearly there is one "V" – single and indivisible.

This is the way in which to tackle the problems that still lie ahead. Uppermost is the need for far vaster opportunities to serve in the armed forces.

In Joe's Spirit – A Mixed Regiment

Two young Navy officers, who attended the Louis-Baer bout for Navy Relief, grasped Joe's hand after the bout and said: "Oh boy we sure would like to have you with us... "I'd be proud to serve under a fighter like you..."

Two white Army lieutenants who used their furlough to see the fight said Joe: "Say we'd like to have you in our regiment all right when you come into the army."

To both of these sincere responses, Joe smiled and said, "Thanks."

Both incidents expressed something that is in the minds of many youth, Negro and white – the desire to end the shameful restrictions upon the opportunity of Negro youth to serve in the armed forces.

This is the American spirit.

Why shouldn't Negro and white Americans fight together? Do they not work together? Are we not fighting for a common cause together? Besides, our nation's history shows we have done so in the past. Crispus Attucks, the first man to fall in our American Revolutionary war, was a Negro. His mates were white. Fifty years ago there were mixed naval units. Negroes served as coxswains, first and second gunner's mates, as well as quartermasters and messmen. What American does not glory in the knowledge that Negro Americans have in each crisis given their last drop of blood for the nation's cause?

Despite the positive steps allowing Negroes to enlist in all branches of the Naval service, Negro youth can only give partial service because Jim Crow still permeates the Navy. But Negro young men and women, fired in the spirit of Dorie Miller and Joe Louis, want to give full service.

If Dorie Miller was able to perform the heroic deed he did, without training, how much better could he accomplish his task – with training? There are millions of Dorie Millers today who want such training to defeat the Axis.

There is need for greater promotion of Negro officers, equal facilities and training of Negro youth in the Army, cracking down on the vicious indignities such as the Fort Dix incident, which result from discrimination in the armed forces.

There is no better way to begin the sweeping removal of the indignities from which Negro youth and the entire nation suffer than to put into effect the growing demand for a mixed regiment.

A mixed regiment of Negro and white soldiers will help our armed forces and our entire war effort. It would help to stimulate Negro-white solidarity boost national unity and strengthen morale both in and outside of the armed forces. It would be greeted by our allies everywhere. It would carry into actual life the constitutional rights of the Negro people for full equality in the armed forces. A mixed regiment would be a slap in the face to the Ku Kluxers and the rest of the Axis fifth column who count on false race hatred and myths of "inferior" and "superior" peoples to divide and conquer us. Many Americans have already demanded that such a step be taken and we are waiting for such action by the War Department. That is the way to put into effect the full meaning of the statements expressed by Army officers, such as Col. Howard Gilbert of Fort Dix, who declared that Joe "is the greatest morale-building influence" that an Army camp ever had.

Joe Unites Us – The Defeatists Try To Divide Us

Yes, the nation is proud of Joe. For Joe is a symbol of everything that is fine and upstanding in American youth. He is a symbol of the character of the American people despite the fact that he is a world champion, having defended his title twenty-one times, scoring nineteen knockouts, his simple dignity, modesty and pride are an inspiration to all Americans. No wonder then that, before the delegates to the Fifth All-Southern Negro Youth Congress, Joe was presented by Brigadier General B.O. Davis with the C. C. Spaulding award for "outstanding service to the nation and the Negro people." Also the Boxing Writers Association voted him as "the man who had done the most in the boxing game in 1940."

His example put to shame the "noisy traitors and bogus patriots" of whom President Roosevelt has spoken. Where Louis unites and strengthens our unity – these advocates of racial disunity and hatred divide and weaken the nation. They are doing the work of Hitler and Hirohito – the Quisling work of the fifth column.

With the insulting, scurrilous attacks upon the Negro people, their newspapers and institutions, the poison-pen artist Westbrook Pegler spreads the "race superiority" ideas of Hitlerism. Such filthy slanders have no place in American public life. Other defeatists work by other methods. Norman Thomas urges a "negotiated" Hitler "peace," distorts the aims of this war for freedom and sows disunity among the United Nations, by slandering our British and Soviet allies. George Schuyler columnist of the *Pittsburgh Courier*, labels this a "white man's war," ignoring the fact that millions of the coloured peoples are fighting for their very existence against the Axis.

Neither the Thomases nor the Schuylers have called for the all-out mobilization of the Negro people behind the war against Hitler. Nor have they urged a single one of the measures necessary to take the offensive against Hitler – the opening of a Western Front in Europe now!! Under the pretext that the main fight is at home, they try to prevent the full mobilization of the Negro people to win the war. John L. Lewis, *The Daily News*, *The Chicago Tribune*, Martin Dies, Representative Howard Smith, Hoover, Gerald K. Smith, Lindbergh, as well as the Hearst press and all their kind, fight against an all-out effort to win the war. When they hold back all-out support to the war, they weaken the entire fight for democracy. By such policies, as well as by the effort to conceal the just and democratic character of this war, they directly aid Hitler in his war against our country. Such people – who by their actions are helping Hitler, though they may pretend to champion the Negro people – are in reality betraying them and their rights to their worst enemies.

Negro youth must reject these defeatists and false friends.

Those Who Fight For Victory

The best and truest friends of the Negro people are the labour movement and all patriotic citizens who want to win the war. *All patriotic Americans must now more than ever, while rallying to their country's defense, take up the cudgels against the sowers of race prejudice, strengthen the unity of Negro and white and champion every just and necessary demand of the Negro people. Thus the anti-Hitler forces of America will advance the fight for full democracy to Negro citizens as part of the fight for victory.*

Among those in the forefront of the fight are the Communists. The Party of Earl Browder and James W. Ford and the Young Communist League are fulfilling their pledge to give their "full energy, devotion, their last drop of blood, their lives" for victory in this war. By fighting today for full participation of the Negro people in the war effort, the Communists are continuing the historic struggle for full equality of the Negro people, exemplified in the Scottsboro and Herndon cases. We Young Communists believe in and practice full equality for the Negro youth. Our organization fights for and serves the nation in every phase of the war effort. As part of the fight for victory, this pamphlet is addressed to all youth, Negro and white. Every young man and woman must heighten participation in the war effort so that we can win victory, which is possible this year, 1942. By buying war stamps and bonds, by participation in the salvage campaigns, in the

different Claudia

blood donor drive of the Red Cross, the USO, by raising food for victory – in short, by doing all the things that help strengthen morale and speed up victory.

Joe Wants To Meet Schmeling In No–Man's Land

"I hope my next fight will be in no-man's land with Max Schmeling," said Joe. All Americans join Joe in this hope. For that's where the real kayo will come against Hitler. Joe is not only a knockout artist. He is an able boxer and recognized universally for his "ring generalship." "Ring generalship" has to do with knowing your opponent's strengths and weaknesses, being alert to deal your opponent the knockout blow.

Today "ring generalship" in the military sense is the concern of all the people. Today, the heroic Red Army holds Hitler in a "corner" on the Eastern front. The Eastern front is the most decisive front of the war. For it is there that the greatest battles are being fought against the main spearhead of Hitler's armies. It is there that our powerful ally, the Soviet Union, is dealing the death blows to the hitherto "invincible" armies of Hitler. The Soviet Union, where over 150 nation-alities live and enjoy the fruits of their labour in complete harmony and equality, has shown to the world its ability to wage total all-out war at the front and in the rear. The Soviet Union has the offensive and initiative today, in its drive on Kharkov. The Red Army's role for all mankind was expressed by General MacArthur on the occasion of its twenty-fourth anniversary:

> "...the world situation at the present time indicates that the hopes of civilization rest upon the worthy banners of the courageous Russian Army..."

But Hitler is not defeated yet. Even now he is planning an offensive to secure the rich oil fields of the Caucasus. We can decide his fate though, if we take the initiative in the West of Europe as the Red Army has done in the East. We have to set up a "corner" on the Western front – now! So that we can all meet Schmeling's pals – the Nazis and help to give them the "haymaker" that is their due.

Hitler doesn't want to fight a two-front war. By his own admission, he is getting a terrific beating by the great Red Army. On the continent of Europe guerilla fighting has reached the stage of open revolt in many places. Yes, Hitler is open for a "right" right now. The defeatists and the Axis fifth column want us to get punch-drunk with wild swings. They want us to play into the hands of Hitler by fighting on many fronts instead of concentrating our blows against the main armies of the axis. But the time is Now, *this year, 1942*! President Roosevelt has said that we must carry the war to the enemy. Winston Churchill said recently that it is better to have an offensive spirit to tackle the enemy and encouraged the growing demand in England and America for a Western front.

Joseph Stalin, leader of the Soviet Union and military genius of the Red Army, has declared that the time is now, this year, 1942. General Marshall, Chief of Staff, has said that our boys must land in France for victory. We want to make every blow count, this year 1942. Let's get out of the clinches of defeat of Singapore; let's avenge Bataan and Corrigidor. Let's make way for victory. We want to make every blow count, this year 1942. Let's make way for victory by boldly moving into the opponent's corner, by taking the offensive on land, sea and air in a mighty invasion on the Western front.

That's the fighting spirit of Joe Louis – that's the offensive spirit of all America! A Western front now! Victory in 1942!

Together, all youth shall build the future and establish a just democratic peace, for with Hitler defeated the collapse of the armies of Hirohito and Mussolini will soon follow. For this purpose and in this spirit all young Americans, Negro and white, must fight and will fight for victory.

On the Right to Self-Determination for the Negro People in the Black Belt (1946)

(A Discussion Article)

to Claudia

The political attacks that are being directed against the Negro people by Big Business have once again placed serious questions before the American working class.

These attacks, reminiscent of post-World War I, are all the more serious because today the main danger of fascism to the world comes from the most colossal imperialist forces which are concentrated within the United States. The perpetrators of these attacks are the representatives of the most reactionary section of monopoly capital and of the semi-feudal economy of the Black Belt. This hook-up, expressed in Congress by the reactionary Republicans and the poll-taxers who draw their power from the oppression of the Negro people and the working class, makes it obvious that the two main forces for democracy are the working class, allied with the Negro people.

In the short period since the war for national liberation, our nation has witnessed a revival of lynchings – three *known* lynchings in the space of three months. This blot of shame lies in America, while we proclaim to the world our "championship" of democracy for other nations!

"fascist-inspired law?"

The two-pronged drive of Big Business to decimate the war-time gains of the Negroes in industry and at the same time to destroy the alliance between labour and the Negro people, the fascist-inspired "race strikes" of American students, the recent attacks on Negro veterans in the South and the closing of FEPC offices in city after city – all this necessitates the greatest political initiative and action by the trade unions and by our Party.

Coupled with this reactionary drive on the economic and political fronts, are the growing Hitler-like incitements of the Bilbos and Rankins. While popular indignation has been aroused by these events, it is obvious that labour must move more aggressively than it has so far on the vital issues affecting the Negro people. *as a nation or on a national level?*

If the alliance, crucial to progress, between the Negro people and labour is to be reinforced and extended, it is necessary to clarify the relationship between the struggle for national liberation of the Negro people and that of the working class against capitalist exploitation and oppression.

In opening this discussion, it must be made clear that the conclusions here arrived at should in no sense be regarded as a condition for the united struggle of the Negro people and the working class for Negro rights. What differences in outlook may be present as regards the thesis here presented must in no way hinder the unity of all progressives in the struggle for the immediate needs of the Negro people.

The basis for this discussion article is the Political Resolution of our National Convention in July, which rejected Browder's revisionist position on the national character of the Negro question. A further basis is the preliminary exchange of opinion registered recently at an enlarged meeting of the newly established National Negro Commission of our Party. At that meeting, it must be stated, that the views expressed revealed varying opinions on our fundamental theoretical approach to the political essence and ultimate aim of the Negro liberation movement in the United States. Similar differences of opinion are indicated in communications, club resolutions and articles submitted to the National Office, which discuss the issue of the right of self-determination for the Negro people in the Black Belt.

It is clear that a deep-going discussion of the subject is necessary. While this article will attempt to discuss some of these views, it is to be hoped that it will be followed by further discussion. The views presented here are my own.

The National Character of the Struggle for Negro Rights

Even the worst enemies of the Communist Party cannot fail to admit that we have been in the forefront of the struggle for equality of the Negro people. It was the Communist Party which fourteen years ago made the name of Scottsboro ring around the world. It was the Communist Party, which was the first, since the overthrow of the Reconstruction governments, to raise in the heart of the South the issue of full Negro freedom.

What galvanized our Party to become the initiator and vanguard of these struggles? It was our understanding of the Negro question in the United States as a *special question*, as an issue whose solution requires *special* demands, in addition to the general demands of the American working class.

It was essentially this understanding that found Communists in the forefront of the struggle to combat the imperialist ideology of "white supremacy" which is today endangering the unity of the labour-democratic coalition and of the working class itself. It was essentially this knowledge that taught white American workers to fight for Negro rights in their own self-interest, to understand that to fight against white chauvinism is to fight against imperialist ideologies and practices of America's ruling class which serves to separate Negro and white workers. It was this understanding that taught Negro workers to fight against petty-bourgeois nationalism – a result of white chauvinist ideology – and to have both Negro and white workers form strong bonds of unity with each other.

It was our understanding of the Negro question as a *national* question, that is, as the question of a nation oppressed by American imperialism, in the ultimate sense as India is oppressed by British imperialism and Indonesia by Dutch imperialism. It was our knowledge, grounded in Lenin's teachings, that every aspect of Negro oppression in our country stems from the existence of an *oppressed nation*, in the heart of the South, the Black Belt.

We knew that the semi-slavery of the Southern sharecroppers; the inferior status of the Negro people in industry, North and South; the existence of Jim Crow in the armed forces; the Jim Crow practices of New York and Chicago, as well as of Birmingham and Tampa; the shooting two months ago of a Harlem child by a trigger-happy cop – all can be traced back step by step to the continued existence of an oppressed Negro nation within our borders.

Wherein do the Negro people in the Black Belt constitute an oppressed nation? To answer this question, we must first determine the characteristics of a nation. Marxist-Leninists hold that "a nation is a historically evolved, stable community of language, territory, economic life and psychological make-up manifested in a community of culture."

The Black Belt, an area in which the Negro people form a majority, came into existence with the growth of cotton culture and plantation economy. As the area of cotton cultivation moved over Westward in the days before the Civil War, so did the area of the plantation that consisted of a white-master family with its slaves.

The Civil War, which abolished chattel slavery, failed either to break up this area of Negro majority or to fully liberate the Negro people within it. Retaining their plantation lands, the ex-slaveholders soon forced to return to these lands of their former slaves as sharecroppers. A series of laws passed by Southern states

– the crop lien laws, the jumping contract laws and so on – prevented and still prevent the free migration of the Negro people. Scarcely less than before the Civil War, is the Black Belt a prison-house of the Negroes; the chains which hold them now are the invisible chains of poverty, the legal chains of debt-slavery and when the landlords deem it necessary, the iron shackles of the chain gang.

The Civil War might have broken the bars of the Black Belt; it did not, for the Northern capitalists, who had gained a united market and field of exploitation throughout the nation as a result of the Civil War, were terrified by the simultaneous rise of Southern democracy, the Northern labour movement and radical agrarian organizations. They betrayed the Negro people and the Southern white masses and turned the South back to semi-slavery.

The migrations of the 1870s, of the First World War and of the Second World War, did not appreciably diminish the proportion by which the Negroes find themselves a majority today in the Black Belt – these are virtually the same. It cannot be said that this majority is accidental, or that the Negro people continue as an oppressed people within the Black Belt by inertia or by choice. They continue so because the sheriff's posse of the twentieth century is carrying on, under new forms, the work of the slave-catchers of the nineteenth. The majority remains a majority by force.

This community in which the Negro people are a majority is neither racial nor tribal; it is composed of a significant minority of whites as well. The territory stretches contiguously westward from the Eastern shore of Maryland and lies within Maryland, Virginia, North Carolina, South Carolina, Georgia, Florida, Alabama, Mississippi, Louisiana, Tennessee, Arkansas and Texas.

Following the Civil War, boundary lines were definitely shaped by the defeated slaveholders to prohibit the full participation of the Negroes and poor whites in political life. If it is true in the North, where certain election districts are "gerrymandered" to prohibit the full expression of the Negro vote (and of the white vote as well), it was no less true of the Black Belt, where the majority of the inhabitants were Negroes and represented its basic core.

As to the other characteristics of nationhood: Have the Negro people, for example, a common language? They have a common language – English. If it be argued that this is the language of the entire country, we say that this is true. A common language is necessary to nationhood; a different language is not. When the American colonies separated from Britain, they had a common language, which was the same as that of their oppressors. Surely no one will argue that our community of language with our British oppressors should have kept us indefinitely in the status of a colonial people.

Is there an American Negro culture? The peculiar oppression of the Negro people and their striving for freedom have been expressed in a native way, in spirituals, work-songs, literature, art and dance. This does not mean that American Negro culture is not part of American culture generally. Negro culture is part of

or root-most current

the general stream of American culture, but it is a distinct current in that stream; it arose out of the special historical development and unique status of the Negro people; no other people in America could have developed this particular culture.

Have the Negro people a stable community of economic life? First, let us discuss what is meant by a common economic life. It is sometimes said that people have a common economic life when they make their living in the same way – they are all sharecroppers, or they are all workers. Actually, a common economic life with reference to a nation or community under capitalism means that the nation or community has within it the class and social relations that characterize society; it has capitalists, workers, farmers and intellectuals, ranged according to their position in the production relations. In this case it means that a Negro must be able to hire a Negro, buy from a Negro, sell to a Negro and service a Negro.

Such class stratification exists among the Negro people in the Black Belt. There is a Negro bourgeoisie, it is not a big bourgeoisie: the bourgeoisie of an oppressed nation never is; it is one of the results of national oppression that the bourgeoisie of oppressed nations is retarded by the oppressors. The market of the Negro bourgeoisie is founded upon Jim Crowism; it functions chiefly in life insurance, banking and real estate. Its leadership among the Negro people is reflected in an ideology – petty-bourgeois nationalism, whose main purpose is to mobilize the Negro masses under its own influence.

By these distinguishing features, therefore, the Negro people in the Black Belt constitute a nation. They are an historically developed community of people, with a common language, a common territory and a common economic life, all of which are manifest in a common culture.

As far back as 1913 Lenin emphasized that the Negro people constitute an oppressed nation. In an unfinished essay on the national and colonial question he made a *direct* reference to the Negro people as an *oppressed nation*, stating:

> In the United States 11.1 per cent of the population consists of Negroes (and also mulattoes and Indians) who must be considered an oppressed nation, inasmuch as the equality, won in the Civil War of 1861–65 and guaranteed by the constitution of the Republic, has in reality been more and more restricted in many respects in the main centres of the Negro population (in the South) with the transition from the progressive, pre-monopolistic capitalism of 1860-1870 to the reactionary monopolistic capitalism (imperialism) of the latest epoch. (V. I. Lenin, *Miscellany*, Collected Works, Vol. XXX, Russian Edition.)

Browder's Revision of Leninist Teachings

In discussing the right of self-determination for Negroes in the Black Belt, we surely cannot ignore the revisionist position taken by Earl Browder, as set forth in his article in *The Communist* for January, 1944, which was presented as a declaration of policy for American Communists. There Browder wrote:

> ... It was in view of the gathering world crisis that we Communists at that time – in the early 30s raised the issue of self-determination. At that time, we necessarily faced the possibility that the Negro people, disappointed in their aspirations for full integration into the American nation, might find their only alternative in separation and in the establishment of their own state in the Black Belt, in the territory in which they are a majority. We raised this as one of the rights of the Negro people, in case the Negro people found this was the only way to satisfy their aspirations.

Browder further wrote: *Integration (vs) separation*

> The crisis of history has taken a turn of such character that the Negro people in the United States have found it possible to make their decision once and for all. Their decision is for their complete integration (into) the American nation as a whole and not for separation.

Browder thus denied that the right of self-determination for Negroes in the Black Belt was any longer an issue, since, according to him, the Negro people had already made their historic choice!

What was the fallacy on which Browder's premise was based?

Browder's fallacy was inherently connected with a false estimate of the relationship of forces in our nation and the world. Clearly, if a rosy future was to be envisioned in which a "peaceful" capitalism would voluntarily relinquish its exploitations, solve its contradictions, etc., the Leninist programme which showed that the very essence of imperialism was the distinction and conflict between oppressed and oppressing nations no longer applied to our country!

Moreover, Browder based his premise, not on evaluating the right of self-determination as it applies to the Negro people in the Black Belt, but on one of its aspects, separation. That he saw fit to discuss the whole question from the standpoint of a "practical political matter," confirms this. His treatment of these two demands as being identical needs examination.

Is separation identical with self-determination? The right to separation is inherent in the right to self-determination whether that right is eventually

Does separation = self-determination?

exercised or not. It becomes a practical political matter only when the concrete objective conditions for that choice are at hand. Therefore, to identify self-determination with separation, or to substitute one for the other, is tantamount to forcing on the Negro people a choice, which they are clearly not in an objective position to make – which, in other words, though a right, is not necessarily a function of their exercise of self-determination!

It is obvious from this that the right of self-determination is not something one can dangle, withdraw, or put forward again as a sheerly objective factor. Either the objective historic conditions of nationhood exist, in which such a right remains inviolate, or they do not. Either the objective conditions exist for the choice to be made by the oppressed nation (either for separation, autonomy, amalgamation, etc.), or they do not. Thus, and only thus, can we approach the issue as a practical political matter.

How then, does the question of integration apply? Are the Negro people demanding integration in American political life? Most certainly they are! But this is no new phenomenon insofar as the Negro people are concerned. Negro Americans have been fighting for integration for over two hundred years. Every *partial* fight – whether expressed in the demand of the Reconstruction leaders, together with the white workers and farmers in the South for land, or in the present day demands of Negroes in Atlanta to enforce the Supreme Court ruling against the "white primary" laws; whether it be the fight against lynching and poll-tax disfranchisement, or the recent successful campaign, conducted in Negro-white unity to re-elect Benjamin J. Davis, Jr., to the New York City Council – is a step towards integration.

But integration cannot be considered a substitute for the right of self-determination. National liberation is not synonymous with integration, neither are the two concepts mutually exclusive.

What does integration really mean? Integration, that is, *democratic* integration, means breaking down the fetters that prohibit the full economic, political and social participation of Negroes in all phases of American life. This does not mean that a merger, or an assimilative process necessarily takes place. In a general sense, the struggle for integration waged today by the Negro people is directed toward achieving *equal rights* – economic, political and social.

But the basic difference, in fact the touchstone of programmatic difference, between the liberals (as well as the Social-Democrats) and the Communists hinges on the application of the programme of equal rights to the Black Belt, and therefore, to the *source of Negro oppression* throughout the country – a difference based on diametrically opposed concepts of the nature of the question.

In the North, the struggle for equal rights for the Negro people is chiefly that of heightening the fight to secure equal participation in every sphere of American life. The problems of the Negro people in the North are akin to those of an oppressed national minority. Particularly here, the fight for equal rights as a

– 66 –

Participation @ enforcement

whole in enhanced by the presence of a large and growing Negro proletariat, in the area of the most highly developed capitalism, as well as by the participation of the advanced workers throughout the country for equal rights for Negroes. In fact, it is the existence of a strong Negro proletariat–represented today by close to one million organized trade unionists – that provides the intimate link between the American working class as a whole and the struggle for emancipation and land for the oppressed Negro people and white workers in the Black Belt.

In the Black Belt the problem is chiefly that of wiping out the economic, political and social survivals of slavery, of the *enforcement* of equal rights. Without the necessary *enforcement* of equal rights for the Negro people in the Black Belt, including social equality, it is folly to speak of integration as being equal to the achievement of national liberation. Hence, equal rights for the Negro people in the Black Belt can be achieved only through enforcement, through their exercise of the right of self-determination. *Hay who?*

The right of self-determination does not exclude the struggle for partial demands; it pre-supposes an energetic struggle for concrete partial demands, linked up with the daily needs and problems of the wide masses of the Negro *Economic country* people and the white workers in the Black Belt. The fight for such partial demands, moreover, is a struggle for democracy. It does not divert or overshadow the working class struggle against exploitation; it is an aid to it.

It is only by helping to interconnect the partial demands with the right of self-determination that we Communists, in concert with other progressive forces, can contribute guidance to the struggle for complete equality for the Negro people.

Certain Contentions Examined

We Communists adhere to the fundamental belief that complete and lasting equality of imperialist oppressed nations and peoples can be guaranteed only with the establishment of Socialism. The aim of Socialism is not only to abolish the present division of mankind into small states, not only to bring nations closer to each other, but ultimately to merge them. But we have never ignored the historical process necessary to the achievement of that goal. Nor can we "postpone" the question of national liberation until Socialism is established or speak solely in general nebulous phrases about national liberation. We must have a clear and precisely formulated political programme to guide our work in the achievement of that goal. For we know that "mankind can achieve the inevitable merging of nations, only by passing through the transition period of complete liberation of all the oppressed nations, *i.e.*, their freedom to secede" (Lenin, *Selected Works*, Vol. V. International Publishers, p. 271).

As Leninists, we are distinguished from the reactionary Social-Democrats in that we reject, even if it is under the name of "internationalism," any denial of the right of national self-determination to the oppressed peoples. For true internationalism, that is, Marxism-Leninism, places the right of self-determination as a basic programmatic point. The "internationalism" of the reformists is nothing more or less than the nationalism of their own respective imperialist rulers, while the national programme of Lenin is an essential part of internationalism. Any "internationalism" that denies the right of self-determination to the subject peoples is false, is a mere cover for imperialist chauvinism.

Our approach is based on proletarian internationalism, which recognizes that the workers of an oppressing nation best fight against national oppression – especially by their "own" bourgeoisie – once they understand that such is the road to realize their own freedom. It is based on the Marxist proposition that "no nation can be free if it oppresses other nations."

Clearly then, those who impute to the Negro people the main responsibility for "accepting" or "rejecting" the principle of self-determination ignore this tenet: they base their conclusions on the subjective factor, instead of the objective and historical conditions of oppression of the Negro people in the Black Belt.

But let us examine some of these arguments. Is it true that the Negro people do not want self-determination; that the Negro people shy away from this concept with abhorrence? Definitely not! It is, of course, quite a different matter if we speak of the Negro people as not being fully conscious of this concept in our terms. But to challenge the deepest desires of the Negro people for the freedom and equality as being other than that of the fullest national self-affirmation is to fail to understand their fundamental aspirations!

What do the Negro people abhor? They abhor the continuation of their actual status in the Black Belt – that of forcible segregation. They abhor Jim Crow from which they suffer in many forms today. They abhor the freedom with which the poll-taxers and feudal landowners, by dividing Negro and white continue their oppression of the Negro people. They abhor the ideology of "white supremacy" which flouts the basic tenets of our Constitution, as the counterpart of Hitler's "Aryan supremacy." They abhor any idea which holds out the perspective, not of full freedom and equality, but of something less than these things. And the slogan of self-determination expresses precisely these aspirations in the most complete sense.

To argue that the Negro people "don't want self-determination," is unwittingly to give sanction to the poll-taxers and feudal landowners in the South to continue exploiting the Negro people and poor whites on the basis that "this is what the Negroes want); it is to argue against a conscious fight by white American workers to help achieve the objective conditions in which the Negro people can freely make their own choice. It is to blunt the struggle for national liberation, to have at best, a bourgeois-liberal approach.

Is it any wonder, then, that the most vehement voices against this principle are not the mass of the Negro people, but the enemies of the white workers and the

*Double consciousness @ double
oppression*

Negro people? The Social-Democrats (and the reactionary mouthpieces of monopoly capital and semi-feudal economy), who advance the ridiculous charge that self-determination would "Jim Crow the Negro people," "Create a Black Ghetto," and other such arguments *ad nauseam*, are exposed in their full light when we examine their real motives. They seek to cover up their denial of double oppression of the Negro people – as wage slaves and as Negroes. They seek to obscure the fundamental character of the status of the Negro people in the Black Belt – which is essentially *national* and rooted in economic and historic conditions of a pre-capitalist nature. Nor can all the piety and wit of Social-Democracy cancel out its real aim–which is to serve imperialism and therefore betray the Negro people and the working class.

Another view holds that the industrialization of the South and new migrations has fundamentally altered the relationship of the Negro people to the land. The proponents of this view maintain that such a development has radically changed the character of the Negro question in the Black Belt from that of oppressed nationhood, if such it was in the past, to that of a class question.

In discussing such views, we should, at the outset, distinguish between the effects of industrialization in the South as a whole and in the Black Belt. The continued existence of economic slave survivals in the Black Belt is a fundamental distinction that must be made in an examination of the characteristics of nationhood among the Negro people. Unless this is done, we shall not be able to understand the problems either of the South as a whole or of the Black Belt in particular.

There has unquestionably been some increase of industrial expansion in the South. The war requirements for victory necessitated the expansion of a number of basic Southern industries, such as steel, coal, textile, lumber and shipbuilding. In addition, new industries, such as aircraft and munitions, were built. Capital investments, however, came primarily from the Federal government. Over $7,000,000,000 were thus expended solely as a war necessity. It is obvious that such investment for expansion of existing plants and the building of new industries no longer exists. The reverse is true – that is, the closing down of plants and a *All* drastic curtailment of industrial production. Thus, it is clear that no trend exists *temporary* at present which would permit one to speak of the industrialization of the South. The trend that was evident during the war was a temporary phenomenon.

By 1944, Mr. D. B. Lasseter of the Atlanta, Georgia, Regional Office of the War Manpower Commission was able to warn us of this trend in summarizing what war orders meant to the South. Taking note of the more than seven billion dollars in prime contracts in six Southern states alone, Lasseter wrote in the *Social Forces* of October 1944:

> At first glance, these factors appear as bright prospects, but there is
> ample cause for anxiety lest this war-inspired prosperity prove only
> temporary. For while industrial activity and facilities have increased

tremendously, there will be great difficulty in maintaining these gains after the war. When the shooting is over the plants responsible for the current boom will shut down entirely, or production will be sharply curtailed. And a glance at the record shows that there is a heavy concentration of this type of industry and activity. The South is packed with Army camps, shipbuilding, airplane and munitions plants further account for much of our industrial development. None of these offers a rosy future as a peacetime investment.

Lasseter added:

> The South faces a grave readjustment. Having had its first taste of prosperity resulting from increased industrial activity, it is slated to lose the source of this prosperity"

It goes without saying that expansion and building of new industries in the Black Belt would, of course, have its influence among the Negro people. Such a process would lead to the extension of the working class base among the Negro people. Instead of de-limiting the national characteristics of the Negro people, it would help importantly to develop the national consciousness of the Negro people and thus accelerate the realization of the aim of self-determination. The extension of the working class base in the oppressed Negro nation is fundamentally the guarantee of the successful forward movement of the national liberation cause of the entire Negro people.

Self-Determination – A Guiding Principle

It is my opinion that we again must raise the right of self-determination for the Negro people in the Black Belt, not as a slogan of immediate action, but essentially as *a programmatic demand*. It might perhaps be argued that, raised in this manner, the slogan is academic and should therefore not be raised at all. Such criticism fails to take into account the difference between a slogan advanced as an issue on the order of the day and a *guiding principle*.

We must place the question in terms of historical perspective, taking into account concretely the stage of the Negro liberation movement today and the present practical struggle for full Negro rights, on behalf of which there must be established both the broadest Negro unity and the broadest Negro and white alliance. Between the current struggles and the programmatic slogan here advanced there is no conflict, but a vital interconnection. The goal of national self-determination should serve as a beacon to the day-to-day struggles for Negro rights and should serve to hasten the realization of the right to self-determination.

Women's Rights

"From 1947–52 – active in national women's movements and united front movements such as the Congress of American Women; National Council of Negro Women"

Autobiographical History

"These special forms of oppression particularly affect the working women, the farm women and the triply oppressed Negro women; but, in varying degrees, they help us to determine the inferior status of women in all classes of society."

International Women's Day and the Struggle for Peace

Introduction

Claudia Jones became a political prisoner for writing and delivering an International Women's Day address which in its original form was titled "International Women's Day and the Struggle for Peace" and republished in pamphlet form by the National Women's Commission, CPUSA as "Women in the Struggle for Peace and Security" (both in 1950). This section on Women's Rights includes that historic essay and contains three (3) other representative essays, all dated from 1949-1953. These essays are more mature and illustrate her gender-related work as an activist and theoretician on women's rights.

In 1947, when the first of these essays appear, she would have been thirty-two years old. "For New Approaches to Our Work Among Women," was actually an internal discussion piece, its title signaling the start of this new Claudia Jones-led initiative when she was secretary of the Women's Commission of the CPUSA but also involved in other women's organizations. All the subsequent essays on women's rights stem from this beginning point even though, of course, they take a variety of different angles, nevertheless to get at a series of core ideas that she saw as relevant. In this essay, we see her challenging the CP hierarchy on race and gender as she takes apart its draft resolution which was supposed to be building a peace coalition. Her position is: Where are women in this? Where are black and working class women? In her first sentence, she states that the resolution did not "sufficiently stress the need to fight for the special social, economic and political needs of the masses of American women." Her argument seems to run that the Party wants to build a mass movement but was not dealing with women substantially. In her view: how could this be when women represented "half the nation." This would be her position consistently and is identified as representing a divergent view from the basic Communist Party position which would have been arguing then that class was prior to gender or race. Jones reversed this paradigm and instead found a variety of ways to argue against this. To reveal how gender fit, Claudia would find theoretical positions within Marxism-Leninism, especially Lenin on the "woman question" to make that argument.

Thus, "For New Approaches To Our Work Among Women," sets the terms for subsequent discussion and can be read as a concept paper which would lay out a few issues: the move to send women back into the kitchen following the war: the inadequate social services; lack of child care and the absence of training programmes to help women get new skills. She references the 1947 establishment of the Women's Commission and speaks to the failure to integrate the work of the Commission into the Party structures because of the absence of a theoretical understanding of the "woman question." In this effort, she counted William Z. Foster, General Secretary of the CPUSA from 1945 as an ally and would consistently refer to his advanced position on women for validation. This is evident in her autobiographical history to him and in her essay; "Foster's Theoretical Guidance to our Work Among Women." In this essay she credits Foster for the founding of the Women's Commission and identifies their common sensitivity to the lot of women in their mothers' poverty and early death. Of interest to the reader will be her identification of the Main Resolution of the 15th National Convention of CPUSA which centred on the "role and importance of women" and uses language identical to Jones (she obviously collaborated on its writing) in the call for increased integration of our women membership in the leadership of the Party on all levels, particularly working class and Negro comrades..." My sense is that this is her resolution; her ideas.

Thus Claudia's activism, writing and thinking on women's rights critiques the weaknesses she saw in the CP around the issues of race and gender. She counters these theoretically: providing information on facts and trends as it relates to women, working with trade unions, avoiding the neglect of black women in particular, providing services which would allow women to do organizational work. She felt then that working class women would respond if the Party would address these weaknesses.

We begin with perhaps the most well known Claudia Jones essay: "An End to the Neglect of the Problems of Negro Women" (1949), which is a wonderful documentation of where women were located in the 1940s and 1950s but which continues to have implications for ongoing arguments which account for black women in a variety of locations. It is perhaps the most important essay on black women in that time- period, laying out the statistics on a range of issues and economic hardships that confronted black women but also providing historical background and information on black woman's status at the time as women, as black people and as workers. And she ends it by challenging white supremacist thinking and the callousness in the treatment of black women and suggests that the responsibility for dealing with this behaviour and its limitations rests squarely with white people. The key issues section is an important summary as it included supporting struggles that are generated by racism, advancing the employment of black women and moving away from the idea even in the party that black women were naturally domestics. She felt that if the CP would deal with the more benign structural and individual racism, inside as it keeps challenging the more extreme forms outside such as lynching, it would be a natural organization for black people. This essay proves that in the Communist Party, Jones advanced a pro-black; pro-women; pro-black women agenda. This is an indispensible essay for anyone studying this period, the history of black feminism and subjects of race, gender and class.

Another essay published that same year, "We Seek Full Equality for Women" (1949), is short but one of my favourites in that it captures her art of black left feminism. She references Foster again but as a lever to talk about how Marxism-Leninism saw the woman question as of course related to woman's relation to the mode of production. Written for a general audience, it is a nice summary of the basics of Marxist-Leninist feminism, outlines the theoretical work that was taking place and the praxis in terms of the organization of state branches of the Women's commission and saw the Communist Party as leading the way to developing a progressive women's movement. "For the Unity of Women in the Cause of Peace" (1951) was organized around the theme of building an international women's peace movement. The other essays in this section were published in various print media: journals like *Political Affairs*, newspapers like *The Worker* and some republished as pamphlets. The famous International Women's Day essay was first a speech then republished in *Political Affairs* and made available in pamphlet form by the Women's Commission.

Claudia Jones' repeated concerns are with the super-exploitation of women, especially the black woman's location in society, the effects of war on women's lives and the need to organize generally but also to create women's peace organizations, the international connections between women and the fact that women make up half the world, which became her theme for a series of journalistic columns in *The Daily Worker*. One sees in Claudia Jones's thinking and activism the back story of a struggle which got lost in the 1970s mainstream Feminist Movement which black women contested consistently, we see with good reason, as it tended to operate too often along the principles of bourgeois feminism, i.e., blaming men only for the oppression of women and not the policies and practices of the states. *Unique brand of feminist (Duplar ? from Alain Locke's Anthology)*

-73-

An End to the Neglect of the Problems of Negro Women (1949)[15]

An outstanding feature of the present stage of the Negro liberation movement is the growth in the militant participation of Negro women in all aspects of the struggle for peace, civil rights and economic security. Symptomatic of this new militancy is the fact that Negro women have become symbols of many present-day struggles of the Negro people. This growth of militancy among Negro women has profound meaning, both for the Negro liberation movement and for the emerging anti-fascist, anti-imperialist coalition.

To understand this militancy correctly, to deepen and extend the role of Negro women in the struggle for peace and for all interests of the working class and the Negro people, means primarily to overcome the gross neglect of the special problems of Negro women. This neglect has too long permeated the ranks of the labour movement generally, of Left-progressives and also of the Communist Party. The most serious assessment of these shortcomings by progressives, especially by Marxist-Leninists, is vitally necessary if we are to help accelerate this development and integrate Negro women in the progressive and labour movement and in our own Party.

The bourgeoisie is fearful of the militancy of the Negro woman and for good reason. The capitalists know, far better than many progressives seem to know, that once Negro women undertake action, the militancy of the whole Negro people and thus of the anti-imperialist coalition is greatly enhanced.

Historically, the Negro woman has been the guardian, the protector, of the Negro family. From the days of the slave traders down to the present, the Negro woman has had the responsibility of caring for the needs of the family, of militantly shielding it from the blows of Jim Crow insults, of rearing children in an atmosphere of lynch terror, segregation and police brutality and of fighting for an education for their children. The intensified oppression of the Negro people, which has been the hallmark of the postwar reactionary offensive, cannot therefore but lead to an acceleration of the militancy of the Negro woman. As mother, as Negro, and as worker, the Negro woman fights against the wiping out of the Negro family, against the Jim Crow ghetto existence which destroys the health, morale and the very life of millions of her sisters, brothers and children.

Viewed in this light, it is not accidental that the American bourgeoisie has intensified its oppression, not only of the Negro people in general, but of Negro women in particular. Nothing so exposes the drive to *fascization* in the nation as the callous attitude which the bourgeoisie displays and cultivates toward Negro women. The vaunted boast of the ideologists of Big Business – that American women possess "the greatest equality" in the world is exposed in all its hypocrisy when one sees that in many parts of the world, particularly in the Soviet Union, the New Democracies and the formerly oppressed land of China, women are attaining new heights of equality. But above all else, Wall Street's boast stops at the water's edge where Negro and working class women are concerned. Not equality, but degradation and super-exploitation: this is the actual lot of Negro women!

Consider the hypocrisy of the Truman Administration, which boasts about "exporting democracy throughout the world" while the state of Georgia keeps a widowed Negro mother of twelve children under lock and key. Her crime? She defended her life and dignity aided by her two sons – from the attacks of a "white supremacist." Or ponder the mute silence with which the Department of Justice has greeted Mrs. Amy Mallard, widowed Negro school-teacher, since her husband was lynched in Georgia because he had bought a new Cadillac and become, in the opinion of the "white supremacists," "too uppity." Contrast this with the crocodile tears shed by the US delegation to the United Nations for Cardinal Mindszenty, who collaborated with the enemies of the Hungarian People's Republic and sought to hinder the forward march to fuller democracy by the formerly oppressed workers and peasants of Hungary. Only recently, President Truman spoke solicitously in a Mother's Day Proclamation about the manifestation of "our love and reverence" for all mothers of the land. The so-called "love and reverence" for the mothers of the land by no means includes Negro mothers who, like Rosa Lee Ingram, Amy Mallard, the wives and mothers of the of the Trenton Six, or the other countless victims, dare to fight back, against lynch law and "white supremacy" violence.

Economic Hardships

Very much to the contrary, Negro women – as workers, as Negroes, and as women – are the most oppressed stratum of the whole population.

In 1940, two out of every five Negro women, in contrast to two out of every eight white women, worked for a living. By virtue of their majority status among the Negro people, Negro women not only constitute the largest percentage of women heads of families, but, are the main breadwinners of the Negro family. The large proportion of Negro women in the labour market is primarily a result of the low-scale earnings of Negro men. This disproportion also has its roots in the treatment and position of Negro women over the centuries.

Following emancipation and persisting to the present day, a large percentage of Negro women – married as well as single – were forced to work for a living. But despite the shift in employment of Negro women from rural to urban areas, Negro women are still generally confined to the lowest-paying jobs. The

Women's Bureau, US Department of Labour, *Handbook of Facts for Women Workers* (1948, Bulletin 225), shows white women workers as having median earnings more than twice as high as those of non-white women and non-white women workers (mainly Negro women) as earning less than $500 a year! In the rural South, the earnings of women are even less. In three large Northern industrial communities, the median income of white families ($1,720) is also 60 per cent higher than that of Negro families ($1,095). The super exploitation of the Negro woman worker is thus revealed not only in that she receives, as woman, less than equal pay for equal work with men, but also in that the majority of Negro women get less than half the pay of white women. Little wonder, then, that in Negro communities the conditions of ghetto-living – low salaries, high rents, high prices, etc. – virtually become an iron curtain hemming in the lives of Negro children and undermining their health and spirit! Little wonder that the maternity death rate for Negro women is triple that of white women! Little wonder that one out of every ten Negro children born in the United States does not grow to manhood or womanhood!

The low scale of earnings of the Negro woman is directly related to her almost complete exclusion from virtually all fields of work except the most menial and underpaid, namely, domestic service. Revealing are the following data given in the report of 1945, *Negro Women War Workers* (Women's Bureau, US Department of Labour, Bulletin 205): Of a total 7½ million Negro women, over a million are in domestic and personal service. The overwhelming bulk – about 918,000 – of these women workers are employed in private families and some 98,000 are employed as cooks, waitresses and in like services in other than private homes. The remaining 60,000 workers in service trades are in miscellaneous personal service occupations (beauticians, boarding house and lodging-house keepers, charwomen, janitors, practical nurses, housekeepers, hostesses and elevator operators).

The next largest number of Negro women workers are engaged in agricultural work. In 1940, about 245,000 were agricultural workers. Of them, some 128,000 were unpaid family workers.

Industrial and other workers numbered more than 96,000 of the Negro Women reported. Thirty-six thousand of these women were in manufacturing, the chief groups being 11,300 in apparel and other fabricated textile products, 1,000 in tobacco manufactures and 5,600 in food and related products.

Clerical and kindred workers in general numbered only 13,000. There were only 8,300 Negro women workers in civil service.

The rest of the Negro women who work for a living were distributed along the following lines: 50,000 teachers, 6,700 nurses and student nurses, 1,700 social and welfare workers, 120 dentists, pharmacists and veterinarians, 129 physicians and surgeons, 200 actresses, 100 authors, editors and reporters, 39 lawyers and judges, 400 librarians and other categories likewise illustrating the large-scale exclusion of Negro women from the professions.

During the anti-Axis war, Negro women for the first time in history had an opportunity to utilize their skills and talents in occupations other than domestic and personal service. They became trailblazers in many fields. Since the end of the war, however, this has given way to growing unemployment, to the wholesale firing of Negro women, particularly in basic industry.

This process has been intensified with the development of the economic crisis. Today, Negro women are being forced back into domestic work in great numbers. In New York State, for example, this trend was officially confirmed recently when Edward Corsi, Commissioner of the State Labour Department, revealed that for the first time since the war, domestic help is readily obtainable. Corsi in effect admitted that Negro women are not voluntarily giving up jobs, but rather are being systematically pushed out of industry. Unemployment, which has always hit the Negro woman first and hardest, plus the high cost of living, is what compels Negro women to re-enter domestic service today. Accompanying this trend is an ideological campaign to make domestic work palatable. Daily newspaper advertisements which base their arguments on the claim that most domestic workers who apply for jobs through USES "prefer this type of work to work in industry," are propagandizing the "virtues" of domestic work, especially of "sleep-in positions."

Inherently connected with the question of job opportunities where the Negro woman is concerned, is the special oppression she faces as Negro, as woman and as worker. She is the victim of the white chauvinist stereotype as to where her place should be. In film, radio and the press, the Negro woman is not pictured in her real role as breadwinner, mother and protector of the family, but as a traditional "mammy" who puts the care of children and families of others above her own. This traditional stereotype of the Negro slave mother, which to this day appears in commercial advertisements, must be combated and rejected as a device of the imperialists to perpetuate the white chauvinist ideology that Negro women are "backward," "inferior" and the "natural slaves" of others.

Historical Aspects

Actually, the history of the Negro woman shows that the Negro mother under slavery held a key position and played a dominant role in her own family grouping. This was due primarily to two factors: the conditions of slavery, under which marriage, as such, was non-existent and the Negro's social status was derived from the mother and not the father; and the fact that most of the Negro people brought to these shores by the slave traders came from West Africa where the position of women, based on their actual participation in property control, was relatively higher in the family than that of European women.

Early historians of the slave trade recall the testimony of travelers indicating that the love of the African mother for her child was unsurpassed in any part of the world. There are numerous stories attesting to the self-sacrificial way in which East African mothers offered themselves to the slave traders in order to save their sons and Hottentot women refused food during famines until after their children were fed.

It is impossible within the confines of this article to relate the terrible sufferings and degradation undergone by Negro mothers and Negro women generally under slavery. Subject to legalized rape by the slave owners, confined to slave pens, forced to march for eight to fourteen hours with loads on their backs and to perform back-breaking work even during pregnancy, Negro women bore a burning hatred for slavery and undertook a large share of the responsibility for defending and nurturing the Negro family.

The Negro mother was mistress in the slave cabin and despite the interference of master or overseer, her wishes in regard to mating and in family matters was paramount. During and after slavery, Negro women had to support themselves and the children, necessarily playing an important role in the economic and social life of her people.

The Negro Woman Worker

The negligible participation of Negro women in progressive and trade-union circles is thus all the more startling. In union after union, even in those unions where a large concentration of workers are Negro women, few Negro women are to be found as leaders or active workers. The outstanding exceptions to this are the Food and Tobacco Workers' Union and the United Office and Professional Workers' Union.

But why should these be exceptions? Negro women are among the most militant trade unionists. The sharecroppers' strikes of the 30s were spark-plugged by Negro women. Subject to the terror of the landlord and white supremacist, they waged magnificent battles together with Negro men and white progressives in that struggle of great tradition led by the Communist Party. Negro women played a magnificent part in the pre-CIO days in strikes and other struggles, both as workers and as wives of workers, to win recognition of the principle of industrial unionism, in such industries as auto, packing, steel, etc. More recently, the militancy of Negro women unionists is shown in the strike of the packing-house workers and even more so, in the tobacco workers' strike – in which such leaders as Moranda Smith and Velma Hopkins emerged as outstanding trade unionists. The struggle of the tobacco workers led by Negro women later merged with the political action of Negroes and whites which led to the election of the first Negro in the South (in Winston-Salem, NC) since Reconstruction days.

It is incumbent on progressive unionists to realize that in the fight for equal rights for Negro workers, it is necessary to have a special approach to Negro women workers, who, far out of proportion to other women workers, are the main bread-winners in their families. The fight to retain the Negro woman in industry and to upgrade her on the job is a major way of struggling for the basic and special interests of the Negro woman worker. Not to recognize this feature is to miss the special aspects of the effects of the growing economic crisis, which is penalizing Negro workers, particularly Negro women workers with special severity.

The Domestic Worker

One of the crassest manifestations of trade-union neglect of the problems of the Negro women worker has been the failure, not only to fight against relegation of the Negro woman to domestic and similar menial work, but also to organize the domestic worker. It is merely lip-service for progressive unionists to speak of organizing the unorganized without turning their eyes to the serious plight of the domestic worker, who, unprotected by union standards, is also the victim of exclusion from all social and labour legislation. Only about one in ten of all Negro women workers are to be found in states having minimum-wage laws. All of the arguments heretofore projected with regard to the real difficulties of organizing the domestic workers – such as the "casual" nature of their employment, the difficulties of organizing day workers, the problem of organizing people who work in individual households, etc., must be overcome forthwith. There is a danger that Social-Democratic forces may enter this field to do their work of spreading disunity and demagogy, unless progressives act quickly.

The lot of the domestic worker is one of unbearable misery. Usually, she has no definition of tasks in the household where she works. Domestic workers may have "thrown in," in addition to cleaning and scrubbing, such tasks as washing windows, caring for the children, laundering, cooking, etc. and all at the lowest pay. The Negro domestic worker must suffer the additional indignity, in some areas, of having to seek work in virtual "slave markets" on the streets where bids are made, as from a slave block, for the hardiest workers. Many a domestic worker, on returning to her own household, must begin housework anew to keep her own family together.

Who was not enraged when it was revealed in California, in the heinous case of Dora Jones, that a Negro woman domestic was enslaved for more than 40 years in "civilized" America? Her "employer" was given a minimum sentence of a few years and complained that the sentence was for "such a long period of time." But could Dora Jones, Negro domestic worker, be repaid for more than 40 years of her life under such conditions of exploitation and degradation? And how many cases, partaking in varying degrees of the condition of Dora Jones, are still tolerated by progressives themselves!

Only recently, in the New York State Legislature, legislative proposals were made to "fingerprint" domestic workers. The Martinez Bill did not see the light of day, because the reactionaries were concentrating on other repressive legislative measures; but here we see clearly the imprint of the African "pass" system of British imperialism (and of the German Reich in relation to the Jewish people!) being attempted in relation to women domestic workers.

It is incumbent on the trade unions to assist the Domestic Workers Union in every possible way to accomplish the task of organizing the exploited domestic workers, the majority of whom are Negro women. Simultaneously, a legislative fight for the inclusion of domestic workers under the benefits of the Social Security Law is vitally urgent and necessary. Here, too, recurrent questions regarding "administrative problems" of applying the law to domestic workers should be challenged and solutions found.

The continued relegation of Negro women to domestic work has helped to perpetuate and intensify the chauvinism directed against all Negro women. Despite the fact that Negro women may be grand mothers or mothers, the use of the chauvinist term "girl" for adult Negro women is a common expression. The very economic relationship of Negro women to white women, which perpetuates "madam-maid" relationships, feeds chauvinist attitudes and makes it incumbent on white women progressives and particularly Communists, to fight consciously against all manifestations of white chauvinism, open and subtle.

Chauvinism on the part of progressive white women is often expressed in their failure to have close ties of friendship with Negro women and to realize that this fight for equality of Negro women is in their own self-interest, inasmuch as the super-exploitation and oppression of Negro women tends to depress the standards of all women. Too many progressives and even some Communists, are still guilty of exploiting Negro domestic workers, of refusing to hire them through the Domestic Workers' Union (or of refusing to help in its expansion into those areas where it does not exist) and generally of participating in the vilification of "maids" when speaking to their bourgeois neighbours and their own families. Then, there is the expressed "concern" that the exploited Negro domestic worker does not "talk" to, or is not "friendly" with, her employer, or the habit of assuming that the duty of the white progressive employer is to "inform" the Negro woman of her exploitation and her oppression which she undoubtedly knows quite intimately. Persistent challenge to every chauvinist remark as concerns the Negro woman is vitally necessary, if we are to break down the understandable distress on the part of Negro women who are repelled by the white chauvinism they often find expressed in progressive circles.

Manifestations of White Chauvinism

Some of the crassest expressions of chauvinism are to be found at social affairs, where, all too often, white men and women and Negro men participate in dancing, but Negro women are neglected. The acceptance of white ruling-class standards of "desirability" for women (such as light skin), the failure to extend courtesy to Negro women and to integrate Negro women into organizational leadership, are other forms of chauvinism.

Another rabid aspect of the Jim Crow oppression of the Negro woman is expressed in the numerous laws which are directed against her as regards property rights, inter-marriage (originally designed to prevent white men in the South from marrying Negro women) and laws which hinder and deny the right of choice, not only to Negro women, but Negro and white men and women.

For white progressive women and men, and especially for Communists, the question of social relations with Negro men and women is above all a question of strictly adhering to social equality. This means ridding ourselves of the position which sometimes finds certain progressives and Communists fighting on the economic and political issues facing the Negro people, but "drawing the line" when it comes to social intercourse or inter-marriage. To place the question as a "personal" and not a political matter, when such questions arise, is to be guilty of the worst kind of Social-Democratic, bourgeois-liberal thinking as regards the Negro question in American life; it is to be guilty of imbibing the poisonous white-chauvinist "theories" of a Bilbo or a Rankin; similarly, too, with regard to guaranteeing the "security" of children. This security will be enhanced only through the struggle for the liberation and equality of all nations and peoples and not by shielding children from the knowledge of this struggle. This means ridding ourselves of the bourgeois-liberal attitudes which "permit" Negro and white children of progressives to play together at camps when young, but draw the line when the children reach teen-age and establish boy-girl relationships.

The bourgeois ideologists have not failed, of course, to develop a special ideological offensive aimed at degrading Negro women, as part and parcel of the general reactionary ideological offensive against women of "kitchen, church and children." They cannot, however, with equanimity or credibility, speak of the Negro woman's "place" as in the home; for Negro women are in other peoples' kitchens. Hence, their task has been to intensify their theories of male "superiority" as regards the Negro woman by developing introspective attitudes which coincide with the "new school" of "psychological inferiority" of women. The whole intent of a host of articles, books, etc., has been to obscure the main responsibility for the oppression of Negro women by spreading the rotten bourgeois notion about a "battle of the sexes" and "ignoring" the fight of both Negro men and women – the whole Negro people – against their common oppressors, the white ruling class.

Chauvinist expressions also include paternalistic surprise when it is learned that Negroes are professional people. Negro professional women workers are often confronted with such remarks as "Isn't your family proud of you?" Then, there is the reverse practice of inquiring of Negro women professionals whether "someone in the family", would like to take a job as a domestic worker.

The responsibility for overcoming these special forms of white chauvinism rest, not with the "subjectivity" of Negro women, as it is often put, but squarely on the shoulders of white men and white women. Negro men have a special responsibility particularly in relation to rooting out attitudes of male superiority as regards women in general. There is need to root out all "humanitarian" and patronizing attitudes toward Negro women. In one community, a leading Negro trade unionist, the treasurer of her Party section, would be told by a white progressive woman after every social function: "Let me have the money; something may happen to you." In another instance, a Negro domestic worker who wanted to join the Party was told by her employer, a Communist, that she was "too backward" and "wasn't ready" to join the Party. In yet another community, which since the war has been populated in the proportion of sixty per cent Negro to forty per cent white, white progressive mothers maneuvered to get their children out of the school in this community. To the credit of the initiative of the Party section organizer, a Negro woman, a struggle was begun which forced a change in arrangements which the school principal, yielding to the mothers' and to his own prejudices, had established. These arrangements involved a special class in which a few white children were isolated with "selected Negro kids" in what was termed an "experimental class in race relations."

These chauvinist attitudes, particularly as expressed toward the Negro woman, are undoubtedly an important reason for the grossly insufficient participation of Negro women in progressive organizations and in our Party as members and leaders.

The American bourgeoisie, we must remember, is aware of the present and even greater potential role of the masses of Negro women and is therefore not loathe to throw plums to Negroes who betray their people and do the bidding of imperialism.

Faced with the exposure of their callous attitude to Negro women, faced with the growing protests against unpunished lynchings and the legal lynchings "Northern style," Wall Street is giving a few token positions to Negro women. Thus, Anna Arnold Hergeman, who played a key role in the Democratic National Negro Committee to Elect Truman, was rewarded with the appointment as Assistant to Federal Security Administrator Ewing. Thus, too, Governor Dewey appointed Irene Diggs to a high post in the New York State Administration.

Another straw in the wind showing attempts to whittle down the militancy of Negro women was the State Department's invitation to a representative of the National Council of Negro Women – the only Negro organization so designated – to witness the signing of the Atlantic Pact.

Key Issues of Struggle

There are many key issues facing Negro women around which struggles can and must be waged.

But none so dramatizes the oppressed status of Negro womanhood as does the case of Rosa Lee Ingram, widowed Negro mother of fourteen children – two of them dead – who faces life imprisonment in a Georgia jail for defending herself from the indecent advances of a "white supremacist." The Ingram case illustrates the landless, Jim Crow, oppressed status of the Negro family in America. It illumines particularly the degradation of Negro women today under American bourgeois democracy moving to fascism and war. It reflects the daily insults to which Negro women are subjected in public places, no matter what their class, status, or position. It exposes the hypocritical alibi of the lynchers of Negro manhood who have historically hidden behind the skirts of white women when they try to cover up their foul crimes with the "chivalry" of "protecting white womanhood." But white women, today, no less than their sisters in the abolitionist and suffrage movements, must rise to challenge this lie and the whole system of Negro oppression.

American history is rich in examples of the cost – to the democratic rights of both women and men – of failure to wage this fight. The suffragists, during their first jailing, were purposely placed on cots next to Negro prostitutes to "humiliate" them. They had the wisdom to understand that the intent was to make it so painful, that no women would dare to fight for her rights if she had to face such consequences. But it was the historic shortcoming of the women's suffrage leaders, predominantly drawn as they were from the bourgeoisie and the petty-bourgeoisie, that they failed to link their own struggle to the struggles for the full democratic rights of the Negro people following emancipation.

A developing consciousness on the woman question today, therefore, must not fail to recognize that the Negro question in the United States is *prior* to and not equal to the woman question; that only to the extent that we fight all chauvinist expressions and actions as regards the Negro people and fight and fight for the full equality of the Negro people, can women as a whole advance their struggle for equal rights. For the progressive women's movement, the Negro woman, who combines in her status the worker, the Negro and the woman, is the vital link to this heightened political consciousness. To the extent, further, that the cause of the Negro woman worker is promoted, she will be enabled to take her rightful place in the Negro-proletarian leadership of the national liberation movement, and by her active participation contribute to the entire American working class, whose historic mission is the achievement of a Socialist America – the final and full guarantee of woman's emancipation.

The fight for Rosa Lee Ingram's freedom is a challenge to all white women and to all progressive forces, who must begin to ask themselves: How long shall we allow this dastardly crime against all womanhood, against the Negro people, to go unchallenged? Rosa Lee Ingram's plight and that of her sisters also carries with it a challenge to progressive cultural workers to write and sing of the Negro woman in her full courage and dignity.

The recent establishment of the National Committee to Free the Ingram Family fulfills a need long felt since the early movement which forced commutation to life imprisonment of Mrs. Ingram's original sentence of execution. This National Committee, headed by Mary Church Terrell, a founder of the National Association of Coloured Women, includes among its leaders such prominent women, Negro and white, as Therese Robinson, National Grand Directoress of the Civil Liberties Committee of the Elks, Ada B. Jackson and Dr. Gene Weltfish.

One of the first steps of the Committee was the visit of a delegation of Negro and white citizens to this courageous, militant Negro mother imprisoned in a Georgia cell. The measure of support was so great that the Georgia authorities allowed the delegation to see her unimpeded. Since that time, however, in retaliation against the developing mass movement, the Georgia officials have moved Mrs. Ingram, who is suffering from a severe heart condition, to a worse penitentiary, at Reedsville.

Support to the work of this committee becomes a prime necessity for all progressives, particularly women. President Truman must be stripped of his pretense of "know-nothing" about the Ingram case. To free the Ingrams, support must be rallied for the success of the million-signatures campaign and for UN action on the Ingram brief soon to be filed.

The struggle for jobs for Negro women is a prime issue. The growing economic crisis, with its mounting unemployment and wage-cuts and increasing evictions, is making its impact felt most heavily on the Negro masses. In one Negro community after another, Negro women, the last to be hired and the first to be fired, are the greatest sufferers from unemployment. Struggles must be developed to win jobs for Negro women in basic industry, in the white-collar occupations, in the communities and in private utilities.

The successful campaign of the Communist Party in New York's East Side to win jobs for Negro women in the five-and-dime stores has led to the hiring of Negro women throughout the city, even in predominantly white communities. This campaign has extended to New England and must be waged elsewhere.

Close to 15 government agencies do not hire Negroes at all. This policy gives official sanction to, and at the same time further encourages the pervasive Jim Crow policies of the capitalist exploiters. A campaign to win jobs for Negro women here would thus greatly advance the whole struggle for jobs for Negro men and women. In addition, it would have a telling effect in exposing the hypocrisy of the Truman Administration's "Civil Rights" programme.

A strong fight will also have to be made against the growing practice of the United States Employment Service to shunt Negro women despite their qualifications for other jobs, only into domestic and personal service work.

Where consciousness of the special role of Negro women exists, successful struggle can be initiated which will win the support of white workers. A recent example was the initiative taken by white Communist garment workers in a shop employing 25 Negro women where three machines were idle. The issue of upgrading Negro women workers became a vital one. A boycott movement has been initiated and machines stand unused as of this writing, the white workers refusing to adhere to strict seniority at the expense of Negro workers. Meanwhile, negotiations are continuing on this issue. Similarly, in a Packard UAW local in Detroit, a fight for the maintenance of women in industry and for the upgrading of 750 women, the large majority of whom were Negro, was recently won.

The Struggle for Peace

Winning the Negro women for the struggle for peace is decisive for all other struggles. Even during the anti-Axis war, Negro women had to weep for their soldier-sons, lynched while serving in a Jim Crow army. Are they, therefore, not interested in the struggle for peace?

The efforts of the bipartisan warmakers to gain the support of the women's organizations in general, have influenced many Negro women's organizations, which, at their last annual conventions, adopted foreign-policy stands favouring the Marshall Plan and Truman Doctrine. Many of these organizations have worked with groups having outspoken anti-imperialist positions.

That there is profound peace sentiment among Negro women which can be mobilized for effective action is shown, not only in the magnificent response to the meetings of Eslande Goode Robeson, but also in the position announced last year by the oldest Negro women's organization, under the leadership of Mrs. Christine C. Smith, in urging a national mobilization of American Negro women in support of the United Nations. In this connection, it will be very fruitful to bring to our country a consciousness of the magnificent struggles of women in North Africa, who, though lacking in the most elementary material needs, have organized a strong movement for peace and thus stand united against a Third World War, with 81 million women in 57 nations, in the Women's International Democratic Federation.

Our Party, based on its Marxist-Leninist principles, stands foursquare on a programme of full economic, political and social equality for the Negro people and of equal rights for women. Who, more than the Negro woman, the most exploited and oppressed, belongs in our Party? Negro women can and must make an enormous contribution to the daily life and work of the Party. Concretely, this means prime responsibility lies with white men and women comrades. Negro men comrades, however, must participate in this task. Negro Communist women must everywhere now take their rightful place in Party leadership on all levels.

The strong capacities, militancy and organizational talents of Negro women, can, if well utilized by our Party, be a powerful lever for bringing forward Negro workers – men and women – as the leading forces of the Negro people's liberation movement, for cementing Negro and white unity in the struggle against Wall Street imperialism and for rooting the Party among the most exploited and oppressed sections of the working class and its allies.

In our Party clubs, we must conduct an intense discussion of the role of the Negro women, so as to equip our Party membership with clear understanding for undertaking the necessary struggles in the shops and communities. We must end the practice, in which many Negro women who join our Party and who, in their churches, communities and fraternal groups are leaders of masses, with an invaluable mass experience to give to our Party, suddenly find themselves involved in our clubs, not as leaders, but as people who have, "to get their feet wet" organizationally. We must end this failure to create an atmosphere in our clubs in which new recruits – in this case Negro women – are confronted with the "silent treatment" or with attempts to "blueprint" them into a pattern. In addition to the white chauvinist implications in such approaches, these practices confuse the basic need for Marxist-Leninist understanding, which our Party gives to all workers and which enhances their political understanding, with chauvinist disdain for the organizational talents of new Negro members, or for the necessity to promote them into leadership.

To win the Negro women for full participation in the anti-fascist, anti-imperialist coalition, to bring her militancy and participation to even greater heights in the current and future struggles against Wall Street imperialism, progressives must acquire political consciousness as regards her special oppressed status.

It is this consciousness, accelerated by struggles, that will convince increasing thousands that only the Communist Party, as the vanguard of the working class, with its ultimate perspective of Socialism, can achieve for the Negro women – for the entire Negro people – the full equality and dignity of their stature in a Socialist society in which contributions to society are measured, not by national origin, or by colour, but a society in which men and women contribute according to ability and ultimately under Communism receive according to their needs.

We Seek Full Equality
for Women (1949)[16]

Taking up the struggle of the Suffragists, the Communists have set tasks, new objectives in the fight for a new status for women. The special value of Foster's contribution is:

The leading role of the Communist Party in the struggle to emancipate women from male oppression is one of the proud contributions which our Party of Marxism-Leninism, the Communist Party, USA, celebrates on its thirtieth anniversary.

Marxism-Leninism exposes the core of the woman question and shows that the position of women in society is not always and everywhere the same, but derives from woman's relation to the mode of production.

Under capitalism, the inequality of women stems from exploitation of the working class by the capitalist class. But the exploitation of women cuts across class lines and affects all women. Marxism-Leninism views the woman question as a special question which derives from the economic dependence of women upon men. This economic dependence as Engels wrote over 100 years ago, carries with it the sexual exploitation of women, the placing of woman in the modern bourgeois family, as the 'proletariat' of the man, who assumes the role of 'bourgeoisie.'

Hence, Marxist-Leninists fight to free woman from household drudgery, they fight to win equality for women in all spheres; they recognize that one cannot adequately deal with the woman question or win women for progressive participation unless one takes up the special problems, needs and aspirations of women – as women.

It is this basic principle that has governed the theory and practice of the Communist Party for the last three decades.

As a result, our Party has chalked up a proud record of struggle for the rights of women. American literature has been enhanced by the works of Marxists who investigated the status of women in the US in the 30s. Its record is symbolized in the lives of such outstanding women Communists as Ella Reeve Bloor and Anita Whitney and others who are associated with the fight for women's suffrage, for the rights of the Negro people, for working class emancipation.

Our Party and its leadership helped stimulate the organization of women in the trade unions and helped activize the wives of workers in the great labour organizing drives; built housewives' councils to fight against the high cost of living; taught women through the boycott and other militant actions how to fight for the needs of the family; helped to train and mould women Communist leaders on all levels, working class women inspired by the convictions and ideals of their class – the working class.

A pioneer in the fight for the organization of working class women, our Party was the first to demonstrate to white women and to the working class that the triply-oppressed status of Negro women is a barometer of the status of all women and that the fight for the full, economic, political and social equality of the Negro woman is in the vital self-interest of white workers, in the vital interest of the fight to realize equality for all women.

But it remained for the contribution of William Z. Foster, National Chairman of our Party, to sharpen the thinking of the American Communist Party on the woman question. Comrade Foster projected in a deeper way the basic necessity for the working class and its vanguard Party to fight the obstacles to women's equality, evidenced in many anti-woman prejudices, in the prevalent ideology of male superiority fostered by the monopolists imbibed by the working class men.

The essence of Foster's contribution is that it is necessary to win the masses of American women for the over-all struggle against imperialist war and fascism by paying special attention to their problems and by developing special struggles for their economic, political and social needs. Basing himself upon the Marxist-Leninist tenet that the inequality of women is inherently connected with the exploitation of the working class, Foster called on the Party and the working class to master the Marxist-Leninist theory of the woman question, to improve our practical work on this question and to correct former errors, errors of commission and omission with regard to this fundamental question.

Foster's special contribution lies in his unique expose of the mask placed on the status of women in every sphere in the US by American imperialism. Comrade Foster exposed the bourgeois lie that women in the US have achieved full equality and that no further rights remain to be won. He shows that the ideological prop used by reactionary propagandists to perpetuate false ideas of women's 'inferiority' is to base their anti-social arguments as regards women on all kinds of pseudo-scientific assumptions, particularly the field of biology.

Any underestimation of the need for a persistent ideological struggle against all manifestations of masculine superiority must therefore be rooted out. If biology is falsely utilized by the bourgeois ideologists to perpetuate their false notions about women, Communists and progressives must fare boldly into the biological sciences and enhance our ideological struggle against bourgeois ideas and practices of male superiority.

In order to meet the tasks projected for a deeper understanding and mastery of the Marxist-Leninist approach to the woman question a special Party Commission on Theoretical Aspects of Work among Women was established.

Reflecting the great hunger for theory on the woman question on the part of Communists and progressives was the one day Conference on Marxism and the Women Question held under the auspices of the Jefferson School of Social Science held in June of this year. Nearly 600 women and men attended. Indicative, too, of how the Party is meeting its tasks in this sphere are the numerous cadre schools which have been held to facilitate the training of women for mass work among women and the training of Communist men on the woman question.

Some 10 Party women's commissions now exist, which, under the leadership and guidance of the Party district organizations, give attention to work among women in the Party and in the mass organizations. It is necessary to utilize the 30th anniversary of our Party to strengthen our mass and Party work and to turn the face of the entire Party toward this question.

This is necessary, first, because without mobilization of the masses of women, particularly working class and Negro women, the fight for peace against a third world war will not be successful. American women and their organizations have given indications in varied ways, that they oppose the Atlantic Pact and are fearful of the implications of the arms pact.

This understanding is necessary, secondly, because of the growing reactionary offensive against the civil rights of the American people, the outstanding example of which is the indictment and trial of the 12 leaders of our Party before a jury having a majority of women.

Finally, this understanding is necessary because without rooting ourselves among the masses of women, without building the progressive organizations of women, such as the Congress of American Women, Women's Division of the Progressive Party, the Negro women's organizations, etc., and without organizing special struggles for the demands of women, we cannot win the women against the reactionary influences of the Roman Catholic hierarchy and the bourgeois ideologists.

By successfully mastering our theory of the woman question, organizing masses of American women and focusing attention primarily on the problems and needs of working class women, our Party can help usher in a new status for American women.

To achieve that end, we must win the women to an over-active fight against imperialist war and fascism. For, in the words of the great Dimitroff, in his famous report, " The United Front Against Fascism:"

'While fascism exacts most from youth it enslaves women with particular ruthlessness and cynicism, playing on the most painful feelings of the mother, the housewife, the single working woman, uncertain of the morrow. Fascism, posing as a benefactor, throws the starving family a few beggarly scraps, trying in this way to stifle the bitterness aroused particularly among the toiling women, by the unprecedented slavery which fascism brings them.'

'We must spare no pains to see that the women workers and toilers fight shoulder to shoulder with their class brothers in the ranks of the united working class front and the anti-fascist people's front.'

In the spirit of the anti-fascist hero of Leipzig, let us rededicate ourselves to the fight for the complete equality of women.

International Women's Day
and the Struggle for Peace (1950)[17]

Women in The Struggle For Peace and Security

On International Women's Day this year, millions of women in the world-wide camp of peace headed by the mighty land of Socialism will muster their united forces to make March 8, 1950, a day of demonstrative struggle for peace, freedom and women's rights.

In our own land, there will be over fifty celebrations. On New York's Lower East Side, original site of this historic American-born day of struggle for equal rights for women, and in major industrial states, such as Illinois, Ohio, Michigan, Pennsylvania, California, Massachusetts and Connecticut, broad united-front meetings of women for peace will be held. "Save the Peace!" "Halt Production of the A-Bomb!" "Negotiate with the Soviet Union to Outlaw Atomic Weapons!" – these are the slogans of women in the USA on International Women's Day.

The Struggle for Peace

The special significance of this holiday this year, its particular meaning for labour, progressives, Communists and for American working women generally, is to be found in the widespread condemnation, among numerous sections of the American people, of Truman's cold-blooded order to produce the hydrogen bomb and to inaugurate a suicidal atomic and hydrogen weapon race.

Not to the liking of the imperialist ideologists of the "American Century" is the growing indication by millions of American women of their opposition to war, their ardent desire for peace, their rejection of the Truman-bipartisan war policy.

As in the Protestant women's groups, many women's organizations are opposed to the North Atlantic war pact, which spells misery for the masses of American women and their families. This development coincides with the policy stand of progressive women's organizations that have been outspoken in demands for peaceful negotiations of differences with the Soviet Union, for the outlawing of atomic weapons, for ending the cold war.

Typical of the shocked reaction to Truman's order for H-bomb production was the statement of the Women's International League for Peace and Freedom demanding that Secretary of State Dean Acheson "make clear by action as well as by words that the United States desires negotiations and agreement" with the Soviet Union. This is necessary, the statement added, to avoid "bringing down upon this nation the condemnation of the world." This organization also expressed its opposition to Acheson's suggestion for the resumption of diplomatic relations between UN members and Franco-Spain, as well as to the proposed extension of the peace-time draft law.

These and other expressions of opposition to the Administration's H-bomb policy by notable women's organizations and leaders merge with the significant grass-roots united-front peace activities developing in many communities. For example, in Boston, as a result of a "Save the Peace – Outlaw the A-Bomb" peace ballot circulated last November, a permanent, broad united-front women's organization, "Minute Women for Peace," has been established. In that city, within ten days, over 6,000 women from church, trade-union, fraternal, Negro, civic and middle-class-led women's organizations signed peace ballots urging outlawing of the A-Bomb. In Philadelphia, a Women's Committee For Peace has addressed to President Truman a ballot to "Outlaw the H-Bomb – Vote for Peace." Similar developments have taken place in Pasadena and Chicago. The wide response of women of all political opinions to these ballots is but an index of the readiness of American women to challenge the monstrous Truman-Acheson doctrine that war is inevitable. Emulation of these developments in other cities, particularly among working class and Negro women, is certainly the order of the day.

Indicative of the determination of women, not only to register their peace sentiments, but to fight for peace, is the coalescing on a community basis, following such balloting, of women's peace committees. The orientation of these committees is to convene women's peace conferences, in alliance with the general peace movement now developing.

The widespread peace sentiments, particularly of the women and the youth in their millions, must be organized and given direction and effective, militant expression. This is necessary, since the monopolist rulers are doing everything possible to deceive the people and to paralyze their will to fight for peace. Particularly insidious agents of the war-makers are the Social-Democratic and reformist labour leaders, the reactionary Roman Catholic hierarchy and the American agents of the fascist Tito gang of imperialist spies, whose main task is to confuse, split and undermine the peace camp.

Hence, a fundamental condition for rallying the masses of American women into the peace camp is to free them from the influence of the agents of imperialism and to arouse their sense of internationalism with millions upon millions of their sisters the world over; to protest the repressive and death-dealing measures carried through against the countless women victims by Wall Street's puppets in Marshallized Italy, in fascist Greece and Spain; to link them in solidarity with the anti-imperialist women, united, 80 million strong in 59 lands in the Women's International Democratic Federation, who are in the front ranks of the struggle for peace and democracy.

In these lands, anti-fascist women collect millions of signatures for the outlawing of the A-bomb, against the Marshall Plan and Atlantic war pact, for world disarmament, etc. In the German Democratic Republic, five million signatures were collected by women for outlawing the A-bomb. In Italy, the Union of Italian Women collected more than 2 million such signatures for presentation to the De Gasperi government. In France, women conducted demonstrations when bodies of dead French soldiers were returned to their shores as a result of the Marshall-Plan-financed war of their own government against the heroic Vietnamese. In Africa, women barricaded the roads with their bodies to prevent their men from being carted away as prisoners in a militant strike struggle charged with slogans of anti-colonialism and peace. And who can measure the capitalist fear of emulation by American Negro and white women of these peace struggles, particularly of the women of China (as reflected in the All-Asian Women's Conference held last December in Peking), whose feudal bonds were severed forever as a result of the major victory of the Chinese people's revolution?

These and other significant anti-imperialist advances, achieved in united-front struggle, should serve to inspire the growing struggles of American women and heighten their consciousness of the need for militant united-front campaigns around the burning demands of the day, against monopoly oppression, against war and fascism.

Reaction's Ideological and Political Attacks Against Women

American monopoly capital can offer the masses of American women, who compose more than one-half of our country's population, a programme only of war and fascism. Typical of the ideology governing this war perspective was the article in the recent mid-century issue of *Life* magazine entitled "Fifty Years of American Women." That "contribution" did not hold out the promise to American women along the demagogic 2000 A.D. line of Truman's State of the Union annual message, but brazenly offered the fascist triple-K (*Kinder-Küche-Kirche*) pattern of war and a "war psychology" for American women!

The author, Winthrop Sargeant, drawing upon the decadent Nazi-adopted "theorist," Oswald Spengler, propounded his cheap philosophy on the expensive Luce paper.

...that only in wartime do the sexes achieve a normal relationship to each other. The male assumes his dominant heroic role and the female, playing up to the male, assumes her proper and normal function of being feminine, glamorous and inspiring. With the arrival of peace a decline sets in. The male becomes primarily a meal ticket and the female becomes a sexless frump, transferring her interest from the male to various unproductive intellectual pursuits or to neurotic occupations, such as bridge or politics. Feminine civilization thus goes to pot until a new challenge in the form of wartime psychology restores the balance.

The real intent of such ideology should be obvious from its barbarous, vulgar, fascist essence. The aim of this and other numerous anti-woman "theories" is to hamper and curb women's progressive social participation, particularly in the struggle for peace. This has been the alpha and omega of bourgeois ideological attacks upon women since the postwar betrayal of our nation's commitments to its wartime allies.

Such ideology accompanies the developing economic crisis and penalizes especially the Negro women, the working women and the working class generally, but also women on the farms, in the offices and in the professions, who are increasingly entering the struggle to resist the worsening of their economic status.

Not always discerned by the labour progressive forces, however, is the nature of this ideological attack, which increasingly is masked as attacks on woman's femininity, her womanliness, her pursuit of personal and family happiness. Big capital accelerates its reactionary ideological offensive against the people with forcible opposition to women's social participation for peace and for her pressing economic and social demands.

None of these attacks, however, has been as rabid as the recent "foreign agent" charge falsely leveled by the Department of Justice against the Congress of American Women [CAW] on the basis of that organization's former affiliation with the Women's International Democratic Federation [WIDF].

Only the most naive, of course, are startled at the attack against this progressive women's organization, whose policies, domestic and international, were always identified with the progressive camp. The CAW leadership, in its press statement, answered the continuing attack of the Justice Department, which demands "retroactive compliance" with the undemocratic Kellar-McCormack Act, despite the organization's disaffiliation from the WIDF (under protest). The statement pointed out that this organization has been harassed from its very birth precisely because of its advanced policy stand and activities for peace, child welfare and education, Negro-white unity and equal rights for women. Incumbent on labour-progressives is the expression of full support for the struggles of women against these and other attacks and for the National Bread and Butter Conference on Child Care to be held in Chicago on April 15-16. The call for this conference indicates a broad, united-front sponsorship that includes CAW leaders and demands use of government surpluses and the diversion of war funds to feed the nation's needy children.

Economic Conditions of Women Workers

Any true assessment of women's present status in the United States must begin with an evaluation of the effects of the growing economic crisis upon the working women, farm women, workers' wives, Negro women, women of various national origins, etc. The ruthless Taft-Hartley-employer drive to depress the workers' wage standards and abolish labour's right to strike and bargain collectively, as well as the wholesale ouster of Negro workers from many industries, was presaged by the post-war systematic displacement of women from basic industry. While women constituted 36.1 per cent of all workers in 1945, this figure was reduced to 27.6 per cent by 1947. Despite this, there still remains a sizable force of 17 ½ million women workers in industry, approximately three million of whom are organized in the trade unions, the vast majority being still unorganized.

The sparse economic data available show that the burdens of the crisis are increasingly being placed on the backs of women workers, who receive unequal wages, are victims of speed-up and face a sharp challenge to their very right to work. Older women workers are increasingly being penalized in the growing layoffs. Close to 30 per cent of the estimated 6 million unemployed are women workers.

Side by side with this reactionary offensive against their living standards, women workers have increasing economic responsibilities. More than half of these women, as revealed in a survey by the Women's Bureau of the US Department of Labour, are economic heads of families. The continued expulsion of women from industry, the growing unemployment of men and youth, as well as the high, monopoly-fixed prices of food and consumer goods generally, are impoverishing the American family and taking a heavy toll on the people's health.

Impoverishment has hit the farmwomen to an alarming degree. Almost 70 per cent of all farm families earned less than $2000 in 1948, when the growing agricultural crisis was only in its first stage.

Women workers still find a large gap between their wages and those of men doing the same work, while wages of Negro women are particularly depressed below the minimum wage necessary to sustain life.

There are increasing trends toward limited curricula for women students and limited opportunities for women in the professions. Employment trends also show increasing penalization of married women workers who constitute more than half of all working women.

The attempt by employers to foment divisions between men and women workers – to create a "sex antagonism" – is an increasing feature of the offensive to depress the wages of women and the working class in general. Male workers are being told that the dismissal of married women and the "return of women to the kitchen" will lead to an end of unemployment among the male workers. But this whole campaign against "double earning" and for a "return of women to the kitchen" is nothing but a cloak for the reactionary, Taft-Hartley offensive against wages, working conditions and social security benefits, with a view to a wide-scale dumping of workers, male as well as female.

It must be frankly stated that there has been lethargy on the part of progressives in the labour movement in answering and combating this insolent demagogy. It should be pointed out that the German finance capitalists also used this demagogic line prior to the rise of Hitler. By perpetuating the lying slogan that "woman's place is in the home," monopoly capital seeks to conceal the real source of the problems of all workers.

Consequently this is a question of attacks, not only against the masses of women, but against the working class as a whole. When we deal with the situation of women workers, we do so, not only to protect the most exploited section of the working class, but in order to rally labour-progressives and our own Party for work among the masses of women workers, to lead them into the emerging anti-fascist, anti-war coalition.

Trade Unions and Women Workers

There is every evidence that working women's militancy is increasing, as evidenced last year in strikes in such industries as electrical, communications, packinghouse and in strikes of teachers and white-collar workers. Have labour-progressives grasped the significance of the vital need for a trade-union programme based on concrete knowledge of the conditions of the woman worker, an understanding of reaction's attacks on her, economically, politically, socially?

Some Left-progressive unionists are beginning to tackle this problem as a decisive one. In New York District No. 4 of UE, splendid initiative was shown by the official establishment of a Women's Committee. Men and women unionists participate jointly to formulate a programme and to combat the growing unemployment trends, especially the ouster of married women and their replacement, at lower wages, by young girls from high schools – a trend that affects the wages of all workers. In this union, also, conferences have been held on the problems of the women workers. Similarly, in Illinois, an Armour packinghouse local held a women's conference with the aim of enhancing the participation of Negro and white women workers; as the result of its educational work and struggle, it succeeded in extending the leave for pregnancy from the previous three-month limit to one year.

But these instances are exceptions and not the rule, and it would be incorrect if we failed to state that attitudes of male supremacy among Left-progressives in unions and elsewhere have contributed to the gross lack of awareness of the need to struggle for women's demands in the shops and departments. This bourgeois ideology is reflected in the acceptance of the bourgeois attitude of "normal toleration" of women in industry as a "temporary" phenomenon. This dangerous, tenacious ideology must be fought, on the basis of recognition that the dynamics of capitalist society itself means the tearing of women away from the home into industry as a permanent part of the exploited labour force. Marx and Engels, the founders of scientific socialism, more than one-hundred years ago exposed the pious hypocrisy of the troubadours of capitalism who composed hymns about the "glorious future" of the family relationship under capitalism; they noted the fact, which many progressives too readily forget, that "by the action of modern industry, all family ties among the proletarians are torn asunder... The bourgeoisie has torn away from the family its sentimental veil, and has reduced the family relation to a mere money relation" (*Manifesto of the Communist Party*).

The absence of a special vehicle to deal with the problems of women workers in the unions has undoubtedly contributed to dealing with these problems, not as a union question, but solely as a woman's question. It is of course, both. But it must be tackled as a special union responsibility, with the Communists and progressives boldly in the forefront. In many instances this approach would improve rank-and-file struggles for wage increases, against speed-up and around other concrete demands, and would also win militant unionists for active participation within the emerging rank-and file movements. In this connection, it is also necessary to examine the just complaints of many women trade unionists, particularly on a shop level, who are concerned over the trend toward fewer elected women officers, and the relegation of women merely to appointed positions, as well as the unnecessary pattern of "all-male organization" union structure on many levels.

This entire question requires that we take into account also the position of the wives of trade unionists.

Indicative of the growing militancy of workers' wives is the role of miners' wives, hundreds of whom, Negro and white, recently picketed the empty tipples in the mining camps of West Virginia in support of the "no contract, no work" struggle of their fighting husbands, sons and brothers. Similarly, in the longshore trade, during the Local 968 strike in New York, wives of workers, particularly Negro and Italian women, played an outstanding role. Likewise, in Gary and South Chicago, wives of steel-workers issued open letters of support for the miners' struggle at the steel plant gates, collected food, etc.

Reactionary propaganda is not at all loath to exploit the wrong concepts of many workers' wives, who, because of political backwardness stemming from household drudgery, lack of political participation, etc., often adopt the view that it is the union, or the progressive movement, that robs them of their men in relation to their own home responsibilities.

Attention to the organization of wives of working men by labour-progressives and Communists therefore becomes an urgent political necessity. And key to avoiding past errors is the enlisting of women themselves, with the support of the men, at the level of their readiness to struggle.

The Equal Rights Amendment

In the context of these developments and attacks upon women's economic and social status, one must also see the recent passage of the Equal Rights

Amendment in the US Senate by a 63-19 vote. The original amendment, sponsored by the National Women's Party, proceeding from an equalitarian concept of women's legal status in the US, would have wiped out all protective legislation won by women with the assistance of the trade unions over the past decades. Objection to the original amendment by labour-progressives and by our Party led to the formation of a coalition of some 43 organizations, including such groups as the Women's Trade Union League, the US Women's Bureau, the American Association of University Women, CIO and A F of L unions, the National Association of Negro Women, etc.

A proper approach to such legislation today must primarily be based on recognizing that it is projected in the atmosphere of the cold war, carrying with it a mandate for drafting of women into the armed forces, for the war economy. Without such recognition, the present Amendment, which now urges no tampering with previously won protective legislative gains for women workers, might serve as an effective catch-all for many unwary supporters of equal rights for women.

Despite this danger, Left-progressives should not fail to utilize the broad debate already taking place to expose women's actual status in law; some 1,000 legal restrictions still operate at women's expense in numerous states; and minimum-wage legislation does not exist for over 1 million Negro women domestic workers. A demand for legislative hearings and the exposure of the reactionary attacks now prevalent in numerous state legislatures against the legislative gains of women workers are necessary to guarantee that no bill for equal rights for women becomes the law of the land without proper safeguards protecting the special measures meeting the needs of women workers. Perspective of a necessary referendum carrying a 37-state majority necessary to the bill's passage should not obscure the possibility that passage of the legislation in its present form, or minus the protective clause, could serve as a means of bipartisan electoral maneuvers for 1950 and the passage of the Amendment in its original reactionary form.

A Rich Heritage of Struggle

Before 1908 and since, American women have made lasting contributions in the struggle for social progress: against slavery and Negro oppression, for equal rights for women and women's suffrage, against capitalist exploitation, for peace and for Socialism. Special tribute must be paid those heroic women who gave their lives in the struggle for Socialism and freedom: Elsie Smith, Anna Damon, Rose Pastor Strokes, Fanny Sellins, Williana Burroughs and Grace Campbell. In this period of the US monopoly drive to war and world domination, reaction pays unwilling tribute to the role of Communist women leaders by its deportation delirium. The present-day struggles of progressive and Communist women merge with the traditions and contributions of such great anti-slavery fighters as Harriet Tubman and Sojourner Truth, of such militant women proletarians as the textile workers of 1848, of such women pioneers as Susan B. Anthony and Elizabeth Cady Stanton, of such builders of America's progressive and working class heritages as Kate Richards O'Hare, Mother Jones, Ella Reeve Bloor, Anita Whitney and Elizabeth Gurley Flynn.

March 8 was designated International Women's Day by the International Socialist Conference in 1910, upon the initiative of Clara Zetkin, the heroic German Communist leader, who later electrified the world with her brave denunciation of the Nazis in Hitler's Reichstag in 1933. Already in 1907, Lenin demanded that the woman question be specifically mentioned in Socialist programme because of the special problems, needs and demands of toiling women. Present at the 1910 conference as a representative of the Russian Social-Democratic Labour Party, Lenin strongly supported and urged adoption of the resolution inaugurating International Women's Day. Thus did the American-initiated March 8 become International Women's Day.

The opportunist degeneration of the leadership of the Second International inevitably reduced the struggle for the emancipation of women to a paper resolution. Interested only in catching votes, the Socialist parties paid attention to the woman question only during elections.

Lenin and Stalin restored and further developed the revolutionary Marxist position on the woman question. Thus, Stalin declared:

> There has not been a single great movement of the oppressed in history in which working women have not played a part. Working women, who are the most oppressed of all the oppressed, have never stood aloof, and could not stand aloof, from the great match of emancipation (*Joseph Stalin: A Political Biography*, p. 65).

Lenin and Stalin taught that the position of working women in capitalist society as "the most oppressed of all the oppressed" makes them more than a reserve, makes them a full-fledged part, of the "regular army" of the proletariat. Stalin wrote:

> ...The female industrial workers and peasants constitute one of the biggest reserves of the working class... Whether this female reserve goes with the working class or against it will determine the fate of the proletarian movement... The first task of the proletariat and of its vanguard, the Communist Party, therefore, is to wage a resolute struggle to wrest women, the women workers and peasants, from the influence of the bourgeoisie, politically to educate and to organize the women workers and peasants under the banner of the proletariat... But working women... are some-

thing more than a reserve. They may and should become ... a regular army of the working class ... fighting shoulder to shoulder with the great army of the proletariat ... (Stalin, *ibid.*)

Women under Socialism

Complete emancipation of women is possible only under Socialism. It was only with the October Socialist Revolution that, for the first time in history, women were fully emancipated and guaranteed their full social equality in every phase of life.

Women in the USSR are accorded equal rights with men in all spheres of economic, state, cultural, social and political life (New Soviet Constitution, Article 122).

But equal rights in the USSR are not just formal legal rights, which, under bourgeois democracy, are curtailed, where not denied in reality by the very nature of capitalist exploitation. In the Soviet Union, full enjoyment of equal rights by women is *guaranteed* by the very nature of the Socialist society, in which class divisions and human exploitation are abolished. In bourgeois democracies, equal rights for women constitute at best a programmatic demand to be fought for, and constant struggle is necessary to defend even those rights that are enacted into law.

In the USSR equal-rights articles in the law of the land are but codifications of already existing and guaranteed reality. No wonder Soviet women express such supreme confidence in Socialism and such love for the people. Their respect for other nations, their profound sympathy with the oppressed peoples fighting for national liberation, is based on the firm conviction that their Socialist country is the decisive factor and leader in the struggle for peace.

Marxism-Leninism rejects as fallacious all petty-bourgeois equalitarian notions. Equal rights under Socialism do not mean that women do not have special protection and social care necessitated by their special function (child bearing, etc.) and special needs which do not apply to men.

Comrade Foster's Contribution

The Communist Party of the USA has many positive achievements to record during the last 30 years in the field of struggle for women's rights and in promoting the participation of women in the struggle against war and fascism.

Outstanding was the recent participation of Party women and of the women comrades who are the wives of the 12 indicted leaders of our Party in the mass struggle to win the first round in the Foley Square thought-control trial. And in the continuing struggle against the frame-up of our Party leaders we must involve ever larger masses of women.

Under Comrade Foster's initiative and contributions to the deepening of our theoretical understanding of the woman question, a new political appreciation of our tasks is developing in the Party. Party Commissions on Work Among Women are functioning in the larger districts and in smaller ones. International Women's Day will mark a high point in ideological and political mobilization and in organizational steps to intensify our united-front activities among women, particularly around the peace struggle. As a further contribution to that end, a well-rounded theoretical ideological outline on the position of Marxism-Leninism on the woman question is being prepared.

Comrade Foster called for theoretical mastery of the woman question as vitally necessary to combat the numerous anti-woman prejudices prevalent in our capitalist society, and the "whole system of male superiority ideas which continue to play such an important part in woman's subjugation." An important guide to the Party's work among women are the following words of Comrade Foster:

> The basic purpose of all our theoretical studies is to clarify, deepen and strengthen our practical programme of struggle and work. This is true on the question of women's work, as well as in other branches of our Party's activities. Hence, a sharpening up of our theoretical analysis of, and ideological struggle against, male supremacy, will help our day-to-day work among women...

Comrade Foster particularly emphasized the ideological pre-conditions for effective struggle on this front:

> But such demands and struggles, vital as they may be, are in themselves not enough. They must be reinforced by an energetic struggle against all conceptions of male superiority. But this is just what is lacking...

An ideological attack must be made against the whole system of male superiority ideas which continue to play such an important part in woman's subjugation. And such an ideological campaign must be based on sound theoretical work (William Z. Foster, "On Improving the Party's Work Among Women," *Political Affairs*, November 1948).

Party Tasks

Following Comrade Foster's article in *Political Affairs*, nine Party Conferences on Work Among Women were held with the active participation of district Party leaders. Two major regional schools to train women cadres were held. An all-day conference on Marxism-Leninism and the Woman Question held at the

Jefferson School of Social Science last summer was attended by 600 women and men. These developments evidence a thirst for knowledge on Marxist-Leninist teachings on the woman question.

But it must be frankly stated that it is necessary to combat all and sundry male supremacist ideas still pervading the labour and progressive movements and our Party. The uprooting of this ideology, which emanates from the ruling class and is sustained by centuries of myths pertaining to the "biological inferiority" of women, requires a sustained struggle. Failure to recognize the special social disabilities of women under capitalism is one of the chief manifestations of male supremacy. These special forms of oppression particularly affect the working women, the farm women and the triply oppressed Negro women; but, in varying degrees, they help to determine the inferior status of women in all classes of society.

Progressive and Communist men must become vanguard fighters against male supremacist ideas and for equal rights for women. Too often we observe in the expression and practice of labour-progressive, and even some Communist men glib talk about women "as allies" but no commensurate effort to combat male supremacy notions which hamper woman's ability to struggle for peace and security. Too many labour-progressive men, not excluding some Communists, resist the full participation of women, avow bourgeois "equalitarian" notions as regards women, tend to avoid full discussion of the woman question and shunt the problem aside with peremptory decisions. What the promotion of a sound theoretical understanding of this question would achieve for our Party is shown by the initial results of the cadre training schools and seminars on the woman question, many of whose students have begun seriously to tackle male supremacist notions in relation to the major tasks of the movement and in relation to their own attitudes.

The manifestation of bourgeois feminism in the progressive women's movement and also in our Party is a direct result of the prevalence of male superiority ideas and shows the need for our women comrades to study the Marxist-Leninist teachings on the woman question. According to bourgeois feminism, woman's oppression stems, not from the capitalist system, but from men. Marxism-Leninism, just as it rejects and combats the petty-bourgeois "equalitarianism" fostered by Social-Democracy, so it has nothing in common with the bourgeois idiocy of "the battle of the sexes" or the irrational Freudian "approach" to the woman question. These false ideologies must be combated by women labour-progressives and in the first place by women Communists. Key participants in the fight against these ideologies, and in the fight to enlist the masses of women for the pro-peace struggle, must be the advanced trade-union women and women Communists on all levels of Party leadership. All Communist women must, as Lenin said, "themselves become part of the mass movement," taking responsibility for the liberation of women.

We must guarantee that women cadres end isolation from the masses of women, by assigning these cadres to tasks of work among women, on a mass and Party basis. The Women's Commissions of the Party must be strengthened. All Party departments and Commissions must deal more consistently with these questions, putting an end to the false concept that work among women represents "second-class citizenship" in our Party. A key responsibility of all Women's Commissions is increased attention and support to the growing movements of youth.

We must gauge our Party's work among women by our effectiveness in giving leadership and guidance to out cadres in mass work, with a view to concentrating among working class women and building the Party. To this end, further, working class and Negro women forces need to be promoted in all spheres of Party work and mass activity.

An examination of our work among women is necessary in all Party districts. There is need of Party conferences on the problems of working women and housewives. The good beginnings of examining the long neglected problems of Negro women must become an integral part of all our future work among women. This arises as an imperative task in the light of the militancy and tenacity of Negro women participating in struggles on all fronts.

Experience shows that a major area of our work should and must be in the field of education, where monopoly reaction and the Roman Catholic hierarchy concentrate in a policy of inculcating militarist, racist, pro-fascist ideology in the minds of our children; of victimizing progressive teachers, of conducting witch-hunts, etc. Where good work has been carried on in this sphere, victories have been won, as in the defeat of reactionary legislative measures directed at progressive teachers. In developing struggles to alleviate the frightful conditions of schooling, particularly in Negro, Puerto Rican, Mexican and other working class communities, Communist and progressive women have an important task to perform and an opportunity for developing an exceedingly broad united front for successful endeavor.

By connecting the struggle against the seemingly little issues of crowded schoolrooms, unsanitary conditions, lack of child care facilities, etc., with the issues of reactionary content of teaching – racism, jingoism, etc. – the political consciousness of the parent masses can be raised to the understanding of the interconnection between the demand for lunch for a hungry child and the demand of the people for economic security; between the campaign for the dismissal of a Negro-hating, anti-Semitic Mae Quinn from the school system and the fight of the people for democratic rights; between the protest against a jingoistic school text and the broad fight of the people for peace.

In keeping with the spirit of International Women's Day, tremendous tasks fall upon our Party. The mobilization of the masses of Americans, together with the enlisting and activation of women cadres, for heightened struggles for peace and for the special needs of oppressed womanhood, is indispensable to the building and strengthening of the anti-fascist, anti-imperialist, anti-war coalition. In working for a stronger peace movement among the women as such, we must draw the masses of women into the impending 1950 election campaign and thereby, on the basis of their experiences in the struggle, help raise their political consciousness to the understanding of the bipartisan demagogy and the hollowness of Truman's tall promises. Large masses of women can thus be brought to a full break with the two-party system of monopoly capital and to adherence to the third-party movement. In the course of this development, with our Party performing its vanguard task, advanced sections among the working class women will attain the level of Socialist consciousness and will, as recruited Communists, carry on their struggle among the broad masses of women upon the scientific conviction that the final guarantee of peace, bread and freedom, and the full emancipation of subjected womankind, will be achieved only in a Socialist America.

For the Unity of Women in the Cause of Peace (1951)[18]

The growing surge for peace among the women of our country fully confirms the premise contained in the Resolution that *"the fight for peace has a special meaning to the women of the country"* and that *"without their full involvement no peace campaign can be effective."*

Why there is this elemental peace upheaval among American women is of course no mystery. For the first time, on the bodies of their husbands and sons, the women experience the price of attempted world domination by an aggressive ruling class, which only a short time ago boasted of "easy" victories and a "push button war."

In thousands of working class homes, in the last few weeks, the *"notification to next of kin"* has meant that a father, son or husband will never return from the Korean plains – 5000 miles away. Even as the Harrisburg, Pennsylvania, mother of the first quadruple-amputee learned, such "slight injuries" are accompanied by callous War Department statements that the soldier's *"morale is excellent."*

Negro mothers and wives are registering alarm, as they become aware that lynching by court martial and wanton shooting of Negro troops in Korea merge with the growth of terrorization of Negro veterans at home, as witnessed in the brutal police lynching of the Negro veteran, John Derrick.

Life is cheap to the brass hats these days. Recently, the *Daily Worker* carried a story with a Peking dateline, in which the chairman of the Peking Red Cross stated that *one-third* of the people killed by MacArthur's troops were children, and forty-five per cent were women! Children at play, women washing on the riverbanks, and peasants working in the fields have been the targets of bombing and strafing by the American armed forces whose so-called "police action" was to bring "freedom" to the "unhappy" Korean people!

With the same cold calculation that planned these barbarous atrocities, US imperialism plans to use the sons of American mothers as "blue chips" in their vicious plot of world conquest, fascism, war and death. Over the radio, Gen. Lucius Clay, the protector of Ilse Koch, and Gen. Mark Clark speak bluntly. Thus did Clark declare: *"in the international poker game we're playing today, we need more blue chips; blue chips are boys with guns in their hands."*

War Drive Places New Burdens on Women

This threatened militarization of American youth, who, according to Federal Security Administrator Ewing, are to be prepared for a *"lifetime of mobilization"* means not only personal grief for American women, the breaking up of family life for young women and cheating them of the possibility of marriage and motherhood, but the loss of loved ones and increased economic hardships.

On the family-sized farms, the farmwomen express deep concern over the fate of their sons in the armed forces. Here, in addition to this general worry, the acute labour shortage, due to the loss of their drafted sons, threatens to drive farm families off the land – since hired labour is made impossible by their shrinking incomes.

In industry, women workers have felt the full blow of the growing war economy – the undermining of their already precarious economic positions due to discrimination, to unequal pay rates, lack of opportunity, etc. They face with special impact the threat of wage freezes, rising prices and additional tax withdrawals from their pay envelopes. Speed-up and ever-rising norms, the Truman threat to increase the hours of work, as well as the growing demands for night work, wreak special havoc with the masses of working women, both as workers and as mothers. And the Negro women – faced with intolerable assaults on their rights and living conditions, and with a practical elimination of the few gains secured in industry during the World War II years – are experiencing growing white chauvinist, Jim Crow obstacles in their efforts to rise above domestic labour which is the lot of millions of Negro women. These harsh economic conditions of Negro and white working women are accompanied by the general male supremacist attitudes prevailing toward all women workers.

But that is not all. Now new economic hardships face the 18 million women workers. Truman's dictatorial National Emergency Decree carries with it a threat to draft women for total war production. Reminiscent of the bestial Nazi attitude toward women, Big Business, in their profit-mad quest for new sources of cheap labour power and resources, seek to emulate the Nazis who likewise drafted "mädchen in uniform" by the millions, reversing their foul slogan that *"woman must be neither comrade nor beloved but only mother,"* and kitchen slave.

These and other problems confronting women in industry make it incumbent on progressives to take the initiative in the fight for the demands of the women workers; to guarantee their integration into the unions; to eliminate the age-old wage differentials and secure equal pay for equal work; and to take special measures to protect the rights of the triply-exploited Negro women workers, as stressed in the main report of Comrade Hall. Side by side with this is the necessity to fight for special social services for women workers, and to wage a struggle for the promotion of women trade unionists to posts of union leadership.

A feature of the growth of *fascization* in any country, Dimitroff told us, is the cynicism expressed toward the feelings and role of women. A recent Mid-Century White House Conference on the Problems of Youth dared to tell American mothers that their "love" can make children "accept worry about war, put up with poverty and make the best of mediocre schooling."

Women Are Speaking Out for Peace

But to these and sundry ideological exhortations directed against women's participation in the cause of peace and social progress, in the struggle to ward off attacks on the living standards of their families, and in defense of the democratic and civil rights of the people, American women are daily giving their answer. They reflect the new moods and express the new possibilities for stopping the war makers. More and more the women are acquiring the consciousness that they will really be to blame if they fail to speak up in defense of their children and their country. That is why they have raised the mass slogans of the camp of peace to end the war in Korea and to bring our boys home.

In the industrial heart of America, a Pittsburgh mother puts an ad in a newspaper simply saying, "Will families of loved ones now trapped in Korea, please call me" and in a single day over 300 mothers responded to this call. Soon, this action is emulated in Akron, Chicago, Detroit and Boston, demanding that Truman bring the boys home. Negro mothers angrily forward letters from their sons in Korea to the NAACP urging speedy intervention against court martial of their sons who are the scapegoats of MacArthur's military disasters. When in the shops, in the packinghouse, electrical and garment industries, working women form the active core of peace fighters who sent thousands of Christmas greeting cards to Truman with the same demands; when in Eugene, Oregon, 84 Gold Star mothers voice the same demands, then here is confirmation of a widespread peace ferment among the masses of working women.

American women have begun to expose the futility and immorality of the A-bomb as a weapon to solve problems between nations. That is why they are beginning to join their voices with that of their wrathful anti-fascist sisters the world over whose role for peace cannot be over-estimated.

American women have begun the embattled cry for peace! And that cry is growing in volume among the innumerable women of the land. This determination to stop war – to impose peace – is growing not only among working-class women, Negro and white, but among Quakers, church women, intellectuals, pacifist groups, every national group and organized section of the women masses, young and old.

A Distinct Women's Peace Movement

Comrades! We must now pose the question: How can we most effectively reach the overwhelming majority of women to *act for peace*? How can we help to convert desire for peace into organization and struggle? How can we help to anchor a women's peace movement, embracing a majority of women, to a working class base which will guarantee it consistency, principle and militancy?

To answer this question, we must pose yet another. Why must there be a *distinct* women's peace movement? Clearly, it is obvious that no mass peace movement is possible among the Negro people without 51 per cent of its population being involved; without its most highly exploited and highly organized sector, the Negro women being organized for peace. No labour peace movement is possible without the millions of women workers decisively represented in the textile, garment, needle, laundry, packinghouse, food and other industries. No working class base can be secured without the organization of seamen's wives, railroad workers' wives, longshoremen's wives, wives of steel workers, miners, etc. No movement for peace can be secured unless large masses of national group and farm women are organized for peace, as well as the specially oppressed Mexican-American and Puerto Rican women.

Yet, we do not find full agreement on the necessity to organize women, as women, in the peace camp. In numerous pre-Convention discussions, in our National Women's Commission, particularly, we have been involved in discussions about the necessity for such a distinct women's peace movement. We all agreed that this perspective must be fully registered and fought for at our 15th National Convention, since it is no secret that the present level of women's peace activity, which represents a new level in our work among women, has developed with little or no help from male comrades. Indeed, they were often guilty of impeding its development. But in the course of our discussions; we found that full clarity did not exist among our women comrades on the character of such a movement. How did this show itself?

Two tendencies emerged in our discussions. First was the tendency which argued that, since an outstanding weaknesses of the past was the failure to build united-front movements among working class and Negro women, it was now necessary to limit ourselves to the organization of a working class women's peace movement. Clearly such a tendency is wrong. It fails to understand the full concept of our Party's united-front peace policy which is to create a movement based on the working class in unity with all other peace-loving peoples. It reflects a lack of faith in the working class women themselves who can and will lead all strata of the women in their struggle for peace. This tendency has "Left"-sectarian implications. For to defeat the war-makers, it is necessary to unite all sections of the women under the leadership of the working women, as it is necessary to unite its broad allies under the leadership of the working class.

Second was the tendency to see the need of bringing into being a peace movement embracing all women. Such comrades argued that the broad masses of women in our land, because of their oppressed social status in present-day society, because of their role as mothers, as the creators of life, are deeply opposed to war and can be won in their majority to peace. However, in presenting this generally sound point of view, the comrades underestimated the need that such a movement be rooted first of all among working class women, Negro and white. This tendency had certain Right-opportunist implications because there was absent the understanding that the sharp turn to the working class, required in all phases of Party work, applied to the field of work among women as well.

In overcoming these wrong tendencies, after considerable discussion our National Women's Commission correctly stressed the primacy of the working class orientation while recognizing the new opportunities which exist to create a broad women's peace movement among non-working class women in every community, and on all levels. Major attention must be given to organizing the millions of workers' wives in basic industry, the millions of working class housewives in industrial cities, the millions of working class and Negro women who can be won on the peace issue and around the struggle for their burning demands.

Organize Working Women for Peace

But this is still not all that needs to be said on the necessity for a distinct women's peace movement. Our comrades often tell us, when we raise this question of the necessity of a working class base for the women's peace movement, that working women are already involved in peace activities in their shops. True enough, we discover, as one comrade reported in the splendid panel on Work among Women, in the New York State Party Convention, that the only peace committee in an upstate electrical plant was organized by women workers – *in the last two weeks.* And this is true of other plants. Working women, who have most sharply felt the effects of the war economy, who face the greatest grief in the contemplated draft of millions of their sons and husbands, of course have risen to spark the fight for peace now finding expression in the shops.

But this does pose a problem, namely, *how can working women participate specifically in the women's peace movement?*

An example of a recent experience in Chicago may be worthwhile as a guide in answering this question. Here, a Women's Committee of the National Labour Conference For Peace was established. This peace committee's role was mainly that of issuing general leaflets which met with little response until they realized that general agitation was not enough; that they had to develop a specific approach to the women, as women. It was then that they issued a leaflet entitled: *Must Babies Die*, which showed the senseless murder of children by the atom bomb and linked the desires of women all over the world – the women of the Soviet Union, China, France, Africa, Latin America, who joined in the world-wide campaign behind the Stockholm Peace Pledge – who want life for their children, not death. The response was immediate. Over 100 working women responded, mostly from the working class communities, expressing their wish to join peace committees.

Our comrades and other progressive women concluded that this experience is a clue to the organization of working women. It showed them that women can be aroused to action, in their specific role as mothers and wives who want peace, so that their children of today and those yet unborn may grow up to manhood and womanhood. But more than that, they also drew the conclusion that working women who have the double task of working in shops and caring for the home and the family can often better be organized for peace in the communities where they live than in the shops. Those women trade unionists who spark the fight for peace in the shops have a duty and responsibility to tie themselves up with the general women's peace movement, providing that working class leadership so essential to greater stability and militancy of the women's peace movement.

The great potential of this distinct women's peace movement is yet to be fully unleashed and can only be unfolded if women are specifically organized as women.

Our responsibility to our own people, to the masses of women, to the anti-fascist women the world over, is to guarantee that we influence and give leadership to this wide peace sentiment expressed by women, to transform that sentiment into a mighty movement for lasting peace and defense of the needs of the children! Broad united fronts can be developed on the issue of the draft, and against the militarization of the 18-year-olds; on ending the Korean war and bringing the boys home; on ending the court martial of Negro troops; on seating the Chinese Peoples Republic in the UN. It is also necessary to unmask the war propaganda of the ruling class, in all its forms. There is a grave lack in the peace movement generally to carry through such an exposure.

In this wise, through the creation of a powerful women's peace movement, American women, Negro and white, will take their proper place in the powerful world peace camp with their peace-loving sisters the world over.

Women the World over Fight for Peace

In over 60 lands, forming a strong sector of the world camp of peace, democracy and Socialism, women are organized in huge federations for peace, security and defense of their children. Led by the Women's International Democratic Federation, the activities of these millions of peace-loving, anti-fascist women to emulate these powerful struggles of their sisters for equality, a happy life for all children and, above all, for a lasting peace.

This *new phenomenon* – of worldwide identification and sisterhood of women – grew out of the years of boundless suffering by women under fascism and during the anti-fascist war. Women, in the technically advanced countries, suffered outrageous degradation. They learned and experienced the lot of their sisters in the colonial and imperialist oppressed countries. Coupled with this was the uprooting of all bourgeois-democratic relationships involving women, the extermination of whole families and generations of families. It was these and other costly experiences that gave rise to the new determination of women throughout the world that never again would they allow the use of their sons for the imperialist slaughter of other nations and peoples.

Impelling these developments is the leadership of the world camp of peace, democracy and Socialism by a *workers' state* – the Socialist Soviet Union, which has exemplified in life its concern for the wellbeing and full equality of women and full protection of children in all spheres. The world-shaking example of free Soviet womanhood, the new freedoms achieved by the liberated woman in the lands of the European Democracies who move toward Socialism, the historic strides – as a result of the Chinese People's Revolution – in the elimination of the feudal bondage formerly experienced by millions of downtrodden women of China – all are decisive contributing factors explaining why there now exists a powerful international anti-fascist, anti-imperialist women's movement.

American women bear a heavy responsibility to the millions of our anti-fascist sisters in the world camp of peace, precisely because the threat to world peace stems from the imperialists of our land. The repeated appeals to American women from the embattled mothers of Greece, Franco Spain and the Marshall-Plan-saddled countries are staunch reminders of the responsibilities women in the United States bear to the world struggle for peace and anti-fascism.

The pro-fascist Department of Justice attacks last year against the international fraternization of women should lead us to conclude that we face a great responsibility, in the sphere of work among women, to the high principles of proletarian internationalism. In great measure, our meeting of that responsibility depends on the support given by labour-progressives, led by our vanguard party, the Communist Party, to the emerging women's peace movement. Through such support, the struggle for the equality of women will merge with the general class struggle of the working class which understands and defends the needs and demands of the masses of women. Support to the peace struggles of women in our country will thereby also help to bring in line with world developments, based on American experience, a new advance in women's status in our country.

A Women's Peace Centre

Comrade Hall properly stressed the necessity for our Party to help nurture, support and encourage the development of such a movement. Already existing in our land is a progressive peace centre of women which should be seen in relationship to the whole perspective of winning and organizing women for peace. The American Women for Peace, represents the centre of coalescing women's peace sentiment, composed of broad peace forces who have identified themselves with a specific women's peace movement. Though not all-inclusive of the peace forces among women, this centre is already playing a signal role in the country. It has led three major actions for peace – on the anniversary of Hiroshima, on UN Founding Day, and on November 28, when Truman brazenly announced he was considering the use of the A-bomb in Korea and Manchuria. On that day, over 2,500 women, on 36 hours notice, appeared before the UN demanding the outlawing of the A-bomb and ending of the inhuman Korean adventure. Here, the splendid initiative and leadership of this women's peace centre was clearly demonstrated.

One should note that this activity has not gone unnoticed by the world camp of peace. The returned women delegates to the World Peace Congress tell audiences everywhere they speak, that the first toast by Soviet Peace Chairman Tikhonov, given on their visit to the land of Socialism, was to the delegation of women who went to the UN on its founding day, *"who got there before the men did."* The regularly issued News-Brief of the Women's International Democratic Federation reported the November 28 women's peace action with the observation that this "was the first news to reach them" of the world-wide outraged protest of women against Truman's madness. In quite a different vein, Eleanor Roosevelt was forced to state demagogically, despite her Red-baiting adjectives, that the November 28 UN women's delegation *"spoke the yearning in the hearts of every woman in the land for peace."*

To expand the unity of women for peace, we must reject concepts which deny the need for a distinct women's peace centre on the grounds that we need a "broader movement and broader forces." These arguments come especially from those who stand on the sidelines, criticizing what exists under the guise that the peace centre is not yet all-inclusive, while doing nothing to reach those "broader forces." On the other hand is the argument that the peace centre is not "militant enough," not sufficiently advanced. This argument reflects a failure to understand that the level of the present activity of this peace centre, which is not anti-imperialist or even anti-fascist but an expression of the general peace strivings of women, is in keeping with *their* present level of experience. It will reach a higher level of understanding and militancy as it expands its activity and especially as it organizes peace committees below, of women from the decisive working class strata. We cannot substitute our own desires for militancy for a broad peace movement, as some of our comrades and advanced progressives sometimes seek to do artificially. If we do that we will be militant by ourselves.

Precisely because this women's peace centre views its task not only as one of serving as a centre of women's peace activities on a minimum united-front basis, but also for stimulating and organizing women's peace committees on a community level, it merits the wholehearted support of Communist and progressive women. Issuance of a splendid regular monthly Bulletin by AWP, *The Peacemaker*, for $1 a year is a splendid vehicle for exchange of experiences of women in the fight for peace. It can serve as an organ which links the women's movement to other developments and trends in the broad labour and people's peace movement. Progressive women everywhere should subscribe to this organ as a major means of assisting its work.

In addition, Communist and progressive women everywhere must give leadership to women in their communities and their organizations on such issues as the terror creating atomic air-raid drills, the inadequate school appropriations, the skyrocketing prices, higher taxes, etc., and other such issues which affect the women and their families. These issues in many instances can serve as the starting point for involving women in broader peace activities.

Negro Women Fight for Peace

In our efforts to help build a peace movement of women, we must once and for all overcome the gap between the influence of the triply oppressed Negro women, expressed in the Negro people's movement generally, and their role in the organized peace movement. We must multiply a thousand fold the leadership of Negro women in the fight for peace. In examining our work in the building of peace committees, our greatest weakness, second only to that of building women's peace committee's in working class areas, is the failure to establish peace committees among Negro women. Can it be claimed that Negro women feel less strongly about peace than do other sections of women? The facts contradict this absurdity. As the wife of William McGee played an outstanding role in the fight against the rising terror and intensified oppression of Negro citizens at home, so it was the wife of Lt. Leon Gilbert whose initiative broke the case of her court-martialed officer husband.

The outstanding peace heroines of the Stockholm Peace Petition campaign were Negro women – Molly Lucas of Illinois and Jackie Clark of California – who were sent as delegates to the Warsaw Peace Congress and had the opportunity to visit the USSR. In Harlem, Bedford-Stuyvesant, Boston's South

End, Philadelphia's 4th Ward and similar areas, thousands of signatures of Negro mothers and wives were affixed to the worldwide petition which called for outlawing as war criminals the atomaniacs who first used the bomb. In all peace delegations of women, almost one-third were Negro women. Why then is there no commensurate movement of Negro women for peace?

Contributing to this state of affairs no doubt was the white chauvinist hesitation to raise the Negro question in the broad labour and people's peace movement, particularly in the context of America's imperialist aggression against the coloured peoples of Asia. Additional reasons may be found in the continued efforts of Negro reformists and bourgeois nationalists to sell the Negro people the idea that this is "their war"; in the whipping-up of false jingoistic moods of contempt even among Negro troops for their Korean brothers; and in reaction's veiled flattery of Negro troops in the early stages of the war – to cover what we now know was tipping their hats to the expendability of Negro troops based on chauvinist contempt for the lives and welfare of Negro soldiers.

Now, more than ever, the Negro people understand the full significance of US military aggression in Korea. They see in the bloody massacre of the people of Korea an extension of the foul white supremacy oppression and contempt for the Negro people and the coloured people of all of Asia. It is therefore possible to organize the broadest type of peace activities among the Negro women. This is necessary in the self-interest of the Negro people. And the merger of this anti-imperialist current with the broader labour, people's, women's and youth peace movements, will greatly strengthen the peace camp as a whole.

In the growing anger of Negro mothers against military lynching by court-martial, in the embittered recognition of Negro mothers and wives that their fighting husbands and sons are dying for a cause that is not their own lies the key to arouse and organize their sentiment for peace. In such activity, a new understanding will arise; they will begin not only to question, as they are already doing, why their sons are expendable, but why it is necessary to fight at all in Korea – why it is necessary to fight in any far-off lands.

A hallmark of the recognition by the American bourgeoisie of the special role women play in the Negro liberation movement is their "courtship" of Negro women. But this "courtship" is to be compared to the white supremacist who prates his superiority, but sneaks into the homes of Negro women, invading their privacy, impugning their dignity and perpetuating their social degradation in our society. Thus did Truman, Acheson, and Dubinsky's Pauline Newman attend the recent national convention of the prominent National Council of Negro Women, in order to align this Negro women's organization with the Truman war programme. The bourgeois chauvinist contempt of Negro women is so great that even the UN appointment of an Edith Sampson is not on the basis of leadership ability of Negro women but admittedly "to counter Russian propaganda."

To fully expose the false and lying purpose of this imperialist courtship, rejected by millions of Negro women, means a sharp unequivocal struggle against the special forms of white chauvinism directed against Negro women.

There is widespread evidence, as shown in experience in the women's peace and other mass movements, also reflected in our Party, that the struggle against the special forms of white chauvinism toward Negro women is not yet recognized as a struggle in the basic self-interest of white women. Indeed this was glaringly evidenced in the shameful white chauvinist remarks of an invited woman comrade to the splendid Women's Panel of the New York State Party convention, who expressed herself to the effect that the Negro women on her PTA board were *"mealy mouthed."* Imagine! Failure of a Negro woman to actively participate in the activity of the PTA is blamed on her and *not* on the crude white chauvinist atmosphere which permeates most of these organizations.

The stifling white chauvinist atmosphere within these organizations stems largely from their overwhelmingly petty-bourgeois composition. It is likewise reflected in the failure to conduct struggles for the social needs of Negro women and their children against dilapidated pre-civil war schools, against segregation within the school system, against the practice of organizing in Negro, Puerto Rican and Mexican communities classes for the "retarded," thus deliberately perpetuating the discriminatory status in the schooling of these children. To state that Negro women, even of petty bourgeois composition, do not themselves conduct such struggles is tainted with white chauvinism. It avoids the prime responsibility of white women to lead in the fight against these appalling conditions.

We can accelerate the militancy of Negro women to the degree with which we demonstrate that the economic, political and social demands of Negro women are not just ordinary demands, but *special* demands, flowing from special discrimination facing Negro women as women, as workers and as Negroes. It means first, to unfold the struggle for jobs, to organize the unorganized Negro women workers in hundreds of open-shop factories and to *win* these job campaigns. It means overcoming our failure to organize the domestic workers who recently won for the first time the begrudging official recognition of the status of "workers" in the social security regulation changes. It means more than a pious sympathy for Rosa Lee Ingram, imprisoned for over 3 years, and a revival of the campaign for her speedy release. It means that we must not allow on the Lower East Side a Settlement House to close because bourgeois Jewish nationalists say: "It was meant for Jewish children and now there are too many Puerto Ricans and Negroes." Yes, and it means that a struggle for social equality for Negro women must be boldly fought for in every sphere of relations between men and women so that the open door of Party membership doesn't become a revolving door because of our failure to conduct this struggle.

Women's Special Issues and Demands

Comrades, I have singled out three main questions in this sub-report flowing out of the splendid report of Comrade Hall, namely: 1) the necessity to develop, strengthen and build a distinct women's peace movement; 2) the rooting of that movement among working women and the wives of workers; and 3) the special necessity to bring the fight for peace to the Negro women.

But we all know that analysis and experiences in struggle, sound though these may be, are not enough. The key to nurture, expand and coalesce these peace strivings of women means the raising of special demands, of special issues and the development of special forms of organization. We have much to learn from the rich experiences of the international anti-fascist women's movement, especially from France and Italy, as well as Argentina and Africa, where a feature of these movements is the distinct peace struggle of women linked with defense of the needs of children.

One of the key issues which grips the heart of every mother and fills her children's hearts with terror are the newly introduced atomic air-raid drills now taking place in the nation's schools. But can it be said that progressive women have grasped the possibilities for peace struggle inherent in the widely expressed new sentiment, which shows that women and particularly mothers are not accepting this programme? Newspaper editorials, the statements of public figures as well as our own knowledge from ties with the people, shows in city after city that despite whipping up of anti-Soviet hysteria, volunteers are not forthcoming and there has *not* been *mass identification* with the civilian defense apparatus. No doubt what contributes to this is that millions of women and mothers cannot see security from war in a civilian defense set-up that is nationally headed by the former Governor Caldwell – a Dixiecrat from Florida and in New York, by the anti-Semite Gen. Lucius Clay and by similar characters in other states.

We can neither encourage false security in a programme which is based on the false idea of the inevitability of war, nor ignore the sentiments which impel response and concern, even though passive, by millions to this programme. We are duty bound, however, to expose the falsity of this programme and the instigators of this programme, the very ones who threaten the use of the atomic bomb.

Let us boldly place the question right side up. Let us tell mothers who are worried about atomic warfare that the only defense – even with shelters, drills and war preparations – is to *ban the atomic bomb*. In many cities children die in congested streets, and mothers have to build living islands of safety with their bodies before a traffic light is installed. Shall we say nothing about such a city spending thousands of dollars on a shelter – which in New York City costs $47,000? Shall we be silent about the use of money for these shelters being built in swanky communities while working class children and Negro children cower in dank pre-Civil War school rooms which need to be torn down?

The cost of a single battleship could provide 325 family-sized dwelling units. Shall this money be used for a false national emergency in which 70 billion is being spent for bombs or shall the money be spent for housing projects and homes?

In addition to this vital issue is the issue of high prices, another weakness of the women's movement. Yet experience shows that this issue of high prices is one of the powerful and effective issues around which women will respond; and in seeing the connection between their immediate demands and the struggle for peace, they will also see a necessity for a change in the political administration that denies to them and their families these basic needs.

Generally on the question of the defense of the needs of children there is need for a new appreciation of the prime necessity of strengthening our support to progressive leadership in the parent-teacher field. In numerous states, it has been the consistent activity of progressive and Communist mothers, whose leadership, together with teachers, has helped to counter the racist witch hunts, has fought disastrous pro-fascist legislation which threatens to penalize progressive teachers, and who have generally challenged the drive to *fascisize* the minds of our children. The fiasco of the Freedom Scroll campaign in Los Angeles and San Francisco, opposed by the parent-teacher movement, is an example of the readiness of women to struggle on these issues. Every city budget hearing, where the axe is being put to school needs, finds women present – aroused and fighting in defense of their children's needs. These and other examples should point up to labour-progressives and our Party the wealth of mass issues to rally women and mothers on; and to the possibilities in struggle to raise their political consciousness on the necessity of the struggle for peace.

Comrades, the politics of the women's movement today is not at all simple but complicated. All that Comrade Hall said relative to skill in tactics is being raised as our women comrades, together with non-Party women peace fighters, grapple with these and other problems. In New England the organization, Minute Women for Peace, is under fierce attack. The bourgeoisie, the state and city officials of New England – the cradle of American liberty – are afraid because the present-day sisters of Molly Pitcher, of Deborah Gannett, of the early textile women strikers for the 10-hour-day are fighting for peace, to preserve liberty. To defeat these and other attacks means to guarantee support to the struggle of these women peace fighters. Involved here is the right of fraternal association with our sisters from other lands which received a severe blow at the hands of the warmongers in the recent period. Winning this struggle also means defending the principle of the right of Communist women to work among, and earn leadership among, the masses of women in order to help dissolve the foul tissue of lies about women's capability and leadership in women's struggle for peace and progress.

Our Party's Work among Women

To help transform women's peace sentiment into a mighty organized movement for peace, security equality and defense of children, means we must change our Party's methods of work and approaches to our own women cadre.

In his report, Comrade Hall stated that:

> "...the worst symptom of male superiority tendencies in our ranks is the speed with which we realized the bulk of our leading women comrades after World War II – and our slowness to correct this error. The new level of work achieved by our women comrades, and the new currents stirring among the masses of women, must be reflected in our Party's new level of understanding of the woman's question. This goes for our entire leadership and membership."

What is necessary to achieve this *"new level of understanding"* in work among women? It means, first of all, recognizing and applying the Leninist concept that Communist women must *"themselves be part of the mass movement of women."* It means the virtual release of dozens and dozens of our women comrades for work among women for peace and to struggle for women's special demands.

In many Party sections a consciousness exists that in order to make it possible for women to participate generally in Party activities, the obstacles to women's full participation must be recognized. Party cadres here understand that because under capitalism, care of children is more than often the sole responsibility of women, and not viewed as a social responsibility, as is the case under Socialism, it is necessary to provide for babysitters to help release women for general Party work. But examination shows that this practice, limited because of its costliness, is not widespread. Nor is the same approach taken to release Party women cadre for work among the masses of women. Coupled with this a general underestimation of work among women is expressed in the practice of taking practically all of our women comrades out of their natural habitat thus robbing them of their mass contracts in PTA's and women's organizations while they function as general Party actives.

Then there is the general male supremacist approach which relegates only certain phases of responsibility to women on the assumption that women aren't ready for top leadership responsibilities on a policy-making level. The fact that in the basic units of our Party, a great deal of leadership is exercised by our women cadres refutes this assertion. But what is required here is the elevation of women to policy-making bodies of the Party organization.

There are literally dozens of women in every Party section who, viewing such practices, ask: How can women function fully in the Party – women with families and children, whose problems cannot be fully solved under capitalism? Of course women can and do function as general Party actives and that is all to the good, but they function as general Party actives, and not among the masses of women. The splendid results shown in not a few communities where women were released for work among women, shows how fully one-half of the Party's effectiveness could be strengthened if our Party leadership on all levels overcomes this general under-estimation of work among women.

Combating Male "Supremacy"

Last summer, when Party reorganization was a prime concern, we learned how costly such attitudes could be. They led to liquidationist trends in our Party expressed in the automatic dropping of women comrades. Male-supremacist attitudes ranged from proposals to pull our women comrades out of mass peace work and work among women generally, to ideas that true security means that women should "protect the kids" by pulling out of Party activity. Here was a case of the intensification of bourgeois feminist notions of what true security is and intensification likewise of male supremacist ideas that "women's place is in the home." When some women resisted, some Party forces even held that women felt the tension more than others even going so far as to hold up as "proof" one woman who had a change of life which is the usual and normal biological manifestation when a woman reaches a certain age!

But true security for the family, including families of Party members, comes in the first place from participation of both male and female members of the family in activity for peace and social progress. True security for the Communist family means not liquidation of women's work but expanding that work on the basis of recognizing that the activization of women generally confounds those who desire to keep one-half of the population in passive acceptance of the false ideas of the inevitability of war and fascism.

Overcoming these male supremacist notions means to recognize moreover that our Party, as distinct from those who hold petty-bourgeois equalitarian notions, fights for the true equality of women. What does it mean? It means fighting for the right of women to enjoy every right and privilege enjoyed by men. Many shout equality in general, but in practice show lack of understanding of the special aspects of equality. The petty bourgeois equalitarian denies the special problems and needs of women. True recognition of the special aspects of equality for women means fighting to squeeze out every concession right here under capitalism relative to fighting women's numerous disabilities and inequalities in the home, on the job, in the community. It means above all fighting for the economic equality of women, because her economic dependence on men in our society, her exclusion from production, makes for a double exploitation of women (and triply so for Negro women) in present-day society. It means support to her special demands, for child-care centres, health centres, etc. It means elevation of women to leadership on all Party levels. It means also taking into account biological differences which contribute to women's special problems. Greater education on what is meant by equality is also needed, with special emphasis, directed as Lenin said, to the men in our Party who should be more self-critical of these weaknesses and who must overcome their patronizing attitudes to women.

Our pre-Convention discussion raised anew the question of the struggle against many male supremacist manifestations which Comrade Foster over two years ago called upon our entire Party to overcome in ideological struggle. We must register that Foster's contribution made for a decisive turn in our approach to the woman question throughout our Party, as particularly reflected in all major reports to this convention and in the stress being placed by our Party leaderships in many districts. But there is no need to be complacent on this question since we must use this new awareness to unfold an even greater ideological understanding that there is a Marxist-Leninist approach to the woman question. This is not just the responsibility of the National Women's Commission which is already overburdened and needs assistance on a national level, which needs establishment on a permanent basis of State Party Commissions on work among women, to serve as powerful arms of Party leadership on state levels in work among women, but it requires the conduct of such an ideological campaign by our entire Party.

For Ideological Clarity on Work among Women

I propose that this Convention instruct our incoming leadership and National Education Department to launch such a campaign starting on International Women's Day, March 8, 1951. IWD should be the occasion for widespread tribute to the role and potentialities of the masses of women, and to inculcate an understanding of the Marxist-Leninist approach to women in society, as a duty and responsibility of all Communist men and women. One such contribution to this end is the forthcoming volume on the woman question (a collection of the writings of Marx, Engels, Lenin and Stalin) which will be published by International Publishers in January and which should receive wide circulation and study.

Proper use of the Women's Page of *The Worker*, under the leadership of Peggy Dennis, now widely read; the organization of friends and readers of *The Worker* to make this page the vehicle of exchange of experiences in the peace and general women's movement, can make this page the avenue to increasing the circulation of the press among the masses of women, particularly among Negro and working class women.

The Draft Resolution's failure to deal adequately with the woman question, overcome now with Comrade Hall's report, consists in the fact that it failed not only to deal adequately with women's role – but with her *oppression* – the crux of the question. It is true that the widespread and justifiable criticism by many of our women comrades of the Resolution's weakness was due to their failure to find a corresponding estimate of work among women on all Party levels. They saw therefore the struggle for women's equality solely as an *inner Party matter*, isolated, as too many of them are from the broad ferment of women for peace. Where women, despite obstacles, plunged ahead, and did not fall into the "battle of the sexes" bourgeois-feminist moods, there recognition of women's full role and contribution to the fight for peace was swiftest. This should point up a great fact: namely, that it is the movement of the women themselves for peace that has forced a new awareness upon our Party and labour-progressive forces everywhere today. A real tribute for this approach goes to Comrade Foster who told us that women must fight for their own liberation, and to women Communist anti-fascist leaders in the international women's movement.

The attention and agreement of the entire Party organization must be won to the solution of, and collective application to these problems. Overcoming of these weaknesses will release the collective talents of our wonderful women comrades to work, write, sing and fight for women's liberation; and they will want to do it not as second-class citizens but as contributors to Party policy and mass work in our clubs and groups.

Promotion of Women Cadres

It is time our Party recognizes the precious capital it has in its women cadres. Important indications of an improved attitude in the Party towards the promotion of women in leadership are seen in many parts of the country. We have the advancement to the State Committee at the recent New York Party Convention of such comrades as Lil Gates, Johnnie Lumpkin and Mercedes Arroya; the splendid leadership of such women comrades as Vickie Lawrence and Anne Garfield in work among women in New York and New England; the recent elevation of Comrade Mollie Lieber West to the post if Illinois organizational secretary; of Grace Tillman to a similar position in Indiana and of Comrade Vi to a leading post in a Southern Party district. We have comrades like Rose Gaulden in the leadership in Philadelphia's 4th Ward, of Dorothy Healy and Bernadette Doyle in key positions in California, of Betty Garnett as our National Education Director, of women Communist veterans like Dora Lipshitz and Rose Baron and that of Martha Stone as District Organizer of New Jersey. We also have emerging Negro women leaders like Mary Adams, the splendid young Party women cadre like Jeanie Griffith and Judy; the inspiring role of the foremost woman leader of our Party, Elizabeth Gurley Flynn and of the great women veterans like Mother Bloor and Anita Whitney. There are other women cadres too numerous to mention.

Inspired and steeled by the powerful science of Marxism-Leninism, which holds the key to the ultimate liberation of women in a Socialist society, where the basis of women's exploitation is eliminated, exploitation of man by man abolished, and the true equality of the sexes achieved, let us resolve at this 15th National Convention of our Party to honour the Jane Higginses whose daily work is a measure of their desire to master Marxist-Leninist theory, to participate in winning a glorious future.

In this struggle, Communist women, by their leadership among the masses of women, and learning from them to fight for their demands, will fuse the women's peace movement under the leadership of the working class and will thereby help to change the relationship of forces in our land in such a way as to make for a new anti-fascist, anti-imperialist people's coalition, advancing through this struggle to Socialism.

Black Political Prisoners and the Defense of Black Activism

The very core of all Negro history is radicalism against
conformity to chattel slavery, radicalism against the
betrayal of the demands of Reconstruction, radicalism in
relation to non-acceptance of the status quo!

"For over 300 years the best fighters of our people
have had a price on their heads"

From "Ben Davis: Fighter for Freedom"

Introduction

The demand that civil rights be the basic assumption for all Americans and an end to segregation would dominate African American political leadership from the mid 1950s up through to the rise of Martin Luther King, Jr. and beyond. But before that, the Communist Party USA would be one of the primary organizations pursuing rights for black people. Claudia Jones, as the earlier essays demonstrate, writing consistently intersected US global foreign policy with the absence of domestic rights for some citizens. She was among the first to critique the development of a US imperialist tendency which as a result continued to come out on the wrong side of national liberation struggles against colonial domination. She therefore always described what the struggle for peace looked like when linked to the needs of black and working class communities. Thus in her essays on peace, the basic desire as identified, was for peaceful co-existence of the USA and USSR and the "basic democratic right of all peoples to choose their own form of government." Along the way she criticized the errors that she saw the CPUSA making and described some of the ways that the demand for black rights at home and the struggle for peace intersected as argued by Benjamin Davis.

Thus her booklet-length essay written in defense of the Communist congressman from Harlem, Benjamin Davis, who was prosecuted and jailed as a political prisoner with the first group of communists, is *Ben Davis: Fighter for Freedom* which is included here in its entirety.

This defense of Ben Davis and by extension all black political prisoners is an interesting piece in that it uses quotes from both black leaders and Biblical verses as sectional lead-ins along with photographs of historic black leaders throughout. The booklet was introduced by Eslanda Goode Robeson, the wife of Paul Robeson who was also targeted by the House for un-American Activities Committee and had his passport withheld thus forcing him to cancel foreign engagements. The many photographs which we are not able to reproduce here tell their own story: Ben Davis and his family, Ben Davis introducing resolutions as a New York City councilman and in various active modes with colleagues, engaged in activist work in Harlem. Photographs of black leaders Frederick Douglass, Sojourner Truth, the first black congressmen, 1869-1877, Harriet Tubman and Jomo Kenyatta are interspersed throughout the text.

The essay details the formation of Ben Davis as a leader, and his early work as a young black lawyer, identifies his contributions and his ideas and interestingly links his and thereby the US struggle for Black rights to other liberation movements, citing in particular Jomo Kenyatta in Africa and Cheddi Jagan in what was then British Guiana and Gabriel D'Arboussier of French Equatorial Africa. Significantly, Claudia Jones provides perhaps the most authoritative documentation of the prosecution of the first group of communist leadership. In the end, she requests amnesty for Ben Davis and for all political prisoners. Importantly as well, the essay provides good detail and listings of the series of Black leaders who were targeted by HUAC during that period and the nature of Black community responses to this targeting.

"Ben Davis – Fighter for Freedom" also gives an early understanding of how imprisonment of its leadership was the major strategy used to destroy the Communist Party USA and to simultaneously attempt to contain Black struggles for empowerment in general. It therefore clarifies the nature of the state's response to Black organizations in the 1960s –the Black Panther Party for example and activists like George Jackson who would suffer a similar fate.

The linking of black activism to communism was an approach that the US governmental machinery used to target Black leadership. These come together well in those Black leaders who used Marxism-Leninism as their ideological mode of analysis as a New York councilman did and as did many other Black leaders at the time. Many felt Marxism provided the best analysis of the conditions of Black people. Still, their orientation and intent would be the advancement and liberation of the black community in the United States. That they were prosecuted and imprisoned for this identified them as political prisoners. Thus an essay like "Ben Davis – Fighter for Freedom" also highlights and foreshadows the growth of the prison industrial complex as it targets Black men and women. Significantly as well, the analyses Claudia uses to defend Ben Davis would also apply to her own defense and it is clear that she recognized this as she built her arguments.

Ben Davis: Fighter for Freedom[19] (1954)

Introduction By Eslanda Goode Robeson

We list many Negro women along with our heroes among the fighters for freedom – from slavery through abolition down to the present – from Harriet Tubman, Sojourner Truth, to Mary Church Terrell. And there are nameless unsung Negro women who have worked in the fields, kitchens, nurseries, factories to supplement the family income when our Negro men have been denied job opportunities and equal pay for equal work. Negro women move into new and dangerous areas with their men when breaking new ground in restrictive housing; they march beside their men on picket lines; they, together with their men, carry the fight against segregation in schools, transportation, etc.

Therefore it is not at all unusual to find a Negro woman, Claudia Jones, writing this pamphlet in defense of our beloved leader, Ben Davis, who is now immobilized in prison. Nor is it at all unusual to find me, another Negro woman, writing this introduction.

Claudia Jones, tall, attractive, warm brown woman, in her late thirties, is a brilliant and dynamic leader. Born in Trinidad, British West Indies, she came to the United States at the age of eight. She was quick and clever at school, but along with five million other young people had to leave school during the depression and go to work. Seeking jobs and on the job, she came smack up against discrimination at every turn. Instead of futile complaining, she determined, as she said in a birthday speech, *"... to develop an understanding of the sufferings of my people and for my class and to look for a way to end them..."* She now holds a position of leadership in the Communist Party and plays a major role in the work for equality for women and for peace. For her beliefs, Claudia Jones was victimized by reaction and prosecuted under the Smith Act. She also faces deportation to her native West Indies under the Walter-McCarran Act.

Ben Davis is in prison because he has the courage of his convictions. I can't imagine a better reason for going to prison. When I was a little girl I used to think that only criminals, bad, wicked, evil people, dangerous to the community, were put in jail. Now I am a woman grown, living in a rapidly changing world, I know that very often, very good, very wonderful people are put in jail because they are dangerous – not to the community – but to the few, sometimes very wicked and corrupt people who are in power in the community.

Ben Davis, who was a chosen and freely elected leader and representative of the people of Harlem who served his constituents and the people of the great city of New York as Councilman honestly, consistently, constructively – reaped the strange reward of a prison sentence for his services. Widespread publicity of so unjust a reward to so just a man will help reveal and destroy the corruption and desperation behind such injustice and persecution. Hence, this pamphlet. The term in prison will not destroy so strong and fine a man as Ben Davis, but will temper and refine the steel and humanity of which he is made.

If anybody should want to know why I, Eslanda Goode Robeson, am writing the introduction to this pamphlet about Ben Davis, an American Communist, now in prison, I will give some of my reasons here and now:

1. First, Ben Davis is an old valued friend of mine and of my family. We are proud to be numbered among his friends. It is an honour that we deeply cherish. We love the man.
2. Second, Ben Davis is an incorruptible leader and representative of the people who has the courage of his convictions. We admire and respect the man.
3. Third, Ben Davis is a militant advocate for the rights of the Negro people and for all American citizens, at a dangerous time when such militant leadership is under continuous and violent attack. We must support and defend the man.

Ben Davis: Fighter for Freedom

Come Now and Let Us Reason Together

ISAIAH 1:18

Together with scores of his closest friends and co-workers, I witnessed the heroic actions of an outstanding people's leader in one of our country's most historic and ominous courtroom scenes three years ago.

It was an unforgettable scene – a scene in which this man, about to be jailed for five long years for his ideas – for merely teaching and advocating these ideas and no actual crime, save perhaps his colour – turned *accuser*.

Ben Davis, towering in stature and spirit, stood in the dock in Foley Square and turned *accuser* as he and his ten colleagues awaited the final legal trappings to an outrageous framed-up case. Ben Davis' prosecutors were moulding a frightful pattern – a pattern of *guilt by association, guilt by stool pigeon testimony, of guilt by frame-up* – which has since been adopted by the McCarthyites of our land to try to frame and outlaw all who hold thoughts and ideas not to the liking of the powers that be.

But even with locked doors and hasty efforts by burly marshals to restrain his speech, Ben Davis' fearful prosecutors could not halt the passionate torrent of his incisive, deadly calm and prophetic words.

For Ben's words spilled out of their carefully guarded cold marble halls, into the streets and shops, factories and farms, alleys and playgrounds, beauty and barber shops and especially into the Negro ghettoes of America – across the seas which border our land.

Asserting his refusal to be intimidated or silenced, and demanding the sentences be completely wiped out, Ben Davis addressed the court on that occasion as his own counsel. And, of the convictions of the eleven Communist leaders (Eugene Dennis, Gus Hall, Henry Winston, Ben Davis, John Williamson, Robert Thompson, Gil Green, John Gates, Jack Stachel, Carl Winter and Irving Potash) under the infamous Smith Act, he declared:

> "The real crime committed is against peace, progress and democracy, against the working class and my people, the Negro people!"

When Ben Davis stated that his people, the Negro people, had never enjoyed full freedom but had experienced the force and violence of Jim Crow life in our country, the cynical presiding judge interrupted and stopped him unceremoniously.

But, Ben Davis, who was not intimidated in the southern lynchers' court in Georgia, when, as a young lawyer of 29, he defended Angelo Herndon – persisted – until his words dinned into our ears and minds and hearts.

Of course, there were *some* differences in the situation. Angelo Herndon was indicted, jailed and convicted for leading a demonstration for jobless Negroes and whites in Georgia and young Ben Davis, who had just hung out his law shingle, joined the legal fight in a cause which was later reversed by the US Supreme Court.

But there were also some striking similarities in these cases. Ben Davis and his Party led the fight and above all the mass struggle to free Herndon from the false charge of "conspiracy" (read: the fight for relief for hungry Negro and white families) against the sovereign southern state of Georgia.

In this northern court of law, Ben Davis was now a seasoned mature political fighter, whom reaction fears, as it does his colleagues because he and his Party, the Communist Party leads the fight for jobs, security, equality and a peace-time economy for labour and all America.

We sat there listening to Ben accusing the bi-partisan court and his prosecutors. Then we listened to two other colleagues of Ben Davis – Eugene Dennis and Carl Winter – make similar impassioned and reasoned protests in which they charged that the rights of free speech, press and assembly were being jailed; the *"peace of our people"* placed in jeopardy and that the whole procedure was *"a denial of due process,"* an *"act of fascism!"*

We rose from the long oak courtroom benches to return their waved goodbyes. But we were to comprehend yet more fully the meaning of their truthful words for the entire nation.

In the figure of Ben Davis and his colleagues that early July morning, you were reminded of the great oration of Frederick Douglass made 102 years ago in Corinthian Hall, Rochester, NY in honour of the forefathers and signers of the Declaration of Independence.

Mourning the denial of liberty to millions of enslaved Negro people and castigating the revolting professions of liberty by those in power, the noble Douglass said, in tribute to those other brave fighters:

> They were peace men; but they preferred revolution to peaceful submission; to bondage. They were quiet men; but they did not shrink from agitating against oppression. They showed forbearance; but that they knew its limits. They believed in order; but not in the order of tyranny... They were great in their day and generation. Their solid manhood stands out the more as we contrast it with these degenerate times.

I'm going to keep on stinging – 'til I awake the conscience of America

Harriet Tubman

Three long years have passed since that bleak July morning when Ben Davis and his colleagues began serving their savage sentences.

Terre Haute prison, where Ben Davis has been for all this time, is like *all* federal prisons, in the United States, a Jim Crow prison.

To fully realize what this means requires knowledge of the prison set-up in our country. In Terre Haute, Indiana, as in all federal prisons, there are not only Jim Crow cells for Negro prisoners, but even a Jim Crow Honour Privilege system exists and meritorious conduct lists, like some employers' lists and some seniority lists are established on the basis of the infamous, time-dishonoured *"separate but equal"* rule for Negro Americans.

Terre Haute penitentiary is one of six institutions of its class operated by the Bureau of Prisons of the Department of Justice. It contains approximately 2,500 prisoners of whom about 250 are Negroes. The Negro prisoners are segregated in the dormitories, in mess halls and in other recreational facilities.

All Negro prisoners, including Ben Davis, are confined to cells which are located in a section of the penitentiary *reserved only* for Negroes. Such segregation and discrimination not only violates the rights of Negro prisoners guaranteed by the Fifth Amendment to the Constitution and the right to be free from cruel and unusual punishment as guaranteed in the Eighth Amendment, but also the laws and statutes pertaining to the government of the United States prisons.

Accordingly, though Ben Davis has met the standard of "meritorious conduct" and his work is classified as "exemplary," he is denied special valuable benefits enjoyed by white prisoners; for example, the door to his cell remains locked during waking hours; he is denied the freedom of a recreation room where there are ping-pong tables and other facilities; access to a library; daily showers after work; the right to engage in conversation with prisoners meeting like standards.

Even in prison, then, the "separate but equal" rule for Negro Americans exists! And this man is not a criminal but a political prisoner jailed for his beliefs!

Is it any wonder that Ben Davis, who has struggled against Jim Crow all his life contemplates a suit against this hateful racist policy? The *Afro-American*, outstanding Negro journal, declared on Davis' suit in an editorial entitled *"Job for Mr. Brownell": "We hold no brief for Mr. Davis' political conviction. But we cannot help but admire his courageous outcry against this denial of elementary justice for men in federal custody."*

Why is Ben Davis in prison – this man who was once a councilman of New York City – the largest city in the world – this man to whom privilege of position from birth was put aside to use his talents and intellectual gifts to serve his people, all labour and the nation?

The Smith Act jailers of Ben Davis told you that he and the other Communist leaders were indicted, convicted and sentenced to brutal prison terms and jailed because they threatened the nation's security.

BUT THEY LIED!
Ben Davis and his colleagues were framed!

The Communists exposed the fact that in the US Southern District Court in Foley Square where Ben Davis and his colleagues were tried, Jim Crow prevails against all prospective Negro jurors and very few workers, Jewish people, or Puerto Rican people ever get a chance to serve on juries.

That this rigged hand-picked jury system deliberately excludes Negroes, Jews and Puerto Ricans and is composed of bankers, manufacturers, corporation executives and big business men and some upper-salary-bracket utility employees only further exposes the contemptible and sordid real life drama in which Ben Davis and his co-workers were tried.

Nor was that all: prospective Negro jurors ran the risk of being accused of *guilt by association* for *knowing* Ben Davis.

I actually witnessed this, when, in the second Smith Act trial in Foley Square of the 13 Communist working class leaders in which I was a defendant, the prosecution, peremptorily threw a Negro off the jury panel, merely because this Negro man *also* attended Morehouse College as did Ben Davis and was *four* classes ahead of Ben Davis!

This Negro juror testified under oath that he had never been in any college clubs with Ben Davis – he being a senior and Ben a freshman at the time. He even testified that he only saw Ben Davis at chapel or spoke to him in passing and subsequently saw him on two other occasions – on a tennis court and once at the Carver Democratic Club in Harlem. But mere *knowledge* of Ben Davis was enough to make that Negro *unsafe* as a juror in a Smith Act trial.

Without even batting an eyelash, the racketeer-associating prosecutor, Myles Lane, told the court:

> *"It seems to me that a man who has been friendly... or was a friend of Benjamin Davis, who was one of the defendants in the first trial... that that itself is sufficient excuse to warrant his being excused for cause."*

This Negro juror was guilty first, *of being a Negro who knew a fighting Negro leader;* second, he was guilty of *being in association with Ben in a segregated southern Negro college* – 4 classes ahead of him; *of meeting Ben in a Jim Crow community* on a tennis court; of once praying *together with Ben in a Jim Crow chapel;* and of *meeting Ben in a Jim Crow Negro political club* of a major political party.

Besides the crass white supremacist inference that this prospective Negro juror could not be relied on to form his own opinion, the prosecutors of Ben Davis also by this act *admitted* that all who really *know* Ben Davis would certainly reject their craven lies that Ben Davis or any of his colleagues, Negro or white, ever advocated the violent overthrow of the United States government. The act of excluding this Negro juror also showed reaction's fear that the Negro people, regardless of political persuasion, will be as ONE when one of their real leaders is under attack – even if the attack comes in the form of oppression by government!

Such admissions, of course, only reflect the old blues-song of our people:

> *"If I got to hate somebody*
> *Rather it be judge and jury*
> *And mean bossman*
> *NOT POOR BLACK MAN LIKE ME."*

We will not be trampled on any longer

Sojourner Truth

None better than the Negro people can understand how it came about that Ben Davis was framed.

A people like ours can easily understand that the Government is perfectly capable of framing fighting Negro leaders like Ben Davis.

The history of more than 300 years of our people stands up to charge America's rulers with unpunished and monstrous crimes.

The crime and frame-ups of Scottsboro and Herndon; the crimes of "Mink Slide"

Columbia, Tennessee, of Cicero and Cairo, Illinois, the Martinsville Seven, Mrs. Rosa Lee Ingram and her two sons, the Trenton Six, Willie McGee, Wesley Wells.

The crime of the Christmas 1952 bombing and legal lynch murder of Harry T. Moore, leading Southern NAACP figure and his wife, Mrs. Harriet Moore.

The crime of the Murder of John Derrick, Harlem Negro veteran and the forever sightless eyes of Isaac Woodward.

The crime of sentencing Lieutenant Gilbert to 20 years by court martial for his refusal to allow Negro soldiers, including himself, to be expendable in Korea.

The crime of the recent attempt to send Dr. W. E. B. Du Bois, our most venerable scholar, to jail as a "foreign agent" on a charge not supported by a single fact.

The crime of the vengeful "house arrest" of Paul Robeson, our most renowned artist, whom the government refuses to give a passport because of his fight for peace and dignity of our people!

The crime of over 5,000 unpunished recorded lynchings.

The crime of genocide – springing from the racist intent to destroy a national or religious group, entire or in part.

The crime of slum housing, of the ghetto, of Jim Crow in our economic, political and social life.

The crime of what a nationally syndicated magazine recently termed "the shame of Sunday morning." To quote the churchman who wrote it: *"There is more jimcrowism in America at 11 o'clock on Sunday morning (in our churches-C.J.) than at any other time!' [Redbook Magazine, December, 1953]*

Yes, a people like ours can easily understand the framing of Ben Davis, Henry Winston and other Negro Smith Act victims on the absurd charge of trying to overthrow the government of the United States!

For over 300 years the best fighters of our people have had a price on their heads!

Frederick Douglass, Harriet Tubman, Sojourner Truth, William Wells Brown and many other Negro leaders all had a price on their heads! The thousands of slaves who fled North and to Canada via the Underground Railway had a price on their heads! And white allies who aided the anti-slavery cause, then as now, were also penalized.

Why is this so?

Because in every period of history, scapegoats have been singled out by reaction – and usually among these scapegoats are the most principled and incorruptible fighters for social progress. They are singled out to terrify and immobilize the people, by pointing to them as an "example" of what will happen to others!

Barely 90 years ago, the slave-owners said: *"Go among the Negroes: find out their marks and scars and make good descriptions and send them to me – and I'll find masters for them. That is the way many, many men were carried back into slavery!"** [*Speech of Charles Langston – Abolitionist, 1858–59, before sentence]

– 129 –

In Hitler Germany, the fascists, improving on this technique, did the same thing. In the process of destroying all democratic rights and gains made by labour and the people for generations, they outlawed the Communist Party of Germany and murdered and jailed countless numbers of its best fighters. The concentration camp and crematoriums claimed thousands of Communists – but also thousands of plain anti-fascists and plain citizens of Germany who considered themselves democrats.

Today, in our country there are those who do not only want to "find masters" anew for our people; they want to rob our people of its honoured and respected leadership – leadership of *any* persuasion who refuse to kowtow with heads tied and knees bowed to satisfy themselves with crumbs from reaction's tables.

Those who so threaten our arduous and heroic struggle for full freedom; for equal citizenship rights in these United States are also those who have enslaved our people for generations; chained us to a feudal-like peonage and share-cropping existence; and who want to rob us forever of the dignity of manhood and womanhood. *They* are the powerful financiers who spawn McCarthy fascism in our country. The same millionaires and plantation owners such as C. L. Hunt and other Texas oil millionaires, who back McCarthy, have made their wealth and super-profits on the misery and exploitation of the Negro people and poor white farmers of the South.

McCarthyism is American fascism. In a McCarthyite America, not only would our people suffer the plight a thousand fold of Mississippi Jim Crow and oppression; of a thousand

Martinsville Sevens; the multiplication of the indignities suffered by Mrs. Rosa Lee Ingram – in a McCarthyite America our people would suffer the fate of the six million Jews who were murdered and exterminated by the fascists in Hitler Germany.

One need only call to witness the legion of our people who have felt the whiplash of the McCarthyite inquisition.

How many prominent Negro churchmen have been falsely listed as engaging in so-called un-American activities? Bishop W. J. Walls, C. C. Alleyne of AME Zion Church; Bishops W. A. Fountain, S. L. Green, Carey A. Gibbs, Frank M. Reid, and R. R. Wright, Jr., of AME Church and J. Arthur Hamlett of the CME Church; Rev. Charles A. Hill, of the Baptist Church, are only a few of the prominent Negro churchmen, who, because of their association with the aims of the common good have been so falsely accused.

How many Negro intellectuals and Negro government workers and Negro trade unionists have felt the blows of the McCarthyite inquisitors? Mrs. Eslanda Goode Robeson, Mrs. Annie Lee Moss, Mrs. Goldie Watson, Dr. Ralph Bunche, Langston Hughes, Doxey Wilkerson, Harold Ward, William L. Patterson, Roosevelt Ward, Attorney George W. Crockett, Jr., Dr. Alphaeus Hunton, Mrs. Mary McCleod Bethune, Dr. Forrest O. Wiggins, Coleman Young, Mrs.

Charlotta A. Bass, Dr. W. A. Fingal and Mrs. J. J. Hannibal, are but a few who have felt the inquisitors' blows.

McCarthyism wars on *all* genuine fighters for Negro rights, not only Communists like Ben Davis and Henry Winston, but on non-Communists and even anti-Communists.

Hence, from the Hitler-like precedent of jailing men like Ben Davis for his ideas – from the whole evil body of anti-labour, anti-Negro, anti-foreign born legislation which can well be termed the legal precedent – *enabling acts* – of fascist McCarthyism has come a pattern: *A "Communist" is one who holds ideas McCarthy and the present GOP administration and other reactionaries do not like or agree with.*

These lessons from history, past and present, teach us how in our country, *"we must remove the weights that doth beset us."*

For this grave new danger – the danger of McCarthyite fascism – besets our path to full freedom. It is a danger which would reverse the new opportunities confronting us as signalized in the recent historic unanimous US Supreme Court decision upholding the NAACP suit abolishing segregation in the nation's schools.

This significant victory can only be implemented and the positive legal decisions of the courts fully realized by our people and their allies, only if there is in existence a really mass movement fighting to reverse the loss of total freedoms being whittled away by reaction's onslaught on the Bill of Rights.

Interracial Actions Suspect

"It is conceivable that any organization working for interracial democracy may be challenged for its campaign against race prejudice, discrimination and inequality"

NAACP Resolution on McCarthyism

Two years ago, a cross section of prominent Negro leaders noted this trend. These leaders, in the spirit of Walker's historic Appeal, issued a call to UNITE TO DEFEND NEGRO LEADERSHIP.*

> *"Things have reached such a state in our country"* their Appeal declared, *"that almost any Negro leader in our country who dares to fight hard for Negro rights is headed for trouble with the law, with 'public opinion' or, with hoodlum assassins. No matter whether these leaders are Communists, non-Communists or anti-Communists, the 'explanation' is most always the same."* [*Appeal of the National Committee to Defend Negro Leadership.]

The 44th NAACP Convention in St. Louis strongly warned against a *"discernible pattern which tends to link advocacy of full equality for Negroes and other minorities to subversion or un-Americanism."*

This important resolution pinpointed "the atmosphere of inquisition whirling unchecked in our nation's capital until it now borders upon the proportions and destructiveness of a tornado."

Still another example of the ominous attempt to control thought and distort truth concerning the Negro people in our country was the US Overseas Libraries ban last year of the works of two well-known non-Communists, Walter White and Gunnar Myrdal (*A Rising Wind* and *An American Dilemma*).

Mr. White's book was found offensive by McCarthy because the NAACP leader observed that *all* Negro soldiers stationed in England in late 1941, except for a single anti-aircraft group, *did only* manual labour.

The fact that protests restored the book to the shelves does not alter the original impulse to ban it.

Even books about laughter – the laughter of our people which hides our pain – the kind of laughter contained in the writings of the Negro poet and writer, Langston Hughes, *Laughing To Keep From Crying* and *Simple Speaks His Mind* irked McCarthy.

A crass example of witch-hunting and book-burning, which goes by the name of Congressional "investigations" was the inquisition attempted by McCarthy when he subpoenaed Mrs. Eslanda Goode Robeson and sought to put on trial her two well-known books, *African Journey* and *Paul Robeson, Negro*.

But when the famous anthropologist and wife of the famed leader, Paul Robeson, appeared, to quote a headline from the *Afro-American*, she proved *"too much for McCarthy."* Among other things Mrs. Robeson pointed out, was that her opinions and her right to her opinions was her own business. Invoking the First and Fifth amendments, Mrs. Robeson also called the McCarthyites' attention to the 15th Amendment to the Constitution, declaring that the Senate Committee headed by McCarthy, by its obvious exclusion of Negro representatives is a *"very, very white committee."*

This significant challenge to the McCarthyites in their very lair, forced McCarthy to retreat!

McCarthy also banned from the US Overseas Libraries *The Races of Mankind* by Dr. Gene Weltfish, (co-authored by Dr. Ruth Benedict) prominent white anthropologist. During the hearing when Dr. Weltfish was interrogated as a "Communist," McCarthy picked up her pamphlet and remarked: *"Just opening at random I find something on page 18 of the book entitled The Races of Mankind which would interest my southern colleagues to some extent. It shows intelligence of Southern whites: Arkansas, 41:55; Northern Negroes: Ohio, 49:50."* (My emphasis-C.J.) Yet, this *very* pamphlet was used during World War II to educate our soldiers and to destroy the Hitlerian myth of Aryan *"white supremacy."*

Similarly, banned from the US Overseas Libraries were such works as: Doxey A.

Wilkerson's *Special Problems of Negro Education*; Dr. W. E. B. DuBois' *The Souls of Black Folk* and other works; Dr. Herbert Aptheker's *A Documentary History of the Negro People and American Negro Slave Revolts*; Howard Fast's *Freedom Road* and his other works.

Ben Davis is in jail because books *he* believes in – books which contain the science of his beliefs – known as Marxism-Leninism – are considered dangerous by McCarthy and the warmakers.

This science, the science of Marxism-Leninism, explains why there is poverty and oppression in the world and how people can change all this in the process of struggle.

It shows furthermore that it is not the Communists who have created class struggle, which existed from the dawn of history, but that Communist fighters help to organize, educate, train and lead the working class to realize its life-long dream of peace, security, equality, dignity and happiness.

It is a barefaced lie that this science is a conspiracy, since its very laws and precepts hold that profound social change evolves *not* as a result of cliques, sects, or groups, but from the movement of the masses, for national independence and freedom, for security against want and poverty, for peace against war, for democracy against fascism.

The Communist Party of the USA the Party of Ben Davis, which adheres to this science, and whose ultimate programme is for Socialism, is first of all the Party of the most advanced class of modern society – the working class. The plainest workers and sharecroppers who suffer most under the capitalist system can quickly understand (if only they were free to hear it!) many things about it that most professors cannot understand. These workers and poor farmers and sharecroppers have a natural basis for understanding this science from their own life experiences of being dispossessed, impoverished and denied elementary necessities of life. They understand that this science is on the side of the future of mankind.

Many honest intellectuals among our people have drawn similar conclusions however, about this science which seeks to resolve the age-old battle not yet ended, between freedom and slavery, between the rights of the toiling many and the special privileges of the aristocratic few.

Dr. Mordecai Johnson, president of Howard University, more than once the target of the un-American Committee's effort to cripple this great Negro institution, in a speech at the 1941 CIO Convention, declared of Marxism-Leninism:

> At the basis of Communism there is this simple and passionate belief: that the scientific and technical intelligence which we have at our disposal in the Western World ... in the hands of men who love the human race, could recognize the entire economic structure of the world so as to overcome the world-wide struggle for existence and build up a working population regardless of race, creed or nationality, which could feed and clothe and house its children without taking anything by violence from the human soul...

> *Communism has its finger on the desire of men and is saying to men all over the world, we have come at last from the ranks of those who suffer, not to make you rich, not to make you powerful, not to place you in a position where you dominate through life, but to fix it so you can sit down with your brothers of every race, creed all over this world and eat your simple bread in brotherly peace and affection.*

The dynamic and principled young Methodist Negro minister, the Reverend Edward D. McGowan, chairman of the National Committee to Defend Negro Leadership, in an address to the historic meeting of the National Fraternal Council of Churches, USA, April 30, 1953 on the theme of the defense of Negro Leadership, said:

> *...To the Negro church has been entrusted the responsibility of translating the hopes and aspirations of the Negro for dignity and freedom into reality. When my grandparents sang the spiritual, 'I Am Going to Eat at the Welcome Table One of These Days,' it is true they meant eternity. But they also meant they were looking forward to a day in time when they would no longer have to eat in the kitchens of white folks but would eat at a table of their own in their own dining room at which they would eat in freedom and with dignity.*

The Rt. Rev. William J. Walls, Bishop of the African Methodist Zion Church, outspoken advocate of peace and brotherhood, himself under attack for his views, truly declared: "*I do not believe these people (the McCarthyites) are afraid of ministers and Communism, they are afraid of religion and righteousness.*"

The sound philosophy of the late Rev. Dr. David V. Jemison of the National Baptist Convention well summarizes these thoughts: "*We want for ourselves, our wives and our children everything that every other man wants for himself and his children. We do not want anything that does not belong to us as human beings.*"

Is this not what Negro fighters from the days of Crispus Attucks and Denmark Vesey fought and died for; is this not what the fugitive from slavery held in his heart when he eluded his captors; is this not what the mothers of our people sang through their freedom songs to us to "*Get On Board That Freedom Train?*"

This is true from Nat Turner who died on the gallows to Ben Davis who is incarcerated in a Jim Crow jail; from Frederick Douglass political refugee from the Fugitive Slave Laws to Henry Winston and James E. Jackson, Jr., political refugees from a fascism-breeding statute – the Smith Act.

Thou shalt not bear false witness against thy Neighbour

Ninth Commandment

One of the main threats the Smith Act represents to our crusade for equal rights as Negroes in this country is that it *censors speech, thought, teaching and advocacy of social change.*

Now, as Negroes, we have got to "teach and advocate" change in the many Jim Crow laws and practices of federal, state and governmental agencies.

But the threat is: that any Negro citizen or organization advocating such changes runs the risk that some paid informer will appear in court or some government hearing to lie and testify that one's intent – *deeds and acts to the contrary* – is to "overthrow the US Government by force and violence."

The Smith Act further makes it a "criminal conspiracy" to teach or advocate or circulate almost any idea which hired stool pigeons can testify imply "intent" to overthrow the government by force and violence, even though as in the case of Ben Davis and his co-workers – *not a single act or deed can be pointed to as showing such attempt at overthrow, simply because there aren't any.*

How then did the government "get" its "evidence?"

Through stool pigeons.

One such stool pigeon received $10,000 for his lying mess of pottage in the case of the second Smith Act trial at Foley Square. He testified to a shocked courtroom, that, if need be, he'd stool on his own mother! In cross-examination by the defense, another stoolie admitted that he recruited members of *his own family* to the Communist Party and then *turned over their names* to the FBI!

In St. Louis, Mo., the revelation that a local minister was a stool pigeon, paid $11,000 for his services, brought almost unanimous condemnation from his congregation. His behavior was so crass that the *St. Louis American*, Negro journal, indignantly contrasted his role to that of "*a partly forgotten little black minister by the name of Rev. Richard Anderson.*" Stressing how way back in 1854 Rev. Anderson pastored the very congregation from which this stool pigeon came, its editorial declared that Rev. Anderson "*remained in his pulpit and openly denied the forces of slavery that had the law of the period supporting them.*"

But nothing so exemplifies the vile role of the informer than the recent startling attempt to dislodge Dr. Ralph Bunche as a "Communist" from his high post as head of the United Nations Trustee Division. Dr. Bunche was forced to undergo the ordeal *of sixteen* hours of investigation before the International Employees Loyalty Board!

The case of Dr. Bunche shows to what depths justice and righteousness have sunk in this country. For on the worthless words of Manning Johnson and Leonard Patterson, two members of the growing profitable profession of *paid* government witnesses – even a man so highly placed as Dr. Bunche was not free from their infamy!

Yet, for their perjury and that of Paul Crouch, a white government informer, the Department of Justice has not lifted a finger to prosecute them! Crouch even had the audacity to boast that the Department of Justice does not dare to prosecute him for perjury since to do so would mean they would have *to amnesty the jailed Communist leaders!*

An example of the worth that can be placed on Manning Johnson, for example, is his brazen admission before the Subversive Activities Control Board that he had no aversion to lying.

As observed in a brilliant column by Cliff W. Mackay, editor, *Afro-American* newspapers, *"...in other words, as long as a lie is wrapped in the flag, it suddenly becomes no longer a lie but a sacred duty. Such is the reasoning of the man who dared point a finger at Dr. Ralph Bunche."*

The man *"who dared point a finger at Dr. Ralph Bunche,"* is the *same* Manning Johnson who testified as a government witness in the Foley Square trial of the eleven Communist leaders. If he is unworthy of belief in the case of Dr. Bunche, is he not likewise unworthy of belief in his testimony against Ben Davis, Henry Winston and their colleagues?

It was stool pigeons of this ilk that brought "evidence" in *all* of the Smith Act trials, which "evidence" was upheld by the courts as I angrily remember, in the case of the eleven Communist leaders and that of my co-defendants in the second Smith Act trial as *"amply justified!"*

The swiftness of the retreat of the McCarthyite inquisitors in the Bunche case is significant. It indicates the widespread and growing revulsion here and abroad to the witch-hunt and the impudence with which the informers violate the Ninth Commandment: *"Thou Shalt Not Bear False Witness Against Thy Neighbour."*

"...Be Not Afraid Or Dismayed..."

David Walker

More than a quarter of a century ago, this thought expressed in these calming and prophetic words in the *Appeal of David Walker,* born of a free mother, rallied thousands of Negro and white Americans to the fight against chattel slavery.

The laws of that day were the Black Codes. Like the Jim Crow and thought-control laws of today – these laws, which replaced the old slave codes, also forbade the teaching of Negroes to read and write and the assembling of Negroes without permission.

A fierce attack descended on Walker's *Appeal* as well as on those who supported or even read it, from the slave and plantation owners. The secret order, of the same cloth as the Ku Klux Klan, was known as the *Knights of the Golden Circle.* The secret order outlined many prohibitions, was the main weapon on the side of the plantation and slave owners and all who challenged this order were termed "subversive" and attacked vehemently.

But Walker's call for unity of the Negro people and his words to *"not be afraid or dismayed"* found an echo in the hearts and minds of the Negro people and their white allies as well as among Negro leaders of both conservative and militant persuasion. It was this kind of people's unity which led to nullification and repeal of these brutal slave codes, which contravened American liberty and subverted the American dream, already sullied by chattel slavery.

Today too, our people are uniting in defense of Negro leadership. And well do we have need for unity and still greater unity?

For in addition to the question of liberty, of the fascist threat to civil rights, which I have earlier discussed, the threat of economic depression, in this richest of all lands, has already descended on our people in a more than 2–1 ratio as witness the growing unemployment lists. Like a long shadow over us, it brings in its train joblessness, starvation, eviction and the return to relief rolls, which are meager enough.

Just as there is an integral connection between the struggle against the twin danger of war and fascism and the struggle for economic security and the fate of Negro freedom, so there is a connection between that struggle and the fight for which Ben Davis and his colleagues were jailed and persecuted.

If there is anything that Ben Davis and his colleagues have been associated with and have vigorously fought for – it is for peaceful co-existence between nations and against atomic war; for a peacetime economy, for extended civil rights, for equality and democracy.

Long before it was popular to do so, Ben Davis and his Party, the Communist Party spoke out against the useless Korean War and the waste of lives of Negro and white youths. For this they were accused of being "unpatriotic" and injurious to the nation's welfare. But can anyone today hold that the Korean War – with its over 100,000 GI casualties and countless Korean dead – was other than a useless war?

It was the Party of Ben Davis that likewise exposed the Korean War as a war against the coloured peoples of Asia – a war with definite racist implications, in which Negro soldiers were especially penalized.

The plain truth is that the American people in their majority ultimately opposed the criminal Korean adventure. They made it plain also they wanted no part of the Nixon-Knowland scheme to send American boys overseas to die for the profits of French colonialism in Indo-China.

It was because they fought for the goal of peace that Ben Davis and his colleagues were jailed and persecuted.

Is a minority Party, like the Communist Party, to be penalized for its scientific understanding of society – and its leaders for their clarity of vision? The truth of their views is being confirmed before the eyes of the whole world.

The great achievement at Geneva, ending the nearly eight year "dirty war" in Indo China, demonstrates the irrepressible will for peace of millions of the world's peoples. This peace heralds the prospect that men, women and youth strive for and believe can be won in our generation.

Were Ben Davis and his colleagues at their posts of leadership today, they would join with the great majority of people who hail this achievement. They would expose the demagogic charge of "appeasement" by those reactionaries who flail against the truce. Davis and his colleagues would join with thousands of progressive and democratic-minded people around the globe who protest new threats to world peace, such as is evidenced in the rape of the great nation of Guatemala whose democratically elected government was recently overthrown by the US-United Fruit-backed puppet, Castillo Armas. Davis and his colleagues would protest the murderous deaths of over 4,000 heroic Kikuyu people of Kenya, East Africa, for their "non-cooperation" with British imperialist perpetuated rule over their homeland and Davis and his colleagues would also oppose the US-backed efforts to remilitarize Western Germany as a threat to world peace.

The pioneering role and contributions of Ben Davis and his Party, the Communist Party, in all of these and other peace struggles, for which they were persecuted and jailed, makes it imperative, now – with the peace will of our people on the rise, with the rising anti-McCarthy movement, that Ben Davis and his colleagues should be freed to give their leadership to further successes for the people's deepest needs and aspirations.

"Out of Such Material Come Saints"

"What about a man who is willing to go to prison for his cause though that cause seems erroneous in our sight? If you were really called to preach and know something about the prophets, you must say, out of such material come saints!"

Dr. J. Pius Barbour, Editor, National Baptist Voice

Ben Davis was not jailed for the big or little lies imputed to him and his Party, the Communist Party – *Ben was jailed for ideas he does believe in.*

One of the very first ideas Ben Davis and his Party believes in is that the Negro people should have full, unequivocal economic, political and social equality – not 20 years hence, not 10 years hence, but *NOW!* This is likewise one of the reasons why Ben and his Party support and stand ready to unite with all organizations of our people or white allies who set on this freedom goal or any aspect of this cherished goal.

Ever since Ben Davis revolted against Jim Crow conditions in his native Atlanta, against Jim Crow education, Jim Crow in the economic, political and social life of Georgia, the Wall Street rulers of our country have been trying to silence his great voice.

Yes, they hate Ben Davis.

When at one point of Ben Davis' slashing testimony in prejudiced, freedom-hating, Federal Judge Harold R. Medina's courtroom, this slick banker and owner of slums leaned over his bench to command, in insulting white supremacist fashion, of Ben Davis: *"Now – be a good boy....."*

Ben flashed back into his teeth:

"I will not be a good boy!"

Reaction has hated Ben and singled him out as a marked man from the moment he refused to *"be a good boy"* and accept the status quo of Negro serfdom, of lynch and mob violence in the South.

Ben Davis' own testimony best exposes the lie that it is *not* the Communists, but those who are continually accusing the Communists of force and violence who are themselves the real perpetrators of force and violence against the Negro people and other sections of the working class in our country.

Here is an exact excerpt of his testimony in his own words:

> *The Court: Mr. Davis, in these speeches that you made, did you at anytime undertake to answer the charge that the Communist Party advocated the overthrow of the Government by force and violence?*
>
> *The Witness: Yes, many times.*
>
> *A (continued): I said about that, that that is just a pure Hiltlerian distortion of our Party in this country. I discussed this very many times and pointed out that this business of charging the Communist Party with force and violence was one of the very strangest things in the world to me. To tell me as Negro about practicing force and violence, as a Communist, when all my life I had been hounded by this both as a Communist and as a Negro well, that just didn't make sense; and that this charge – of force and violence – usually comes from fascist sources and that it is usually uttered against the Communist Party, in order to hide the real forces of force and violence, who are the Ku Kluxers, the terrorists and the lynchers and the police brutes who attack the Negro people and who attack other sections of the working class in this country. That is the way I answered that question."*

This is why they went out to get him; to silence this great tribune of American democracy, of our people, the Negro people of all the oppressed, Negro and white.

Go and Do Thou Likewise

Luke 10:37

Ben Davis was born *"on the other side of the tracks"* in Dawson, Georgia, September 8, 1903.

His grandmother was born a slave as were a couple of his aunts and uncles. His father, an editor and publisher, was a member of the Republican National Committee – whose election was greeted by burning crosses of the KKK on his front lawn. This campaign, for months of terror by the KKK against his home, hastened the early death of his mother.

When about six years of age, he attended for a few weeks a segregated "tumble-down rural school in Dawson, Georgia."

Ben also attended Summer Hill Public School, a public Elementary school in Atlanta. But because provision for public education for Negroes ended at the sixth grade in Georgia, at that time, his parents sent him to Morehouse College and then to Amherst where he "did well in studies... did a little debating, belonged to the glee club and orchestra, played the cornet in the band and the violin in the orchestra. And other varied campus activities."

After graduating in 1921, from Morehouse Academy, the equivalent of high school and later Amherst, where he received his Bachelor of Arts degree in 1925, Ben went to Harvard Law School and took his law degree in 1932.

After graduating from Harvard, at 28 years of age, Ben returned to Atlanta to practice law and was admitted to the Georgia Bar in 1932. Two months later came what he describes as "a turning point in my life."

Ben Davis was just starting out – with the advantage of a Harvard Law degree. He might, if he "knew his place," have achieved what success is possible for a Negro in the South and a considerable degree of material comfort.

But Ben Davis believed in justice. He believed that the Constitution applied to his people – equally with all others. That is how it came about that he offered his services to the International Labour Defense and became Herndon's lawyer.

That trial did a lot to change the course of his life. Describing that trial Davis said together with his client he "suffered some of the worst kind of treatment against Negroes. The judge in the case referred to me as a "n – – " and a "darky" all the way through the case and to my client... treated me in such a way that I could see before me the whole treatment of the Negro people in the South where I had lived all my life.

"The fact that I had been a little luckier than the average Negro and in some ways, the average white, to have gotten such an education, was not at all effective in shielding me from what the Negroes had to suffer whether they were labourers or whether they were doctors or lawyers or men of wealth. ...I considered what I could do at that moment that would enable me to hit the thing, this lynch system, this Jim Crow system. I considered that the best thing I could do was to join the Communist Party because that would hurt most, and so I did."

Ben did plenty of "hurt." As an associate of the International Labour Defense, headed by William L. Patterson, he participated in the now famous legal and mass defense of the framed nine Scottsboro Negro youths. He entered the defense of the Atlanta Six, Negro and white, who faced a conspiracy charge similar to Herndon. He helped edit the *Southern Worker*, which also meant in this land of "free speech" trying to find printers to print the paper.

In 1935 Ben became editor of the weekly *Negro Liberator* in New York City, then wrote for the *Daily Worker* and moved up to its editorial board. He ran for Congressman-at-large in 1942 and got 50,000 votes. In 1943 he was elected to the New York City Council with over 40,000 votes. In 1945, he was elected again to the Council – *with more votes from white people than voted for Rankin in Mississippi* – with 63,000 votes. His programme was simple in words: *"Make New York City a city without discrimination and injustice."*

Of his programme in the City Council Ben told the Court: *"I was there to represent the working people of New York City and I could do that by doing everything to stop the plunder of the big financiers and to stop their use of the City Council for their own interests."*

From this clear statement of beliefs, the Court thought it had found something partisan. *After all, it asked, wasn't Davis there to represent everybody?*

Ben replied dryly that since the monopolies were few and the working people and consumers pretty nearly represented everybody, he was satisfied with representing *"pretty nearly everybody."*

Ben Davis is a man who chose to risk many things and now finally his very freedom to represent and defend *"pretty nearly everybody"* against the privileged very few.

There has not been a single case of injustice that Ben Davis has not raised his voice and pen against.

Whether it has been the defense of the honour and dignity of Negro womanhood, against legal lynching, or whether it has been his fight against the deathly rat-traps and tinder boxes in which some of our people live; whether against police brutality and terror which rides on well-groomed horses in the Harlem ghetto; or against the monopoly owners of our homes, our jobs and the very plots which claim our bodies in death which are Jim Crowed, Ben Davis' fearless and uncompromising voice has assailed the people's enemies.

An example of successful adoption of measures he proposed when a city council legislator, was the measure urging the New York City Congressional delegation to support enactment of pending Fair Employment legislation, for anti-lynch and anti-poll tax legislation.

Today with the job gains of Negro Americans, formerly strengthened by federal fair employment safeguards, almost a memory, can one truly imagine what Ben Davis' voice would mean demanding FEPC passage as against the shameful failure of the 83rd Congress to uphold a single election promise to enact any civil rights legislation?

Other measures Davis fought for and in some cases secured adoption were such varied measures as: granting the demands of merchant seamen for an increase of their basic wage rate; opposition to anti-labour legislation in Congress, jobs for all at trade union wages without discrimination; full job equality for Negro women; equal pay for equal work for women workers; increase in the New York City teacher salaries; greater monetary appropriations for our schools, increased state aid to New York City for education; appointment of a

Negro to the New York City School Board; measures to protect the safety and lives of our kids in the antiquated structures called schools in the working class, Negro, Puerto Rican, Italian and Jewish communities.

Also, for restoration of the five cent fare on all subway and bus lines; demands for bans on biased textbooks and the lifting of bans on such books as authored by Mark Twain, Robert Louis Stevenson, Howard Fast and other outstanding writers; whose writings are feared. Davis urged restoration of progressive teachers to their posts and the exclusion of biased white supremacist and anti-Semitic instructors in our schools; cancellation of tax exemption to housing and redeveloping companies which practice discrimination against persons because of creed, race, colour and national origin.

The magnificent fight finally achieved to break Jim Crow in Stuyvesant Town was led by Ben Davis during his four-year tenure in the City Council of New York for which he earned the enmity of the real estate lobby and Metropolitan Life Insurance Company.

If today, New Yorkers celebrate Negro History Week, it is due to the consistent and the unflagging role of the Communist Party to set the record straight as to the heroic history of our people and to Davis' unanimously adopted measure in January 1944, to have New York's mayors proclaim this anniversary.

And if, when the baseball diamond, catching the shadow of the season's first ball, shiningly rings with the fan's plaudits for Negro athletes, a modest part of that struggle can be credited to Ben Davis and his Party.

If today the birthday of that scientific genius of Tuskegee, George Washington Carver, is officially proclaimed in New York by the mayor, it also is the result of a resolution introduced by Ben.

Ben Davis also fought the antecedents of the vicious McCarran and Walter-McCarran anti-foreign born legislation restricting West Indian immigration. He condemned such measures as a product of the whole reactionary campaign of hysteria against all of the foreign born, Negro and white, as well as against the Negro people, at the expense of West Indians first, the great majority of whom are staunch and militant fighters in this country (as well as in the Caribbean from whence their rich history springs) for Negro rights and full democracy.

And above and through it all was Ben's consistent record for international friendship and peace between nations based on negotiation of differences for national independence and freedom of all national and colonial oppressed peoples, for trade and cultural exchange between East and West.

Together with the late Hon. Peter V. Cacchione, first elected Communist legislator, Ben Davis' role as a fighting leader and people's legislator can be no more honourably termed – *tribunes of the people!*

But even this inadequate record does not give a full insight into Ben Davis, man, people's leader and proud Communist.

To get that one must seek out the people – they who know him, who have felt his hand, know his wisdom and have heard his great voice raised against oppression. We must seek out the people and listen to their voices.

A Little Part of You and Me

"When jail doors close behind him in the not too distant future, Benjamin J. Davis, convicted Communist, will take with him into his cell a little part of you and me."

Walter White (*The Progressive*, Nov. 1950)

They *are legion* who while *not* agreeing *in toto* with Ben Davis or the Communist Party, do agree that Ben Davis is a man of principle. They *do* agree that this man's fearless devotion to principle is to be respected. They *do* agree that one more day in jail is too long for Ben Davis who should never have been jailed for his ideas.

Two years ago, 13,000 people from Ben Davis former district in Harlem, signed petitions demanding presidential amnesty for Davis and his colleagues. Now, if a man is to be judged, as the old saying goes, *"by the company he keeps,"* he can best be estimated by the opinions of his contemporaries. From the day of Ben Davis' jailing and since that time, angry voices have been lifted among our people and our leaders as well as among white allies, to loose him and let him go!

Listen to their Voices:

"Ben Davis is a burning and shining light in these days of Cadillac leadership; he takes his place with the saints of old who went to jail for their opinions."
Reverend Dr. J. Pius Barbour

"Nobody considering Ben Davis as a man and a leader could by any stretch of the imagination think of him as guilty of anything but what this nation ought to reward and give the broadest chance for development. They need not necessarily follow him in all his opinions, but they must applaud the man, who, having the chance to be idle and careless, becomes busy, thoughtful and devoted and gives his life to the great cause of changing the methods of production and distribution of wealth in this country and in the world"
Dr. W. E. Burghardt Du Bois

"I stand firmly at the side of the convicted Communist Eleven. What happens to them is a deep concern of every American... Shall we defend our true heritage or shall we allow ourselves to be destroyed by American fascism parading as defenders of the democratic faith?"

"Our powerful answer must be that Ben Davis may continue his fine contribution. Together with that answer must be provision and demand for arrest of judgment based on the true traditions of American justice."

"I am proud to say these few words for my dear friend and associate – Ben Davis."

Paul Robeson

"There is this... that must be admired about DuBois, Robeson, Ben Davis and others. They are not taking it lying down. Ben Davis is in prison... Robeson has sacrificed... DuBois has fought without let up for over half a century and at 85 he is determined as ever. Some day when truth gets a hearing, America, regardless of colour, we will honour them."

J. A. Rogers, Negro Historian

"It is time for non-Communists to drop their prejudices and do something and do it quickly or we will all be bound hand, foot and body."

"Negroes in the South are overthrowing the government of white supremacy every hour and we intend to continue doing it. There was a law saying Negroes couldn't vote. And we have been overthrowing that kind of government. When the government starts putting people in jail because it doesn't like their ideas then the liberties of 15 million Negroes are at stake".

"Harry T. Moore was sent to his death by a bomb and Benjamin J. Davis was sent to prison for the same reason. We cannot recall Harry T. Moore. But the American people can recall Ben Davis."

Mrs. Modjeska Simkins, Editor,
South Carolina Lighthouse and Informer.

Numerous other prominent individuals have spoken out against the Smith Act. Among these are: Hon. Judge Hubert L. Delaney, Roscoe Dunjee, Editor of the Oklahoma *Black Dispatch*, Bishop William J. Walls, Dr. J. Pius Barbour, Editor, *National Baptist Voice*, Bishop C. C. Alleyne and others. Such widely differing political forces such as the CIO, AFL, independent unions, Americans for Democratic Action, NAACP, churchmen, cultural leaders, educators and other prominent figures here and abroad, while themselves non-Communists and even anti-Communists, are alarmed over the threat to free speech by the jailing of Communists under the Smith Act. And two eminent Negro lawyers, Richard Westbrooks and Earl Dickerson of Chicago, in an historic *amicus curiae* brief urged reconsideration of the US Supreme Court 6-2 conviction of Ben Davis and his colleagues.

By Their Fruits Ye Shall Know Them

Matthew 7:20

Ben Davis is not the only Negro leader who has been attacked by reaction as we can plainly see.

But Ben Davis, Henry Winston, National Organizational Secretary of the Communist Party and the other Negro Communists under attack, were illegally seized, persecuted and harassed by reaction because they represent the most advanced sector of Negro leadership who link the Negro freedom fight to that of the working class and to the fight against war and fascism.

Reaction so fears the impact of Negro Communist leadership on the struggle for Negro freedom in our country, that an integral part of their anti-Negro offensive is the drive to jail and remove from leadership *all* leading Negro Communists in our country.

Today, Henry Winston, born in Hattiesburg, Mississippi, is a political refugee from the persecution of his country's government – a political refugee because he dared to expose and challenge the Jim Crow system of men like John Rankin from his hometown – a political refugee, because he dared along with his colleagues to expose and challenge the Korean War and because he proposed a system of society which would eliminate economic crises.

James E. Jackson, Jr., leading Negro Communist of Virginia, is similarly a political refugee. In a splendid pamphlet, written last year by his wife, Mrs. Esther Cooper Jackson, entitled *This Is My Husband*, Mrs. Jackson, mother of two children, wrote:

> *"They accuse my husband of taking his "dangerous ideas" out of books of "foreigners" like Stalin and Lenin...*
>
> *"... No, it is not dictation from any foreign source which caused my husband to dedicate his life and talents to the struggle for a new social order. Rather in the course of the struggle for a better life he discovered the answer to the problems of our times which have grown as an integral part of the history of our country. That these ideas have been adopted in other lands simply indicates that mankind, facing common problem, eventually arrives at common answers."*

For dedication of their lives to realizing the answers to the common problems of mankind over 115 Communist and working class leaders, 13 of whom are Negroes, have been arrested under the Smith Act.

These include, besides Ben Davis and Henry Winston, Pettis Perry of California and New York, Claudia Jones of New York, James Jackson, Jr. of Virginia, Thomas Dennis, Michigan, Ben Carreathers, Pittsburg, Pa., Al Murphy of Missouri and Alabama, Thomas Nabried, Philadelphia, PA, Robert Campbell of New York and Ohio, Paul Bowen of Seattle, Washington, James Tate of Connecticut and Claude Lightfoot of Illinois.

The ruling class of our country well understands the historical significance of the rise of Negro Communist leadership in the United States. It is a leadership whose ideas and perspectives are based upon the scientific principles of Socialism, upon the conviction that full economic, political and social equality for the Negro people can only be won fully allied to the cause of the working class.

This new leadership arose in the [19] 20s, grew rapidly in the [19] 30s and strengthened its ties with the Negro community. Even today, held deep in the hearts of thousands of non-Communist Negro people, are memories of the struggles waged by the Communists against hunger, homelessness, joblessness and the misery of the Hoover depression.

What is more, the numerous and brilliant contributions made to the cause of Negro freedom – in the economic, political, social and cultural fields, by Negro and white Marxists have been recognized in all parts of the country by the Negro people.

Today, the very meaning of any serious leadership in the fight for Negro rights brings one into opposition with the foreign and domestic policies of government.

Ask yourself: Can anyone support the great national liberation struggles of the peoples of Africa – without facing the accusation of being a *"Communist?"*

Can anyone fight for the right to live in homes of our own choice-as in the Trumbull Homes in Illinois – without facing mob violence and the accusation of being a *"Communist?"*

Can one invoke the First or Fifth Amendment, without the accusation of being a *"Communist"* who *"hides"* behind the *"protection"* (!) of the Constitution?

Whether in writings, speeches, or needed organization endeavors, *any* Negro leader who pursues *any necessary manifestation of leadership* is labeled "subversive," "communistic," "undesirable", "aliens," or "dangerous troublemakers."

Thus it is clear that while Negro leaders active in the Communist Party are singled out for special prosecution, the attacks extend far beyond the Communists. But in the struggle for full citizenship rights many different forces must unite for victory.

"In the shouting out times
In the stand up and be counted days
Do you turn your heads
Are you afraid?"

When things get thick Some gents then out

An Old Saying Of The Negro People

There have not been a few such gents and ladies who have so thinned out when the going got rough. They are among those who figuratively prefer the safety of their scalps and can down their troubled consciences, if they have any, by avoiding the rising glances of concern by our people who increasingly judge our leadership by their incorruptible and unpurchaseable characters.

Well, let us ask ourselves:

> Then, there are those who tell us that to be radical and black means
> three strikes against us, or to be black and red is even worse.

Essentially this argument is one which counterposes patriotism to the nation's
welfare; loyalty to radicalism, *real loyalty*, to jingoism.
Well, let us ask ourselves:

> Do not our people have a *right to have* radicals?
> Yes – a *right!*
> Do not our people have the *right to seek some radical solution* to their
> highly oppressed status?
> And have a *right to be radicals?*
> It would surely *seem* they have.

The very core of *all* Negro history is *radicalism* against conformity to chattel
slavery, *radicalism* against the betrayal of the demands of Reconstruction, *radicalism*
in relation to non-acceptance of the status quo!
Is there a conflict between being *radical* and *being loyal* to one's country?
History can best answer this question. For the history of our people is rich in
example that because the oppression of our people comes from the ruling class,
the very *survival* of our people required nonconformity to preserve the dignity of
manhood and womanhood.
For example, when in 1850, Frederick Douglass said: *"that the whole framework of
the American government is radically at fault"** [*Herbert Aptheker, *A Documentary History
of the Negro People*] was he not expressing a radical thought? Was he being disloyal
to the Negro people, to democracy, to the interests of the vast majority of the
American people?
Or when Charles Langston, Negro secretary of the Ohio Anti-Slavery Society
told a US Court in 1858 about to jail him for violating the Fugitive Slave Act: *"I
know that the courts of this country, that the Governmental machinery of this country are
constituted as to oppress and outrage coloured men,"*(Aptheker) was he not expressing a
radical idea fundamentally in the interests of the country?
When Sojourner Truth, demanding equality for Negro women told the First
National Women's Rights Convention in Seneca Falls: *"I have borne five children and
seen most all sold off into slavery and when I cried out with a mother's grief... none heard... And
aren't I a woman?"* (Arthur Fauset, *Sojourner Truth*) was she disloyal to the laws of the
land, which not only denied legal, political and social rights to white women, but
triply discriminated against Negro women?
When President Buchanan sent US marshals to Frederick Douglass' home to
arrest him after John Brown's heroic effort, in order to question him as to his

knowledge of the event, was Douglass not radical in writing from Canada that: *"I have no apology for keeping out of the way of these gentlemanly US marshals. ...I have quite insuperable objections to being caught by the hands of Mr. Buchanan."* Douglass also wrote from Canada he would never *"assume the base and detestable character of an informer."*

Now, Douglass may have disconcerted the slave owners, but *"only base and detestable characters"* owe loyalty to exploiters and oppressors!

We can conclude as a result of these examples that the entire history of the Negro people has been one of *radical* solution to a sorely oppressed status. We can also conclude that the finest patriots of the Negro people – Harriet Tubman and Frederick Douglass, Sojourner Truth and David Walker, Nat Turner and Denmark Vesey, Ben Davis and Henry Winston – those who have been assailed as radicals-are the staunchest fighters against slavery and Jim Crow, for freedom and equality. We can also conclude that the oppressors of the Negro people are the betrayers of the American nation. When, finally, we remember that history teaches that the only organized effort to overthrow the US government through force and violence came from that class holding the Negro people in slavery, we can better judge who is truly loyal to America!

Who is loyal to America and its democratic traditions? James Byrnes: governor of South Carolina, who equates the role of the NAACP and KKK, correctly assailed by Thurgood Marshall as *"fascist McCarthyism rampant with racism"*?

Or Ben Davis – whose eloquent voice against Jim Crow scathes Byrnes and all the racists even from behind prison bars?

Yes, To Believe In Negro Freedom Means To Be Radical!

I believe with Ben Davis and his colleagues that this thought – Marxist-Leninist thought – contributes mightily to correcting the many evils in our society through peaceful effort.

You may not.

BUT you will agree that to disagree with a man's thoughts is no reason to jail him.

Instead of using his great talents and enthusiasm of deeply-held beliefs, Ben Davis is thrust into jail.

It is a disgrace to this country that Ben Davis ever went to jail or that he is kept there now.

Ben Has no Fear...

"Ben has no fear. The fear he said is from those who don't know what the future holds. He is at long last a free man.

His is the freedom of the man who has been subjected to persecution and can still stand up and say: 'I've taken all they can throw at me. I have not been conquered!'"

Attorney George W.Crockett*

[*Attorneys George W. Crockett, Michigan, Harry Sacher, New York, Abe Isserman, New Jersey, Louis McCabem Philadelphia, Penna and Richard Gladstein of California, were all counsel for the eleven Communist leaders]

In these inspiring words, Attorney George W. Crockett summed up his impressions of Ben Davis following an early visit to him in Terre Haute Jim Crow prison.

After describing Ben's "high spirits," his "loss of quite a bit of excess poundage" and the difficulties which Davis and the other jailed Communist leaders have experienced, such as the denial of correspondents requested, a few of whom were won after a fight, Crockett wrote of Davis' concern with prison Jim Crow.

The heinous practice of discrimination against men in federal custody forced Ben Davis *even in prison to* continue the fight for which he has dedicated his life against Jim Crow and segregation. He is planning court action.

Davis' action lays bare one of the genocidal practices of prison life in these United States in general and *for* Negro Americans in particular. This "brazen practice" of prison Jim Crow is another stench in the noses of democratic Americans and further exposes the hypocritical prattling of our State Department of a *"free America in a free world."*

Nor is this all that Ben Davis has done even while incarcerated in Jim Crow jail. Despite a serious illness last year in prison which required hospitalization for nearly 5 weeks, Davis once again testified in the Pittsburgh Smith Act case of Steve Nelson, Andy Onda, Ben Carreather, James Dolsen, Irving Weissman and Bill Albertson. In brilliant, clear testimony, permeated with calm confidence, after being jailed for two years, his truthful accusations could not be answered by the prosecutors of his ideas and that of his Party. For this heroic stand and his refusal to name names of workers to his prosecutors, Davis was again sentenced for contempt and drew two additional months to be served separately, not concurrently, from his present five-year sentence. *But Ben would not endanger the security of Negro and white workers who would face vilification and persecution in these days of anti-Communist hysteria from the McCarthyite fascist witch-hunters.*

Now, were Ben Davis an ordinary prisoner, he could, *after* February 21, 1954, be released anytime prior to March 1, 1955 – the date of his conditional release.

But the government seeks to use a further detainer – another charge – not tried at the time of his first indictment – the *charge of making it a crime to be a member of the Communist Party of the United States.*

– 149 –

The recent arrest of the outstanding Illinois Communist Negro leader, Claude Lightfoot, under the membership section of the Smith Act is directly related both to this detainer and to the spreading move by government for police state powers yet attempted in this country. Deliberately framed under Section 2 of the Smith Act, Attorney General Brownell seeks to get a conviction and set a precedent to make membership in the Communist Party a crime. A conviction under this additional unconstitutional section would widen the thought control dragnet. Lightfoot was held under the excessive bail of $30,000 in a Chicago jail.

What is more, the dangerous precedent set in the closing days of the 83rd Congress in which for the first time in our nation, a political party, the Communist Party, was virtually "outlawed" amidst legislative chaos, terror and irrational procedure, without benefit of public hearings or full debate indicates the serious growth of fascism in the country. The arbitrary criteria in this *bill of attainder* for determining who is and who is not a Communist as anyone who "thinks" or acts" as a "Communist" is a logical climax to the Smith Act jailing of men and women for their political ideas. This bill is a dagger aimed at the heart of the trade union movement, providing it as it does for the licensing of trade unions, even as was done under Hitler's decrees. Such is the real iron fist behind this measure to curtail the rights of labour, the rights of the Negro people and all Americans.

Thus, through these two new attacks, the Attorney General and Department of Justice attempting something even the US Supreme Court has so far denied. These new moves, to which there is wide and growing opposition, by the nation's press, labour, civil rights organizations and the Negro people's movement should spur the fight for amnesty for the Smith Act victims because it further exposes the whole crude frame-up character of the Communist trials and the jailing of Ben Davis and his colleagues.

Ben, Davis gets a "Hearing"

A Federal Judge, member of the Federal Parole Board, described Ben Davis as the *"most intelligent"* prisoner he had ever interviewed and that he had found him a *"sincere and fundamentally honest man."*

A white Southerner by birth, the judge also told Ben Davis that any parole action in his case would be held up pending a full Board hearing in Washington, DC.

Accordingly, a delegation headed by Paul Robeson, outstanding artist and life-long friend of Ben Davis; John Abt, Davis' present attorney; Mrs. Dolly Mason, community leader; Cyril Phillips, New York businessman; Rev. Kenneth Ripley Forbes of Philadelphia and Dr. Marcus Goldman, former Government geologist, appeared at a Federal Parole Board hearing February 11, 1953.

Their pleas were that Davis had served more than one-third of his sentence in the federal prison of Terre Haute and was now eligible for parole. Among other things raised by Robeson in a press conference was the tremendous sentiment for Davis' release in the Negro communities. Rev. Forbes said he communicated to the Board a feeling in the Negro communities throughout the nation for Davis' release.

Robeson further pointed out that in the recent Smith Act case involving the 13 Communist leaders, Judge Edward J. Dimmock had set the top sentence at three years, stating that Congress did not intend to apply the five-year sentence to conviction for "conspiracy to advocate."

Despite their pleas, the Parole Board, while listening politely, in a later decision, turned thumbs down on Davis' release.

Still another delegation went in February of this year to Brownell's office. The delegation in this case was headed by William L. Patterson, National Executive Secretary of the Civil Rights Congress, who was forced to serve a vindictive three-month sentence for not being able to produce *lost* names of his contributors to the Treasury Department; James W. Ford, National Executive Secretary, National Committee to Defend Negro Leadership; and Miss Louise Jeffers, Executive Secretary of the Harlem Committee to Free Ben Davis. This delegation presented petitions urging Davis' freedom and also left a memoranda [sic] with Senator Langer, Chairman of the Senate Judiciary Committee, which outlined the discriminatory practices suffered by Davis and other Negro prisoners in Terre Haute federal prison and demanded action by this Senate Committee.

Despite numerous petition campaigns, which have found a receptive echo and numerous anxious inquiries as to why Ben Davis is still in prison – HE *IS STILL NOT FREE!*

With every ounce of strength
I shall continue to fight for the people

Benjamin J. Davis

In these words, Ben Davis opened his farewell speech to the people of his community and all his former constituents the night he spoke for the last time before his jailing in Harlem's famed Dewey Square.

The square was jammed with people and placards urging *"Repeal the Smith Act!" "Free the Eleven Communist Leaders." "Stop Thought Control"* and home-made signs scrawled *"Ben, We Love You."*

Some people had clenched fists and tears of anger were in their eyes.

But Ben Davis continued to speak:

> *"The sun of liberty is rising all over the world..."* He talked of the unbreakable fraternity which we have with the peoples of Africa, Asia, the West Indies, Europe, Latin and South America, who are

achieving national independence and freedom, as well as with the peoples of the Soviet Union whose nation has wiped out racial discrimination and made it a crime. Ben spoke of our bonds with the people in the wide world who fight for peace, equality, national independence and security against atomic wars and for friendship between nations.

And Ben said: *"I'll be back on these Harlem streets some day; I know I will..."*

...On the streets of Harlem one finds many people who know and remember Ben Davis for his fight for the people's needs.

Here is a woman who remembers, how, when evicted, it was Ben Davis and his Party, the Communist Party, who were among the first to fight against her eviction, helped put her furniture back in her house. Here is a bartender who asks, as you open a paper, the *Daily Worker*, of which Ben Davis was publisher before he was jailed, *"How is Ben?"*

Here is a Negro woman, whose sad eyes contrast strangely with the strong lines in her stern face. I recognize her as the mother of one of the five bereaved families from whom death claimed five victims, three of whom were children and who lived in a firetrap in Harlem. That was in January, 1947, when there were 45 deaths in one month from slum housing in the Harlem-Puerto Rican Washington Heights area. *"How is Mr. Davis?"* She presses your hand meaningfully.

Here is a Negro minister who, when you talk to him, quotes the Scripture: *"Smite Down the Shepherd and the Sheep Will Be Scattered!"* to show his understanding of Ben's jailing.

Here is a white couple who knew Ben and who ask: *"What can we do to help free Ben Davis?"*

Two youths, Negro and white, striding arm in arm - they seem like students - come up and say in the bright tones of youth: *"We Must Free Ben Davis!"*

Yes, we can hear his voice! Even from behind prison bars, Davis' fearless voice scathes racist Jim Crow!

And because it is the supreme evidence and continuation of his entire life's fight for his people, for all the oppressed, it is all the more resounding.

It is resounding, because it is *one* with the Negro leaders of the South who rallied in 15 states against the McCarthy tactics of the Jenner Committee, condemning them as a blow against the entire Negro community of the nation.

It is *one* with all those who fought to save Ethel and Julius Rosenberg and who fight to free Morton Sobell from a living death sentence of 30 years. It is *one* with the millions here and abroad who kept Wesley Wells from execution in the California gas chamber and who fight to free Mrs. Rosa Lee Ingram.

It is *one* with all our people who fight in these coming elections for an anti-

McCarthy, pro-labour, pro-democratic Congress, for extended Negro representation, for peace, security and democracy!

It is *one* with all our people and our allies who fought and *won* reversal of the "separate but equal" doctrine of southern school's Jim Crow. And who fight to realize implementation *now* of the Supreme Court's ruling.

It is *one* with our brothers and sisters in the South, in Atlantic itself, in Ben's birthplace, in Dawson, Ga., who asked: *"What are you doing to get Ben Davis out of prison?"*

Ben Davis' voice and his fight for freedom is *one* with Jomo Kenyatta of Africa; Cheddi Jagan and Burnham of British Guiana; with Gabriel D'Arboussier of French Equatorial Africa; with all the valiant men and women fighters of all creeds and nations who fight for liberation and national independence in all parts of the world.

They've jailed Ben Davis. But his ideas are still abroad. It is Ben Davis himself who can best express his ideas from ladders on the streets of Harlem, in the broad arena of political and legislative struggle, in unity meetings with his people, Negro and white and with white allies, and in the councils of his own Party. Until Ben Davis can do so, the McCarthyites and the racists will have a strong weapon with which to spread fear and subversion.

Will you answer Ben's confidence that he will be back on the streets of Harlem — and all the broad highways of the nations of the day--soon?

The one answer – the one response to Davis' fight against prison Jim Crow and his jailing for his ideas is contained in the word – *AMNESTY!*

The fight to free men and women jailed for unpopular political beliefs by presidential amnesty is a great American tradition. There have been numerous cases of political amnesty in our country. Andrew Johnson's Republican Administration granted amnesty to conscientious objectors of World War I. President Harding freed Eugene Debs, famed Socialist leader and other political prisoners as a result of a mass campaign which forced their freedom. And similar amnesty decrees were issued by President Calvin Coolidge.

Surely – there is need for unity of all democratic-loving Americans to free Ben Davis-to demand amnesty for all political prisoners. Especially true of the Negro people as a whole, who first understand that the jailing of Ben Davis, *in the prime of his life*, is the jailing of a part of our historic struggle for full citizenship rights in these United States!

FREE BEN DAVIS NOW!

Amnesty For Ben Davis And His Colleagues Now!

To sing the hallelujah of the famed Negro *spiritual:* We *must* free *him for* he "bears our burden in the heat of the day!"

The Caribbean
and Caribbean Diaspora

"If then, our Caribbean Carnival has evoked the
wholehearted response from the peoples from all the
Islands of the Caribbean in the new West Indies
Federation, this is itself testament to the role of the arts in
bringing people together for common aims and to its
fusing of the cultural, spiritual, as well as political and
economic interests of West Indians in UK and at home."

"A Peoples' Art..."

Introduction

Essays on the Caribbean and Caribbean Diaspora

Claudia Jones' arrival in London in December 1955, began a new phase in her
more direct self-definition as a Caribbean woman. Her presence in London
indeed gave shape to the Caribbean Diaspora in England. The mass migration of
Caribbean people to England, iconized in the 1948 HMS Windrush, which
carried on it the calypsonian Lord Kitchener, continued unabated until the
Commonwealth Immigration Act of 1962 which created more stringent
conditions for Caribbean entry into the UK. By 1958, Claudia Jones had founded
the *West Indian Gazette and Afro-Asian Caribbean News*, the first major black newspaper
in England and through it launched the first Caribbean Carnival in England in
1959. Her major involvement in the London community came following the
Notting Hill race riots in 1958, which marked the high point of white residents
violent attacks on Caribbean migrants. The creation of a public march,
accompanied by musicians and pan men, in Portobello Road in 1958, where there
is now a plaque marking this event aimed to demonstrate to the London white
community that Caribbean people had come in peace but also to infuse the joy
of Caribbean life in a cold and unfriendly England. The first identified Caribbean
Carnival was held on January 30, 1959, at St. Pancras Town Hall, London. Two
plaques have been placed on the corner of Portobello Road and Tavistock Square
and at the Carnival Village in Powis Square, London W10 at the 50th anniversary
of the carnival in 2008 identifying Claudia Jones as founder of the London

Carnival. The plaque on Portobello Road, unveiled by the High Commissioner for Trinidad and Tobago and the mayors of Kensington and Chelsea marked an interesting coming together of recognition of Claudia for her contributions to the Caribbean and British communities. A stamp in her honour was also issued in October of 2008.

The bulk of her thinking and writing on the Caribbean appear in the various editorials of the *West Indian Gazette and Afro-Asian Caribbean News* which she edited from 1958 until her passing in 1964. However, two major essays on the Caribbean are available and are included here along with her statement in the Souvenir booklet for the Caribbean Carnival 1959. The first "American Imperialism and the British West Indies," was published in 1958 and is a good summary of the developments and critique of the process which was leading to the failure of the West Indian Federation. A great deal of the arguments she makes in this essay have been evident in the loss of control of a variety of resources (oil, bauxite, aluminum) to US and British transnational corporations like Texaco. She correctly identifies the role of the Caribbean colonies for the British and US imperial interests and the Anglo-American rivalry for control of the Caribbean and the struggles that leaders like Dr. Eric Williams faced as they tried to shape a Caribbean national identity. She also cites the work of John La Rose, a leading trade union activist from Trinidad who would also have a similar but even more sustained critical role in the shaping of the cultural and political life of Afro Caribbeans in England throughout the 1960s up to his passing in 2006. La Rose for example would be a member of the Caribbean Artists Movement, lead the International Book Fair of Radical Black and Third World Books (1982-1995) and through New Beacon Books and the George Padmore Institute would carry the baton of supporting and developing black intellectual thought for over five decades. It is helpful then to see Claudia Jones as one significant actor in a stream of political-intellectual activists from the Caribbean in order to fully put her contributions into context.

The second essay included here was the introduction to the Caribbean Carnival souvenir booklet of the first carnival in 1959 and is titled, "A People's Art is the Genesis of their Freedom." Here she references the warmth of Caribbean culture now being transplanted into British soil and gestures to the Notting Hill and Nottingham events as the "matrix binding West Indians in the United Kingdom together." She was of course referring to the racist riots against Caribbean people's presence in England which had sparked the need for the Carnival and the collaborative efforts of the Caribbean Carnival Committee which had made it happen. The title of this short introductory essay has been quoted often so it is important to have the full text available in this collection. For one thing, it provides good documentation on the thinking that went into the first carnivals and the love of Caribbean culture and its people that she was demonstrating by these means.

The third essay included in this group was published in 1964 in the African

American journal *Freedomways* then edited by John Henrik Clarke is; "The Caribbean Community in Britain." It is perhaps the first major essay on the Caribbean Diaspora in England and should no longer be overlooked in Caribbean migration studies, as it is perhaps the first documentation of what the Caribbean community looked like in that time period. It provides the demographic statistics, the sources of the migration and where the population was establishing residence. It identifies the role of the Commonwealth Immigrant Act of 1962 in curtailing migration and links it to the McCarran-Walter Immigration Law of 1952 under which Claudia herself had suffered. It also identifies the economic and social problems that Caribbean people faced once they arrived in London. In looking at the future, she identified the two pathways for the Caribbean, that of the socialist Cuba and the other the colonial Caribbean beset by a combination of British and US imperialisms. She calls these two paths to national liberation. One sees these two paths still in process even today with the Cuban approach standing still as one model; most Caribbean nations following the second option.

Another interesting point that can be made about the two longer essays is the extent to which she maintained an intellectual link with the American and African American communities even after she left the USA. This is also mirrored in her meeting with Dr. Martin Luther King in London and her parallel to the March on Washington, held in London at the same time.

The essays on the Caribbean and her editing of the *West Indian Gazette and Afro-Asian Caribbean News*, as indicated, mark Claudia's full immersion into Caribbean culture in the diaspora. They reveal another, though intensely brief (nine-years), productive period in her life, in which she turned her full attention to Caribbean and Pan African subjects and contributed to the advancement of the socio-cultural and economic life of the black community in England.

American Imperialism and the British West Indies (1958)[20]

The election on March 25th of the first Federal Assembly in the West Indies marks a new political stage in the history of the Caribbean.

This period will also witness the advancing role of American capital investment in the forthcoming West Indian Federation. Increasing United States economic penetration is not, of course, unrelated to the struggle of the West Indian people for full political and economic independence.

Bearing in mind only highlights: there is the Texaco Oil purchase of Trinidad oil, the growing US investments in Jamaican bauxite and in British Guiana's aluminum deposits. Clearly the West Indian Federation is already heavily mortgaged to US export capital.

Nor does it appear that this indebtedness to Uncle Sam worries John Bull unduly. Seemingly a sort of family arrangement has been worked out to prevent the burgeoning freedom struggle of the West Indian people from too rapid advancement or "getting out of hand." While the outward political responsibility remains with Britain, increasingly Washington controls the economic basis of the Federation.

This crucial interconnection was clearly shown when a *London Daily Express* staff reporter wrote that in talks he had had last October in Washington, a State Department official had pointed out that while American trade is less than half the West Indian trade with Britain, it is growing at a faster rate. And he added:

> The islands' 3,000,000 people offer a reservoir of cheap labour to attract more American capital. A mighty American naval base mushrooming in Trinidad is encouraging the whole dollar flow to the West Indies. The US Defense Department makes no bones about it – the Trinidad base is now regarded as the Caribbean keystone to the Panama Canal. American forces are going to be there for a long time to come and businessmen look on the Trinidad base as a guarantee of military and political stability for the future.

This rather bald face analysis likewise underscores the scandal of Chaguaramus, the Federation's capital site chosen after examination of other locations by a West Indies Commission. The United States blandly refused to cede Chaguaramus – site of the US Trinidad base – despite questions in the Commons as to the original legality of the Churchill-Roosevelt 99-year lease (no legal authority exists for this and the other US military bases in Antigua, St. Lucia and the Bahamas); despite special talks in London last summer between West Indian leaders and British and United States representatives; despite angry criticism of West Indian leaders that not even a by-your-leave request was ever made to the people of Trinidad as to the use of their land; despite an uproarious clamour of protest by important sections of the West Indian and British press criticizing the usual US high-handedness.

The growth of American economic and political influence in the West Indies was facilitated by the establishment in 1942 of an Anglo-American Caribbean Commission, renamed the Caribbean Commission in 1946. Presumably its function was "to advise and consult" the governments concerned on matters pertaining to "labour, agriculture, health, education, social welfare, finance, economics, etc." But with the help of this Commission, American monopolists have been seizing possession of the natural resources of the West Indies. For example, in 1955, they received the right to exploit the resources of Jamaica. Dominion Oil, a subsidiary of Standard Oil of California, operates in Trinidad. In 1955, Reynolds Metals started mining bauxite in St. Ann's Bay, Jamaica. These projects are financed by the United States government which, in 1951, advanced $1,500,000 for this purpose through the Economic Cooperation Administration. Some idea of the inroads made by American monopolies into the British position may be gleaned from the fact that while British Union Oil spent one million pounds since 1950, prospecting for oil in Barbados, when oil was found, the concession was obtained by Gulf Oil of Pittsburgh.

For Britain, the West Indies is not only a source of cheap food and raw material; it is also a market for her manufactured products. Britain holds a predominant position in West Indian trade. Between 1948-51, she took 43.8 per cent of the total exports of the area and supplied 37.2 per cent of her imports. British trade superiority is facilitated by the imperial preference system. But despite all obstacles, American business has penetrated this market. The United States, as of 1955, was taking 7.1 per cent of the exports and supplying 17.5 per cent of the imports of the West Indies.

American capital has also penetrated West Indian agriculture. The notorious United Fruit Company owns extensive plantations – in Jamaica alone, 15,000 acres. Through the Royal Bank of Canada and the Canadian Bank of Commerce, which have branches on all the big West Indian islands, American capital exercises its influence on the economic affairs of all the British colonies.

Anglo-American Rivalry

Anglo-American antagonisms have particularly been reflected around the Federation issue – with Washington distinctly pooh-poohing it. Washington opposes any idea of strengthening Britain's position in the Caribbean. The US, moreover, has systematically encouraged opposition to the British Federation plan by neighbour states in the Latin and Central American Republics and by encouraging the opposition of certain sections of the West Indian bourgeoisie.

The danger of the new West Indies Federation falling into the pit of US imperialist domination cannot be sounded too often. For, faced with the immense task of solving the economic problems of the West Indies (the problem aptly termed by Labour Minister Bradshaw as the "lame foot" of the Federation) many of the present national leaders in the West Indies look increasingly to the US for salvation, based on a one-sided estimate of the relative progress of Puerto Rico and on the hope of a growth of tourism from Americans. A third factor explaining why the dangers of US imperialism are not fully grasped is the leaning among the West Indian masses towards the more prosperous United States – masses in revolt against British imperialism which they see as their ever present and age-old enemy.

Still a fourth factor is the view of many bourgeois-nationalist West Indian leaders that they can thus tactically bargain between the two imperialisms for greater benefits for the West Indies. Thus, as recently reported in the *London Times*, the Chief Minister of Jamaica, Norman Manley, publicly denounced the "parsimonious" handouts of the British Government to the Federation. He also criticized the saddling on the Federation of the military contribution of 325,000 West Indian dollars for the West Indian Regiment. Dr. Eric Williams, of Trinidad, has spoken in similar terms. A 200-million pound loan requested as a minimum for a 5-year period to launch the Federation has not yet been agreed to or satisfactorily settled by the British Government. Yet a recent issue of *Trumpet*, official organ of the People's National Party, the government partly in Jamaica, revealed that Jamaica received from the USA a loan of $34 millions – more than the total granted by the Colonial Development Corporation to all the West Indian islands.

Mass Struggle

The struggle of the West Indian people for the right to live and work and for national independence has taken on greater intensity in recent years with the spread of the national liberation movement in the colonial world. It is also one of the evidences of the deepening crisis of the British Empire under the growing influence of the liberation movement in the colonies.

Six times since the end of the war the British found it necessary to send punitive expeditions to "restore law and order" in the West Indies. In 1951, when Negro strikers in Grenada (pop. 80,000) demanded that their wages be increased – from 36 to 54 cents a day! – two cruisers, a gunboat, marine and police units went into action. In 1955, following the victory of the Peoples Progressive Party in British Guiana, British Tommies and gunboats invaded British Guiana, deposing its legally elected legislators headed by Dr. Jagan and revoking its progressive Constitution as a "Communist-inspired coup." But four years later the people of Guiana, in a victorious mandate despite a party split, re-elected Jagan and the PPP now holds important elected ministerial posts.

Only a few weeks ago, as witnessed in Nassau, Bahamas, the same step was taken when a general strike exposed the shocking conditions under which the 90 per cent of the coloured population live.

The West Indian people have not taken lightly the extensive exploitation of their resources and human labour. Record profits have been declared by domestic and foreign capital interests in the sugar, oil and bauxite industries.

But there have been many instances of working class resistance: strikes among port workers in Jamaica, the workers of St. Vincent have been heroically struggling to win concessions from arrogant landlords in sugar. Throughout the West Indies, teachers, match workers, waterfront workers were aroused to defend their interests. In Barbados, printers and port workers were locked in struggle with the powerful Advocate Printers. In British Guiana the PPP victory forced revocation of reactionary laws which restricted the movement of their leaders. In Trinidad, store clerks, sugar, oil and educational workers have similarly displayed commendable class consciousness in defending their interests in the face of menacing threats from employers and government.

These and other examples make it necessary to be mindful of the astute observation of Mao Tse-Tung – namely, that imperialism is not prepared to permit the independent development of any new capitalist state, is out to stultify it, make it impossible for the native capitalist to carry out the bourgeois-democratic revolution. We know, of course, that as its foundations totter, imperialism seeks more flexible methods of governing the colonies and seeks to devise new means to camouflage its rule. Central then to Britain's desire to revise the status of her West Indian possessions is the spread of the national colonial liberation movement and the deepening crisis she finds herself in.

The New Federation

Exactly what will the Federation mean to the West Indies? To begin with, except for British Guiana, British Honduras and the Bahamas, the remaining 10 British colonial units, composing approximately 3 million people will be federated into a new national structure. This national structure will be comprised of an appointed or nominated Council of State. A bi-cameral legislature will consist of a nominated senate of 19 members and a House of Representatives of 45 members. The House is to be elected based on population with Jamaica, representing one-half of the Federation's population, having 17 members; Trinidad 10; Barbados 6 and 2 each from Grenada, St. Lucia, St. Vincent, Antigua, St. Kitts, Dominica and one from Montserrat.

A Supreme Court of the Federation is to be established, having original jurisdiction in specified federal or inter-unit matters. It will also have jurisdiction to hear appeals from unit Courts of Appeal and recourse may be had to this court by British Caribbean territories not members of the Federation.

This new federal structure will in no wise substitute for self-government in each unit, where territorial constitutions, already hobbled and proscribed by colonial administrative restrictions, must constantly be improved by the increasing struggles of the people and their political representatives.

Indicative of the measure of this struggle are the constitutional changes in Barbados where since October 1957, a Cabinet Committee excluding the Governor is the main instrument of Government. Similar changes have taken place in Jamaica, where, since November 1957, the Peoples National Party has been successful in its fight to put power in the hands of its Chief Minister and to exclude the Governor from the Council of Ministers. But responsibility for criminal affairs will still remain within the control of the appointed Attorney-

General. Although the Governor will not normally appear in the Council of Ministers, he will still have the right to summon Special Meetings, to preside at them and he will still retain his wide Reserved Powers.

The impact of these advances on other islands was recently summed up when the Bahamas Federation of Labour in the recent general strike demanded: "We want to be governed like our brothers in Trinidad, Barbados and Jamaica."

Still another example of the fight for broader party representation was the sweeping election victory of the Peoples National Movement, headed by Dr. Eric Williams in Trinidad, when the PNM was allowed to name two of the nominated members, thus creating a constitutional precedent.

But these examples are the exceptions rather than the rule. At present in most of the units there exists Legislative Councils of both Nominated and Elected Members and officials. All the Governor-Generals hold wide Reserved Powers, as will Lord Hailes, new Governor-General of the WI Federation, who took office January 3, 1958.

It is no accident in the face of this undemocratic system that for years the chief demand of the West Indian political movement and particularly its advanced sectors has been for greater internal self-government for each unit based on wholly elected legislatures.

Conflicting Views

So tenacious has been this key demand that it has now extended to the Federation itself. Some West Indian ideologists however, have counterposed self-government to Federation – as though the two concepts are mutually exclusive. Such, for example, is the view of W.A. Domingo, outstanding student of West Indian affairs. In his pamphlet, *British West Indian Federation-A Critique* Domingo urges Jamaicans to reject Federation outright – primarily on the grounds that as the largest and most populous of the West Indian islands, she can easily achieve self-government without being hampered by the underdeveloped economies of the Leeward and Windward islands, dependent as they still are on grants-in-aid which are to be curtailed after the first five years of the Federal Government. He further holds that "to equate federation with self-government obscures the real issue – the right of every colonial people to seek and win control of their political life."

But no one who advocates a federated progressive West Indies *equates* these concepts. In fact, those who have consistently fought for a progressive federation structure have always accompanied this demand with one for autonomy of the island units as well. Besides, how can the unity of a people who have similar cultural and historical experiences be held to be violative of "a right" of self-determination if, in seeking to control their political life, they strengthen their ties with others similarly situated? We can assume that Domingo's arguments, like other pre-Federation critics, had as their aim, that of modifying the present federation structure. But to base one's arguments largely on the pragmatic grounds that Britain considers the West Indian colonies as "financial liabilities" and that they are of "no strategic value to England today," that Britain will "grant self-government" to the West Indian colonies, because of the "proclaimed official British policy to grant independence to the colonies" flies in the face of a fundamental, scientific assessment of imperialism today.

Still other political ideologists, including some progressives and even some adherents of Marxism, have denounced the current Federation proposals as a "fraud" and appear to be resisting its arrival.

Such approaches appear to be utterly unrealistic politically. For while serious limitations hedge the new federal structure, can it be denied that it is a political advance over the previous colonial status of 300 years?

Basically, the struggle for the free West Indian market by both the foreign and local bourgeoisie is what has given the movement for Federation its urgency. John La Rose, leading Marxist of Trinidad's West Indian Independence Party, in his Report to the Second Congress of that Party, in July 1956, places it this way:

> The basic economic law of West Indian life which gives this movement such urgency is the struggle for the free West Indian market by both the local and foreign bourgeoisie (interlocked and not interlocked) caused by the inability of the markets of the local territories to satisfy the capacity for expansion and exploitation engendered by capital accumulation in their hands.

Both the foreign and native commercial bourgeoisie have expanded their interests beyond the confines of territories...

Both local and foreign banking and insurance institutions of finance capital (like Bookers Trading concerns, Barbados Mutual, etc.) have expanded their interests beyond the confines of a single territory... besides the activities of foreign banking and insurance institutions.

Both the local and foreign industrial bourgeoisie have expanded beyond the confines of a single territory, e.g., shirt manufacturers, biscuit manufacturers, gin and rum manufacturers, edible oil manufacturers, citrus juices, time clocks, cement manufacturers exporting to British Guiana, Barbados, Grenada, etc., and vice versa. Even at the level of small agricultural producers, e.g., Grenada, St. Vincent, this need is felt and exists as a powerful urge to Federation.

While not all political forces in the West Indies are prepared to formulate immediate demands they are nevertheless broadly united on the aim of Dominion Status. Thus it seems that here once again is reflected the inevitable process of development which cannot be halted – the quest for full national independence.

Consequently, the chief programmatic demand to overcome the limitations advanced by progressive and socialist minded forces in the West Indies include:

1. International self-government for the Federation entailing a wholly elected
    Parliament (a nominated Senate is a retrograde step), full cabinet status
    based on the Party principle with the elected Prime Minister wholly
    responsible and restriction of the Governor-General's power to represen-
    tation of the Sovereign as is the case of Ghana, or a republication form of
    government, as in India, with the Crown as the head of the Common-
    wealth.
2. Civil liberties embracing the entire Federation including freedom to travel,
    freedom to organize and to discuss.
3. Protection of rights of minorities for cultural and other forms of
    development.
4. For full national independence for the West Indies.

Despite the serious limitations it would be fundamentally wrong to assess the
forthcoming Federation as being simply the brainchild of the Colonial Office. To
understand the significance of this development it must be realized that what is
taking place in the West Indies is the unfolding of the classical bourgeois-
democratic revolution, with, of course, its own special features.

Leadership of the national political movement is today in the hands of middle-
class intellectuals who either come from the class of the national bourgeoisie, or
are representative of their interests.

Because federation of the West Indies occurs at a time when the local capitalist
class is developing, every nuance of the federal structure is, naturally, tempered
by their influence. Motivated firstly by their own desire for improved status and
a desire to be free of their inferior colonial status, essentially this influence is
anti-imperialist and anti-colonial.

What unites the *all-class* struggle of the West Indian people is opposition to
foreign imperialism. This stage of political development in general coincides with
the historic aim and dream of the West Indian working class, its militant industrial
and agricultural workers, who in the 30s hoisted the banner of Federation, with
Dominion status and self-government for the units, to their standard. These and
other demands have today been incorporated into the political platforms of the
present national political parties and movements in the islands.

It is important to stress that leadership of the national political movement has
passed relatively recently into the hands of the national bourgeoisie.

Prior to World War II, leadership of the national movement was in the hands
of the working class, arising from the upheavals during the mass strikes of
1937–38. The working class spearheaded the mass struggle; their leaders won
their confidence through their selfless and courageous actions. This was the
period in which trade unionism rapidly developed in the Caribbean and a new

sense of power was felt by the workers.

There then emerged the Caribbean Labour Congress, a united West Indian people's anti-colonial movement for Federation with Dominion status and self-government for the units. It comprised an all-class coalition in which the working class shared leadership with other anti-imperialist classes including important sections of the national bourgeoisie.

But this development was split and declined.

Basic to the answer as to how this decline and split arose was the "divide and rule" tactics of imperialism, which, fearful of this forward development, facilitated the separation of the Right-wing from the Left-wing in accommodation with some of the bourgeois national leaders.

True, imperialism, faced with the mounting pressure of the national liberation movement is seeking to develop the national bourgeoisie as a reliable bulwark to protect its interests for as long as possible even after national independence is won. But India's experience proves that that does not always work.

The working class was also handicapped in that it lacked a scientific approach to the national and class struggle, in many instances pursued sectarian policies and consequently lost leadership to the developing middle-class intellectuals.

It is this background, given briefly, which largely accounts for the hesitations which have marked sections of the working class and socialist-oriented groupings in the West Indies in definitely committing themselves to the present Federation.

Here, a distinction is made between the justified reservations shared by all sections of West Indian opinion and the imperative task of the working class and its advanced sector to play its indispensable role in carrying forward the movement for West Indian national independence.

To sit it out, instead of entering fully as leading partners in the national struggle for independence is to abdicate a contribution they alone can make. The working class and the Left in such a role can encourage the progressive tendencies of the national bourgeoisie. It can steady the middle-class intellectuals towards firmer anti-imperialist stands (criticizing where necessary but not from outside this development).

Trade-Union Activity

A most imperative conclusion appears to be the need to co-ordinate and strengthen trade union activity. In recent months support for the idea of a united militant trade-union movement on a federal scale has been underway in the West Indies. Such a trade-union movement would not only help to facilitate independence and national unity but would be the instrument for achieving improved living standards, higher wages and in general defense of the workers' rights against pressure by US and British capital. Such a united trade-union movement would have a decisive effect on the policies of the two main federal parties – the West Indian Federal Labour Party and the Democratic Labour Party, who will contest seats for the Federal Assembly.

Together with improved living standards and economic advancement is the need for expanded educational development. Educational standards in the West Indies are today frightfully low – too low to fulfill the needs of a country aiming at nationhood.

A prime necessity is the development from the working class itself of a class-conscious cadre and leadership. This is especially important because of the mistaken conception current among West Indian intellectuals that political parties in the West Indies do not represent social classes. Buttressing this false theory is the fact that all mass parties in the West Indies have to rely on support of the working class.

Political pressure and leadership by the Left has already vitally affected the national political movement in the West Indies. One such contribution has been their pointing up the contrast between Soviet economic aid with no strings attached and the historic significance of Bandung. Advocacy of such policies can help change the pace with which the national bourgeoisie and middle-class intellectuals press for full national independence in the West Indies.

While at this juncture the bourgeois national struggle is directed against foreign imperialism, without doubt as the development of the national bourgeoisie takes place, the internal class struggle will grow in importance and scope.

All political observers would do well to follow the course of West Indian development; in Britain this course has been forced on all political forces anew with the presence of 80,000 West Indian immigrants now resident in Britain – the largest immigration of colonial people in recent years. Faced with impoverishment and unbearable conditions and barred by the infamous racially biased Walter-McCarran immigration laws which retards West Indian immigration to100 persons a year from all the West Indies to the USA, they have trekked in thousands to Britain, where they are confronted with an extension of their problems as colonials in a metropolitan country in the form of colour prejudice, joblessness, housing shortages, etc.

Progressive and Communist forces in Britain, mindful of their own responsibilities and of the greed of the US imperialist colossus, are advocating economic assistance to the West Indies; solidarity with their trade-union and other struggles and full national independence for the West Indian people.

A Peoples' Art is the Genesis
of their Freedom (1959)[21]

Rarely have the creative energies of a people indigenous to another homeland been so quickly and spontaneously generated to such purpose as witness the work of the Caribbean Carnival Committee of 1959 set up last November under the sponsorship of the *West Indian Gazette*.

It is as if the vividness of our national life was itself the spark urging translation to new surroundings, to convey and to transplant our folk origins to British soil. There is a comfort in this effort not only for the Carnival Committee and the *West Indian Gazette*, for the fine artists participating in our Carnival who have lent of their talents here, but for all West Indians, who strain to feel and hear and reflect their idiom even as they strain to feel the warmth of their sun-drenched islands and its immemorable beauty of landscape and terrain.

There is of course another cause to be assessed to their response to those who have filled St. Pancras Town Hall. That reason is the event of Notting Hill and Nottingham – an event which was the matrix binding West Indians in the United Kingdom together as never before –determined that such happenings should not recur.

If then, our Caribbean Carnival has evoked the wholehearted response from the peoples from all the Islands of the Caribbean in the new West Indies Federation, this is itself testament to the role of the arts in bringing people together for common aims and to its fusing of the cultural, spiritual, as well as political and economic interests of West Indians in the UK and at home.

A pride in being West Indian is undoubtedly at the root of this unity; a pride that has its origin in the drama of nascent nationhood and that pride encompasses not only the creativeness, uniqueness and originality of West Indian mime song and dance – but is the genesis of the nation itself.

It is true to say that pride extends not only to what the West Indians have proudly established in the culture of the Caribbean but to the treasury or world culture.

In the midst of our revelry let us remember that it is a world on eve of conquest of Space – tribute to man's unconquerable quest for adventure, achievement and mastery over Nature and himself. Our multi-racial culture should be the fount, helping the universal quest to turn the instruments of science everywhere for the good of all mankind, for the freedom of all the world's peoples, no matter what the pigment of their skin, for human dignity and friendship of all peoples everywhere.

If our Carnival is a triumphal success, it is not only as a result of the inspired spirit that has permeated its preliminary activities from its inception, but also the moral and material support given generously by our friends and neighbours in the British Isles representing tangible evidence of their goodwill.

For me and the management of the *West Indian Gazette* and to all of the Carnival Committee I say a deep thank you. It would be unfair for me not to tell you that we have still another determination, that is, to make the *W I G Caribbean Carnival* an annual event. In that endeavour, we know we can count not only on – the artists, the décor, the committee heads, our friends and neighbours but many who we have not yet reached.

May the aim of our mutual efforts to help build the *West Indian Gazette* and above all in that endeavour help to extend the already acknowledged cultural influence of the Caribbean throughout the Commonwealth. And may that be the leaven to weld still more firmly the brotherhood and unity of West Indians and other peoples of colour as well as the friendship for all peoples that will be the fruit of this cultural exchange.

The Caribbean Community in Britain (1964)[22]

Over a quarter of a million West Indians, the overwhelming majority of them from Jamaica, have now settled in Britain in less than a decade. Britain has become, in the mid-1960s, the centre of the largest overseas population of West Indians; numerically relegating to second place, the once superior community of West Indians in the United States.

This new situation in Britain, has been inimitably described in the discerning verse of Louise Bennett, noted Jamaican folklorist, as, "Colonization in Reverse."

Immigration statistics, which are approximate estimates compiled by the one time functional West Indian Federation office (Migrant Services Division) in Britain, placed the total number of West Indians entering the United Kingdom as 238,000 persons by the year 1961. Of these, 125,000 were men; 93,000 women; 13,200 were children; and 6,300 unclassified. A breakdown of the islands from which these people came, showed that during the period of 1955-1961, a total of 142,825 were from Jamaica; from Barbados, 5,036; from Trinidad and Tobago, 2,282; from British Guiana, 3,470; from Leeward Islands, 3,524; from the Windward Islands, 8,202; and from all other territories, the sum total of 8,732.

Distribution of the West Indian population in the United Kingdom indicates that by mid-1962, over 300,000 West Indians were settled in Britain. The yearly immigration and the growth of community settlement illustrate the rate of growth of the West Indian settlement. For example, the emigration of West Indians to the United Kingdom in mid-1955 totalled 24,473 and by 1961, this figure soared to 61,749. Corresponding to the latter was the fear of family separation due to the then impending Commonwealth Immigrants Act.

In the industrial city of Birmingham, by mid-1955, 8,000 West Indians formed the community there, while in mid-1962, this figure stood at 67,000. Similarly in London, where in Brixton the largest settlement of West Indians exist; the mid-1955 figure of 85,000 had by 1961 grown to 135,000.

West Indians were also to be found in the North of England (Manchester, Nottingham, Wolverhampton, Derby and Leeds) and in such cities as Cardiff, Liverpool, Leicester, Bath, Oxford, Cambridge and in other provinces. *What constitutes the chief features of this unprecedented migration to Britain? To what factors may we ascribe this growth of overseas West Indians away from their original homelands?*

Emigration from the West Indies has served for over two generations as a palliative, a stop-gap measure to ease the growing economic frustrations in a largely impoverished agricultural economy; in which under colonial-capitalist-imperialist relations, the wealth of these islands is dominated by the few, with the vast majority of the people living under unbearable conditions.

It was the outstanding Cuban poet, Nicholas Guillen, who noting a situation (also observed by other West Indian writers) in which the young generation, most of it out of work, 'chafing at the bit,' seeing as their only hope a swift opportunity to leave their islands, lamented thus: "Scant, sea-girt land, Oh, tight-squeezed land "

Indeed, as with all migrant populations here is mirrored in extension the existing problems of the nations and territories from which the migrants originally spring. West Indian emigration to the United Kingdom is no exception to this phenomenon. Furthermore, this emigration, as with many other Afro-Asian peoples, has occurred almost immediately prior to the achievement of political independence in two of the largest of the West Indies islands. *It is because prospects have not yet qualitatively improved for the vast majority of the West Indian workers and people, inhibited by the tenaciousness of continued Anglo-American imperialist dominance over West Indian economic life, that this emigratory movement of people from the West Indies continues.* History will undoubtedly evaluate this development as, in part, attributable to the demise of the West Indian Federation and the consequent smashing of wide hopes for the establishment of a united West Indian nation in which freedom of movement would have absorbed some of our disinherited, disillusioned and unfilled people who were compelled to leave their homelands in order to survive.

Up to a decade ago, West Indian immigration was directed to America rather than to Britain. But this was sharply modified when, in 1952 the United States

Federal Government enacted the racially-based McCarran-Walter Immigration Law, which unequivocally was designed to protect the white "races' purity" and to insure the supremacy of Anglo-Saxon stock; limited to 100 per year, persons allowed to emigrate to the United States from each individual Caribbean territory. Henceforth all eyes reverted to Britain. This is not to imply that West Indian Immigration to Britain was wholly non-reciprocal. Another influence was that post-war Britain, experiencing a brief economic boom and full employment, needed overseas and cheap labour to staff the semi-skilled and non-skilled vacancies, the results of temporary postwar economic incline. Britain sought West Indian Immigration as an indispensable aid to the British economy; to the British economy; indeed, encouraged it!

The presence of West Indian immigrants (who together with other Afro-Asian peoples total nearly a half million people) represent less than one per cent in an overall Anglo-populous of 52 million. But even this small minority has given rise to a plethora of new sociological and analytical works such as "Newcomers"; "Coloured Immigrants in Britain"; "The Economic and Social Position of Negro Immigrants in Britain"; "Black and White in Harmony"; "Coloured Minorities in Britain"; "Colonial Students"; "Report on West Indian Accommodation Problems in the United Kingdom"; "Race and Racism"; "Dark Strangers"; "They Seek a Living, and the Like".

Extreme manifestations of the racialism which underlies the present status of West Indians in Britain were graphically witnessed in late 1958, when racial riots occurred in Notting Hill and Nottingham. These events, which followed the as yet unsolved murder of a St. Vincentian, Mr. Kelso Cochrane, claimed world headlines. Clashes even occurred between West Indian and other Afro-Asian migrants with white Britons. The firm handling of the provocateurs by the authorities, following the wide protests of immigrants, labour, communist and progressive forces and the intervention of the West Indian Federal leaders, for a time quelled the overt racialists and the "keep Britain white, fascist-propagandists." But the canker of racialism was now nakedly revealed. It exposed also the smugness of official Britain, who hitherto pointed to racial manifestations in "Little Rock" and Johannesburg, South Africa, but continued to deny its existence in Britain.

Today, new problems, underscored by the Tory Government's enactment and recent renewal of the 1962 Commonwealth Immigration Act (one which ostensibly restricts Commonwealth immigration as a whole, but in fact, discriminates heavily against coloured Commonwealth citizens) has established a second-class citizenship status for West Indians and other Afro Asian peoples in Britain. Accompanying the general social problems confronting all new migrant workers, West Indians, stemming as they do in large measure from African origins, are experiencing sharper colour-bar practices. In common with other workers, the West Indians take part in the struggle for defense and improvement of their working and living standards. But the growing intensity of racialism

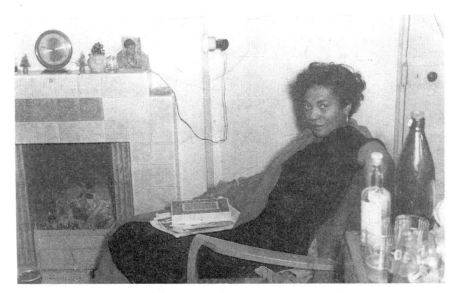

A relaxed Claudia Jones has a drink in a social setting in London.
(Date unknown)
(WIG Photo/Schomburg)

forces them, as it does other Afro-Asians, to join and found their own organizations. In fact, their status is more and more a barometer of British intentions and claims of a so-called "Multi-racial Commonwealth." As put in one of the recent sociological studies of the absorption of a West Indian migrant group in Brixton, financed by the Institute of Race Relations and the Nuffield Foundation:

> Now that the whole equilibrium of world power is changing and the Commonwealth is, by virtue of conscious British policy, being transformed from a family based on kinship, to a wider multi-racial familia, the presence of coloured immigrants in Britain, presents a moral and a practical challenge. The people of these islands face the need not only to reformulate their views of Britain's role and status in such a Commonwealth, but also to apply the new relationships in their dealings with coloured Commonwealth migrants here at home. And not only the colour-conscious migrants themselves, but the newly-independent Afro-Asian countries and the outside world as a whole, show an inclination to judge Britain's good faith in international relations by her ability to put her own house in order.
>
> From *Dark Strangers*, by Sheila Patterson

The Commonwealth Immigrants Act

Far from heeding the advice even of sociologists whose studies themselves show a neo-colonialist bias in its precepts (the study is full of pragmatic assertions that xenophobia is the "norm" of British life and hence, by implication "natural," etc.), the Tory Government has shown utter disdain for putting its own house in order.

Faced with the coming general elections in October, having suffered from local government defeats, mounting criticism rises towards its ruinous domestic and foreign policies. Internally, these range from housing shortages and a Rent Act which has removed ceilings on rentals to the failures of providing new houses; high interest rates on loans to the rail and shipbuilding closures, mergers and the effects of automation.

The external policies of the present British Conservative Government also suffer similar criticism. As a junior partner its supports the United States imperialist NATO nuclear strategy, continuing huge expenditures for colonial wars in Malaysia, North Borneo and Aden. Its subservience to US imperialism is also demonstrated in the case of its denial of long over-due independence to British Guiana, on whom it is imposing the undemocratic system of Proportional Representation which aims further to polarize and divide the political life in British Guiana in order to depose the left-wing, thrice-elected People's Progressive Party under Dr. Cheddi Jagan. As an experienced colonizer, shopping around for a scapegoat for its own sins, the British Tory Government enacted in 1962, the Commonwealth Immigrants Act. The Act sets up a voucher system allowing entry only to those who have a job to come to. Some of its sections carry deportation penalties for migrants from the West Indies, Asia and Africa, whom it especially circumscribes. Its passage was accompanied by the most foul racialist propaganda perpetrated against West Indians and other Afro-Asians by Tory and fascist elements. Thus, it coincided with the futile efforts then engaged in by the British Government to join the European Common Market. It was widely interpreted that these twin events demonstrated the dispensability in Britain's eyes of both the needs of the traditional market of the newly independent West Indian territories for their primary products and the labour supply of West Indians and other Afro-Asian Commonwealth citizens. On the other hand, the doors would close on Commonwealth citizens, while open wide to white European workers.

The pious and hypocritical sentimentality accompanying the "bills" passage was further exposed when the Tory legislators removed the non-Commonwealth Irish Republic from the provisions of the Act, revealing its naked colour-bar bias. The result, following a year of its operation, showed that eighty to ninety per cent of all Indian and Pakistani applicants were refused entry permits; and West Indian immigration dropped to a little over 4,000, qualifying for entry. The latter occasioned cautious queries whether the West Indians had either turned their backs on Britain or had become bitter with the Act's passage.

What the figures showed, of course, was that the main blow fell as intended, most heavily on the *coloured* Commonwealth citizens. So much for the facile promises of the then Home Secretary, now Britain's Foreign Minister, Mr. R.A. Butler, that *"we shall try to find a solution as friendly to these people as we can and not on the basis of colour alone."* (my emphasis: C.J.)

All Tory claims that the Act would benefit either Britain or the immigrants are, of course, easily refuted. The most widely prevalent Tory argument was that coloured immigrants were "flooding Britain." At the time of the Act's passage, the 1961 British population census showed a two and a half million increase, during the very period of the growth of the immigration of West Indians and Afro-Asians and this increase was easily absorbed by the British economy. The coloured migrant is less than one in every hundred people. Yearly emigration of Britons shows that for every single person entering Britain, *three* leave its shores.

The shibboleth that "immigrants take away houses and jobs," when viewed in light of Tory responsibility for high interest property rates and the Rent Act makes this claim likewise ludicrous. As for new houses, there is no evidence that West Indians or other coloured immigrants have taken away any houses. Allowed largely only to purchase old, dilapidated short-lease houses, it is the West Indian building worker, who helps to construct new houses, he makes an invaluable contribution to the building of new homes.

Even the usual last retort of the racial ideologists that West Indians and other coloured citizens "lower moral stands" also fails to stand up. The world knows of the exploits of Christine Keeler and the British Ministers of State, an event which occasioned a calypso in the widely-read *West Indian Gazette*. There has been no notable increase in jobs as a result of this Act. In fact, rail and shipbuilding closures, mergers and automation, continue apace. It is widely admitted that withdrawal of coloured workers form transport, foundries and hospital services would cause a major economic dislocation in Britain and that they continue to make a contribution to the British economy. Vic Feather, leading trade union official reiterated strongly, this view at an all-day conference recently in Smethwick, a Birmingham suburb, where a local election campaign slogan was that to elect Labour meant *"having a nigger for a neighbour."* One finally observes regarding the asserted economic social burden of the migrant, that a "tidy" profit has been made by the Ministry of National Insurance from contributions of the surrendered cards of thousands of immigrants who returned home after a few years in Britain.

In the eyes of the world, the Tory record does not stand any better when it is known that nine times they have blocked the Bill to Outlaw Racial Discrimination by the Labour member for Parliament from Slough, Mr. Fenner Brockway. The main provisions of this bill would be to outlaw discrimination in public places, lodgings, inns, dance halls and other leases; and also put penalties on incitement to racialism. The Bill has now gained the support of the

Labour leadership who promised if they achieve office to introduce such a measure (although there are some indications that it may be watered down), as well as from leading Liberal MPs and even from some Tory MPs. Thus, there has been witnessed a reversal of the former open-door policy to Commonwealth citizens and speciously to coloured Commonwealth citizens. The result of all this has been a new degrading status and sufferance accorded to coloured immigrants who are likewise saddled with the responsibility for Britain's social evils.

There is a reluctance on the part of virtually all sections of British public opinion to assess the fundamental reasons for the existence of racial prejudice. The citizens of the "Mother of Democracies" do not yet recognize that the roots of racialism in Britain are deep and were laid in the eighteenth and nineteenth centuries through British conquests of India, Africa and great parts of Asia as well as the British Caribbean. All the resources of official propaganda and education, the superstructure of British imperialism, were permeated with projecting the oppressed colonial peoples as "lesser breeds," as "inferior coloured peoples," "natives," "savages" and the like—in short, "the white man's burden." These rationalizations all served to build a justification for wholesale exploitation, extermination and looting of the islands by British imperialism. The great wealth of present-day British monopoly-capital was built on the robbery of coloured peoples by such firms as Unilever and the East Africa Company to Tate and Lyle and Booker Brothers in the Caribbean.

These artificial divisions and antagonisms between British and colonial workers, already costly in toll of generations of colonial wars and ever-recurrent crises, have delayed fundamental social change in Britain and form the very basis of colour prejudice. The small top section of the working class, bribed and corrupted and benefiting from this colonial robbery have been imbued with this racialist "white superiority" poison. On the other hand progressive opinion rallied with the migrants' protests at the Commonwealth Immigrants Act, for the Labour Party leadership had voted in opposition to its enactment; yet allowing its subsequent renewal to go unchallenged, for fear of losing votes in the coming general elections. Labour offered the government an unopposed passage on the condition that it agree to place the Act with new and improved legislation drawn up "in consultation" with the Commonwealth countries.

The government, which had itself, tried this tactic before, to the negative response of West Indian and other affected Commonwealth Government, refused to give these assurances. The Labour MPs voted against its renewal, but not before they made clear, to the dismay of the overwhelming majority of immigrants, that they too, stood for "quotas" and "controls." In essence, this stand does not differ in principle from the attitude of the Tory Government and the provisions of the Commonwealth Immigrants Act. With the sole exception of the British Communists, who completely oppose the system of "quotas" and "controls" for

Commonwealth immigration, all other political parties have capitulated in one or another way to this racialist immigration measure. A recent statement of the Executive Committee of the British Communist Party declared its opposition to all forms of restrictions on coloured immigration; declared its readiness to contest every case of discrimination; urged repeal of the Commonwealth Immigrants Act and called for equality of access for employment, rates of wages, promotion to skilled jobs, and opportunities for apprenticeship and vocational training. It gave full support to the Bill to Outlaw Racial Discrimination and pledged its readiness to support every progressive measure to combat discrimination in Britain. It also projected the launching of an ideological campaign to combat racialism, which it noted, infects wide sections of the British working class.

Some Issues Facing Coloured Immigrants

That the Tory colour-bar Commonwealth Immigrants Bill has been enacted at the time when apartheid and racialism is under attack throughout the world from the African Heads of State, at Addis Ababa, to the half million Civil Rights March on Washington; from the United Nations and world criticism of South Africa and the demand for application of economic sanctions, to the condemnation of apartheid and Jim Crow racialist practices in the US; bespeak the fantastic blindness of Britain's Tory rulers even to Britain's own national interests. But as with every exploiting class, as the example of Hitlerism shows, faced with a radical movement of the masses against their rule, they seek to split and divert this anger onto a false "enemy."

Added to the second-class citizenship status foisted by such a measure, West Indians and other Afro-Asians are confronted in their daily lives with many social and economic problems. Forming several settlements in various cities, the overwhelming majority are workers, with a scattering of professionals. There are 3,000 students.

Throughout Britain, the West Indian contribution to its economy is undoubted. As building workers, carpenters, as nurses, doctors and hospital staffs, in factories, on the transportation system and railway depots and stations, West Indians are easily evidenced. Lest the younger generation be omitted (without commenting here on the social mores "guiding" the cultural orientation of today's youth) one of the most popular current pop singers is a 16 year- old girl from rural Jamaica.

Indicative of their bid to participate in the political life of the nation was the recent success of a West Indian doctor on the Labour ticket as London County Councillor for the second time in an area composed, though not solely, of West Indian migrants. For the first time many thousands of West Indian and Afro-Asian voters have registered and will be eligible to vote. It is not accidental therefore as reflected in an article entitled "The Colour of Their Votes" in a leading Sunday periodical, that speculation is growing as to how they will use their vote. One such article entitled "The Colour of Their Votes" concluded that they would vote "according to colour" but in consonance with their class interests. But this observation is only a half-truth. For the common experience of all Afro-Asian-Caribbean peoples in Britain is leading to a growing unison among these communities as they increasingly identify an injury to one as being an injury to all. When added to this, one marks their pride in the growth of national liberation achievements from the lands of their origin and among other nationally-oppressed peoples, they are likely to be influenced by this bond as much as by their particular mode of production. Most pre-election polls have indicated their leaning, if critical, towards Labour and other Independents.

Many acute problems face West Indians who seek jobs and shelter. There is as yet no overall veritable picture of West Indians' skills. Results from sample polls are given here, bearing in mind the West Indian economic colonial background, to indicate scales in skills. One such poll revealed that of 608 persons sampled for their skills, by their own characterization, the results among West Indians were as follows: Professionals-1 per cent; other non-manual-13 per cent; skilled- 46 per cent; semi-skilled-13 per cent agricultural-12 per cent. In a further breakdown the professional and other blackcoated workers predominated in the migrant groups from Trinidad and Tobago, while skilled workers were more numerous from Jamaica and Barbados. Considerable down-grading of skills frequently occurs and many unskilled workers have been unable to acquire skills, many from rural areas having formerly no industrial experience at all. But even where qualifications exist, many find it difficult to obtain jobs commensurate with their skills. Some employers have a secret quota system for the employment of coloured workers, based on the chauvinistic view that "too many coloured workers" even if qualified, will "rock the boat." Others, even when inclined to take on coloured workers, have had to face English workers, in some cases, trade unionists, who have a definite policy of keeping out coloured workers. Even Government Employment Exchanges accept orders from employers not to submit "coloured" applicants for work. But this too, is being resisted and demands are being made for the ministry of Labour to rescind these instructions.

In the background is the country-wide pattern of industrial-labour relations; the traditional view of "keeping the labour force small," the better to bargain with the employers and the real fear by trade unionists that non-union labour will undercut wages. Then too, there is the ambivalent right-wing trade union view, which seeks to reconcile the principles of trade union brotherhood and non-discrimination with the antipathies of a large and vocal proportion of its rank-and-file members.

Even in the early stages of the present West Indian immigration to Britain, struggles had to be waged for the acceptance of West Indian workers into the jobs they now hold. In the transport system, despite the agreements between the British Transport System and the Barbados Government to train and employ workers, sharp struggles by progressive trade unionists, led by Communists, had to be waged for hiring and upgrading of West Indian workers, for their right to work in booking offices, or as shuttle-plate workers in railway depots or for West Indian women to be employed as "clippies" or bus conductors.

Many of these gains are today under fire. A recent vote by the London busmen served notice that they opposed the hiring of any more West Indian workers. What is more, a growing "Blacklist for Jobs" exists, as an article in the *Sunday Observer* states. The article noted that thousands of West Indians born and educated in Britain will "not be content to do shift work on buses" in a society which, "despite their high academic levels treats them as less than human beings," (the article detailed the difficulties experienced by school-leavers particularly in white-collar jobs). In banks, sales staff, insurance companies and newspaper staff, a policy of "tokenism" is operative. As one executive put it: *"If you have one in an office and she's pleasant, she fits in, but you put two or three there and you may find yourself losing some of your white staff."* Facing stiff competition for jobs, they have it both ways: if undertrained and if efficient, (the too-well-trained, may be rejected) in either case, they may face a colour-bar.

Excluded from skilled jobs and forced into lower paid ones, still another disability must be faced in the field of housing accommodation. In addition to the problems occasioned from the general housing shortage, the West Indian immigrant and other coloured Commonwealth citizens are widely rejected as tenants of advertised flats and lodgings on the basis of a colour-bar and are obligated to pay higher rents, even than white tenants. *"So sorry, No Coloureds, No children," "Europeans Only," "Whites Only,"* signs dot the pages of advertised flats and lodgings. A "colour-tax" meets the West Indian purchaser of property, often inferior lease-hold ones. No wonder estate agents and unscrupulous landlords, some of them coloured themselves, had not been averse to exploiting for huge profits of this housing shortage. "Rachmanism" is a synonym in present-day England for this type of practice, alluding to the fortunes made by the man so named in North Kensington in the very area of racial riots of a few years ago. Through exorbitant rentals, resale of properties, the shortage of housing is widely exploited and the West Indian, Afro Asian as well as white workers are the victims.

A Commons inquiry is now pending since the revelation of collusion of estate agents with Big Business when a restrictive colour-bar covenant was discovered in Loriel Properties on whose board of directors are two Tory Cabinet Ministers, a leading Conservative Member of Parliament, who led the racist attack in the House of Commons on the Commonwealth Immigration Act. This company has shareholders among the nation's leading universities at Oxford and Cambridge and most of the other directors hail from The Establishment. Thus, the real origin of colour-bar practices and policies stems from the City's imperialist financial barons to whom it is highly profitable, both ways. The Commons inquiry, it should be added, has been initiated by Mr. Fenner Brockway who has nine times tabled his anti-discrimination bill to ban discrimination in public housing, leases, inns, pubs, hotels, dance halls, etc. These and other examples more than confirm the urgency for this type of legislation in present-day Britain. Education policy is yet another field in which inroads are being attempted by the racial propagandists. Stemming from their central campaign, now sanctioned by the Commonwealth Immigration Act to oust West Indian Immigrants from Britain, they have fastened on the growth of communities where children of Afro Asian-Caribbean immigrants are at school. Encouraging the idea of schools segregation, they have attempted the organization of parents to get them to move their children to other schools. In Southall for example, where, in two wards 5,000 Indian families live, this type of segregation propaganda began to make headway and the local Council, despite the relatively good stand of the Board of Education began to weaken. Following an appeal however, from the Education Committee to the Minister of Education, Sir Edward Boyle told 400 parents, "there will be no segregation in our schools." This basis was adopted to spread the children over several schools so that there will be no more than one-third Indian children in the schools. Despite this, new calls are being heard for establishment of separate classes for coloured children on grounds of "language difficulties," despite the well-known adaptability of children to become bi-lingual. This approach is being strongly resisted by West Indian, Afro-Asian, educational and progressive groups in Britain. For it is feared that such a wedge may establish an American "Jim Crow" pattern of "separate but equal education," an animal, (as we have learned from the Negro liberation struggles that just don't exist). This fear was confirmed anew when a recent White Paper issued by the Commonwealth Conservative Council suggested that children of immigrant parents be regarded as "immigrants" despite being born in the United Kingdom.

Consequently, whether as tenants waging anti-discrimination struggles; clubbing together to purchase homes to house families the large majority of whom were separated for years until the necessary finances were raised; whether as workers fighting for the right to work, or to be upgraded; or as cultural workers engaged in the attempt to use their creative abilities to stage, screen or television, or to safeguard their children's right to an equal education; or as professionals, students, or in business pursuits, the West Indian immigrant community has special problems, as a national minority. While the workers are heaviest hit, the disabilities cut across class lines.

Future Perspectives

Conscious therefore of the need for alleviation of their second-class citizenship, determined to live and work in human dignity as is their natural right, the resourceful West Indian migrant, in common with all peoples involved (either consciously or not) in anti-imperialist struggles, are also thinking about their ultimate direction. That they are only now at the stage of tentatively formulating their view may be ascribed to three main factors: 1) to the constant pressure and concern with daily problems of survival, 2) to the groping in their own minds for the fundamental significance of their national identity and, 3) to the lack of an organized perspective for a progressive, united West Indies at home. Linked to the first factor is the urgent necessity to organize and unite the West Indian community in Britain around their fundamental demands. The level of organization in Britain is not yet commensurate to fulfill this urgent need. The West Indian worker, in common with all workers, is confronted with the necessity to engage in struggles, supported by their allies, for his own survival in a new environment. This also means engaging in the general struggle for peace, trade unionism, democracy and social change. While clinging strongly to his own roots, he is mindful of the conditions at home and the reasons for his emigration and mindful too, of the disabilities which face him there. But his economic situation is relatively better and he views as a practicality that his children will grow up in England. If to this is added the recognition that as with all migrations, this too, will form a permanent community, it is only natural that steps should be taken to implement the recognition: that with permanency comes the growth of new institutions with all its accompanying aspects.

It is true, of course that some measure of organization exists. West Indians are organized largely in social and welfare groups in the United Kingdom, established originally to meet the needs of incoming migrants. Only a smattering have thus far joined political movements or play an active role politically. This is undoubtedly attributable to the false twin ideas that they should only become politically active with their "return home," or the apolitical view that they should eschew politics. More fundamentally, it is traceable also to the lack of previous political activity at home and the fact that for most West Indians their political baptism is occurring in their new environment. There exists such organizations as the Standing Conference of West Indian Organizations, a council composed of fifteen social and welfare groups in London boroughs, as well as Freemason Lodges in areas of large West Indian settlements. There are also similar organizations existing in the Midlands, all of which have close supervision by the Migrant Services Division of the Jamaica, Trinidad and Tobago, Barbados, Leeward and Windward Islands government offices in Britain. In addition there are a growing number of inter-racial committees and groups engaged in dealing with the problems of West Indians and other migrants, besides the students organizations.

There are also special organizations based on island origins beginning to develop. The Church forms a centre for many religious West Indian groups, choirs and the like. Yet questions are now arising as to whether these organizations fully meet the present needs of this community. This is evidenced in the concern being expressed by West Indians, as to whether integration in British life should be the sole aim in Britain or whether the self-organization of West Indians should not likewise be emphasized. Questions are being posed too, as to how to harness the national identity of West Indians towards this end.

An interesting example of attempts to concert these trends among West Indians on the basis of reliance on their own efforts, was shown in Bristol last year, when in midst of the MCC-West Indian Test Match tour, a young university student graduate led a successful struggle following threats of a bus boycott by West Indians when one of their number was refused a job by the Bristol Bus Company. Here was witnessed too, the classical intervention of "do good" liberals who "advised" the young West Indians militants not to be too "hotheaded" and themselves sought to designate who were the "good boys" and the leadership to be followed. But this ruse didn't quite succeed. Their action, widely publicized in the press was won when following the intervention of the then High Commissioner for Trinidad and Tobago, Sir Learie Constantine and Mr. R. C. Lindo, Jamaican High Commissioner, supported by Mr. Robert Lightbourne, Jamaica Minister of Trade and Industry, trade union and student groups, the bus company climbed down and revoked its stand.

A major effort designed to stimulate political and social thinking has been the launching, six years ago, of the progressive news-monthly, the *West Indian Gazette*. This newspaper has served as a catalyst, quickening the awareness, socially and politically, of West Indians, Afro-Asians and their friends. Its editorial stand is for a united independent West Indies, full economic social and political equality and respect for human dignity for West Indians and Afro-Asians in Britain, for peace and friendship between all Commonwealth and world peoples. It has campaigned vigorously on issues facing West Indians and other coloured peoples. Whether against numerous police frame-ups, to which West Indians and other coloured migrants are frequently subject, to opposing discrimination and to advocating support for trade unionism and unity of coloured and white workers, WI news publications have attempted to emulate the path of progressive 'Negro' (Afro Asian, Latin American and Afro American) journals who uncompromisingly and fearlessly fight against imperialist outrages and indignities to our peoples. *The West Indian Gazette* and *Afro Asian Caribbean News* has served to launch solidarity campaigns with the nationals who advance with their liberation struggles in Africa and in Asia. The present circulation and readership of the WI publication, would be larger, but for the usual welter of problems faced by most progressive journals. A campaign of support for financial aid among its readers and friends has recently been launched to help its expansion to a weekly and to establish its own printing plant. It counts among its contributors and supporters, many West Indian writers, who live in England, trade unionists and members of Parliament.

Underlying what may be termed "the search for a national identity," is the concern of West Indians to understand their historical and cultural heritage. This concern, which arose with establishment of the now defunct West Indian Federation, has become more widespread. The consequent polarization of West Indians into Jamaicans, Trinidadians, Barbadians, Grenadians, etc., has certain unrealities in England where existing problems among West Indians are shared in common. A consequence of emigration to England, has been that Afro-Asians and West Indians have come to know one another as they might not have previously, separated by the distance of their homelands.

Here, reference is not to some pseudo-intellectuals who, ignorant or unaware of a scientific definition of nationhood, deny the lack of a national identity on the spurious grounds of lack of a separate not common language. But rather to the leadership need to acquaint West Indians with their own history and by a social interpretation of that history, better to arm them for future struggles by imparting a pride in their origins, struggles and future. This lack of historical perspective is at root, as Dr. Eric Williams correctly noted, from a society which eulogized the colonialist and whose knowledge of West Indian history was limited to that of Anglo-Saxon conquests, Sir Walter Raleigh, Captain Morgan and the feats of royalty. The task remains to enhance the knowledge of the true history: of the Morant Bay anti-slavery rebellion, the glorious Maroons, the early anti-colonial struggles of Captain Cipriani, or of Critchlows trade unionism or of the significance of the movement towards closer West Indian federation, all of which early struggles created the preconditions leading to the contemporary struggle for nationhood, which thus is something less than that for which West Indian patriots fought and dreamed. Such an understanding would likewise help to create awareness of the need for support and aid to the bitter struggle being waged for British Guianese independence against US imperialist intervention which fears social change along Socialist lines.

Related finally to the continued lack of an organized perspective for an advancing West Indies, is the indication of floundering in West Indian political life since the Federation demise. The present political parties in the Caribbean advocating a Socialist alternative, the only ultimate course for the West Indies, are still small and ineffective. But they represent the hope of the future, if only because they challenge the perspective of the present bourgeois-nationalist leaders, who heading a titularly independent West Indies continue to proclaim their reliance on the West, not only geographically, but in political and social aims even to the shame of all West Indians, and Jamaicans in particular, of the unprecedented offer of Jamaica's soil for a US nuclear base.

Such advocacy may ultimately inspire West Indians at home and abroad to leap the shoals of struggle necessary to transform the economy of the West Indies and consequently to establish a socialist West Indian nation that will play its role in the community of nations.

Such a perspective would win inspiring participation among West Indians in Britain, who adjure the gradualist view voiced by many of their Ministers that the pace of West Indian advancement will be "slow" and that the West Indian immigrant would do well to consider themselves primarily citizens of Britain and to cease to worry about their national identity. This idea is likewise based on the view held toward immigration by many bourgeois nationalist West Indian politicians who encourage migration as a "safety-valve," fearing the growth of Militancy for social change, at home, more than they do the loss of their most valuable citizens.

A special importance attaches itself to the Caribbean, where there is evidenced the two paths to national liberation: either the path of obsequiousness to US imperialism and neo-colonialism or the high road to Socialist advance as exemplified by Socialist Cuba. Particularly in the Caribbean, where United States imperialism threatens socialist Cuba; infringes on the national sovereignty of all Latin American peoples; intervenes in the internal affairs of British Guiana and Panama; and whose pretensions of a "free America in a free world" stands exposed before the massive hammer blows of the mounting Negro liberation struggle, which, as shown in our merged protest, Afro Asian and Caribbean peoples, held a Solidarity March to the US London Embassy, in support of the Negro peoples' demands, the struggle for national liberation proceeds with singular emphasis.

[Note:"Claudia Jones was writing on this with her available knowledge in the 1960's. Since then the accurate details have been provided by historians like Peter Fryer in *Staying Power: The History of Black People in Britain Since 1504* (Pluto, 1984) – the authoritative source. Kelso Cochrane was from Antigua and died 17 May, 1959 according to Fryer".]

III
POETRY
"There are some things one always remembers"

Writing out of Containment: Finding Beauty in Creativity

Introduction

Claudia Jones used poetry as Audre Lorde[23] suggests to "give form to her feelings." As such, the writing of poetry accompanied intense moments in her life, gave outlet to her pain and expressed her feelings around emotionally charged situations. These included of course her incarceration, but also her departure from friends and also when she encountered Russia and China for the first time and wanted to express her emotions about those experiences. The range of poems then, (only fifteen available) capture these moments of intensity and give us another view of these life struggles. The first two included here are 1950s poems, "Elms at Morn" and "Morning Mists," both dealing with aspects of nature ostensibly but also using these encounters with nature to express the difficulties of state persecution. "Elms at Morn" accompanied a letter to John Gates, editor of the *Daily Worker* and was published on November 8, 1950.[24] The poem describes the reality of imprisonment. This and the poem that follows are both written with images of sadness at physical confinement juxtaposed with those of nature which communicate something larger than human frailty.

While incarcerated in Alderson, she produced the group of poems, all dated in 1955, the year of imprisonment. They include "Clay Sculpture," "For Consuela – Anti-Fascist," "Lament for Emmett Till," "For Elizabeth Gurley Flynn." Looking at them, especially the ones for Emmett Till and Consuela, one sees why she expressed concern that the guards were not going to have her leave with them. These are the poems that are described as being memorized and re-written on the train on the way back to New York. The deportation poem, "Paean to the Atlantic" captures the crossing and describes the pain of exile but also the excitement of seeing new places. Finally, poems like "Radiant Season," "There are Some Things One Always Remembers" and "To a Dear Friend on her Birthday" reflect on life passing by and the aging process. The last three poems, "Paen to the Crimea," "Storm at Sea" and "Yenan – Cradle of the Revolution" detail her travelling to Russia and China, those socialist destinations that she had always dreamed of visiting.

The Elms at Morn
(1950)

Barbed wire fence surrounds me
And the fog rolls slowly in
The elms stand tall and stately
And the maples crowd them in

The mops are on the porch my dear
And Frances sits beside me
Lois smokes a cigarette
I am in an awful net

Morning Mists

Deep in my heart I know beyond the mists
Lies Morning – that full blown with morn
Will waken free from list of rest
That comes with dawn.

I know as well that this dense film
Will soon recede though not from whim
As surely as it rolls now in
To shroud all seed with covering.

While this I know, my heart rebels
At screens that shut off sunlight's beams
My thoughts rise too like tinkling bells
To welcome shafts of light in seams.

Ere as I write bright rays peep through
Their fiercer power pierce this dew
Strengthen born of atoms held at bay
Simulation of man's will to cast all doubt away!

To Elizabeth Gurley Flynn[25]
(1955)

I think I'll always see you everywhere –
At morn – when sunlight's radiance bathes all things like verse
Proclaiming man, not beast,
Is king of all the universe.

I'll see you in young shooting sprouts
That sneer at weeds – age-gnarled in doubt
Of users who defile in epithet,
A life well-lived in service, built from strife.

I'll see you too at noontime
When the sun in orbit
Flings its rays like thyme through skies on days that hurt
Causing you to weld anew full courage spurt

I'll see you oft at twilight's dusk
Before the sun will fade
I'll conjure up your twinkling laugh
Your eyes so much like jade.

I'll see you in the dark of night
When Nature seeks her rest
Except the reedy crickets
Who muse in watch, I guess.

I'll think of you forever
And how your spirit rings
Because your faith leaps as a flame
Sweet nurture to all things

Of all the times I'll miss you most
Is when I'm least aware
Because you will intrude I know – Upon my inner ear
Beloved comrade – when from you I tear –
My mind, my heart, my thoughts, you'll hear!

For Consuela – Anti-Fascista*26
(1955)

It seems I knew you long before our common ties – of conscious choice
Threw under single skies, those like us
Who, fused by our mold
Became their targets as of old

I knew you in Jarama's hills
Through men and women drilled
In majesty, whose dignity
Rejected shirts and skirts of dimity.

I heard you in Guernica's songs
Proud melodies that burst from tongues
As yet unknown to me – full thronged
With Liberty.

Anti-anti-fascistas!
That was your name
I sang your fame
Long 'fore my witness of your bane of pain

I saw you in the passion-flower
In roses full of flame
Pure valley lily, whose bower
Marks resemblance to your name.

Oh wondrous Spanish sister
Long-locked from all you care
Listen – while I tell you what you strain to hear
And beckon all from far and near

We swear that we will never rest
Until they hear nòt plea
But sainted sacrifice to set
A small proud nation free

*   Dedicated to Blanca Consuela Torresola, now serving 4 years in the Federal Reformatory for Women
    in Alderson, W. Va, USA and who, upon completion of this sentence faces an 140 year jail term in
    her native Puerto Rico for her heroic participation in the struggle for Puerto Rican independence.

O anti-fascist sister – you whose eyes turn to stars still
I've learned your wondrous secret – source of spirit and of will
I've learned that what sustains you heart, mind and peace of soul
Is knowledge that their justice – can never reach its goal!

Clay Sculpture[27]
(1955)

Molecules long hidden lay
In Earth, rich-aged with Time
Dust of the ancients stamp the way
Of peoples, rich in rhyme.

I've held in hand unmolded piece
Unformed and pliant blob
And wondered as I rolled and ceased
What form would start to throb.

I've marveled how its contents rare
Are snared in secret lime
How Nature hid in tablets here
Past History in its prime.

But most of all when turning 'round by hand this property
I turn the lock on all mankind's recorded history
For here lies proof supremely clear that bold humanity
Can storm all doors through toil and will – if they but see!

Lament For Emmett Till[28]
(1955)

Cry lynch- murder!
  – Sear the land
Raise fists – in more than anger bands!

Mother, mother – you who bore
Son from womb of sorrow know
White washed justice sure will reap
More than it can ever sow…

Uncle, uncle who stood
Firm-hand-in jim crow dock of wood
Facing lynchers eye for eye
Meeting sadism of parading child

People, people, you who swore
Vengeance for this brutal hour
Make your unity soar above strife
To swiftly avenge Young Emmett Till's life!

Ship's Log – December 19, 1955

December 19, 1955
My dear Daddy:

Remember I promised to send to you my Ship's Log so that you may see how we spent our Crossing – on this first transatlantic crossing of mine. I shall retype it exactly as I wrote it.

December 9, 10 p.m. Ship Time

Ship Diary or Log

We plow through the high seas and tonight, a short while ago, on Observation Deck of this magnificent ship, I peered thru the deck panes to see the mighty ocean spill its foam against her stern. Foam whiter than whitecaps that I have seen in Southampton, L.I. or on the Hudson – the white lights of phosphorus was all around illuming the darkness of the wide expanse which is the Atlantic. Now she veers and rattles. We must hug rails as we did when we went to dinner at seven to eat English lamb roast, mint juice or sauce, iced pineapple, salad and a fat baked potato, vanilla ice cream, tea with lemon (for Millie) cream for me. Our cabin is sumptuous and comfortable – something of a tribute to man's inventive genius to conserve space – and to the unfolding and rising promise of international visits, exchange and culture for the world's peoples. On the high seas for England, I find memories crowd (as they will continue, I know) on me. Long after more than 50 of my closest colleagues and friends and neighbours, Negro and white and their children, my father, my sister and others left, the room was full of their presence. We must yet meet the test of good travelers. The cradle of the deep sometimes jerks you sharply – sometimes like a lullaby rocks and caresses you as our Queen ship plows the ocean deep. Tomorrow – the first morning of my exile for my independent political ideas – we will see its beauty at dawn. Folders of Shakespeare's country – of Sussex, Manchester, Clyde etc., that we collected and the Gen. Information bulletin (so we don't call a Commodore a Purser etc.) and all the marvelous places I will see beckons and excites me – but tonight my mind, heart and thoughts are still in the land I belong to and know and its people with whom I have worked and struggled with for social progress – tonight my mind and heart and deepest thoughts are with my comrades – the finest representatives of the people of the United States of America. They are with my magnificent family whom I love and miss.....

P.S. On my dressing-table too, are radiograms of love and best wishes for happy bon voyage from Tracty, Joe, Dorothy Rose, Blanch Freedman, Nemmy another from Stretch which we centre on our dressing table, another's from Maude Katz and wires received earlier from the Magil's who sum up these greetings: "What is an ocean between us; we know how to build bridges." December 10, 1955

Ship Log
Written aboard the Queen Elizabeth 10:45 PM ship time

(I write my poem to the sea – it burst from me after churning inside all day...) I call it....

Paean to the Atlantic

To watch your ceaseless motion
Your foam and tideful billows view
Is but to gleam your beauty
Of immemorial hue
Oh, restless wide Atlantic
Path of nations old and new
Asylum path of peoples
Bound to social progress true

I stand awe-struck before you
As swiftly league on league
You cradle us to lands – accrue
Of mankind's search for freedom's clue

To understand your motion
Is to reason why like you
Millions move towards ascension
Nurtured by your ancient dew

There Are Some Things One Always Remembers[29]
(July 9th 1958)

There are some things one always remembers...
The hurts – especially the little ones
The cruelty of cruelness, the harshness
Of reality.

These are the things one should
forget – staunch the hurt, mend the
rip of heartbreak...

But one remembers till
It hurts remembering too...

The plans, the buds of forgotten dreams...
The fleetness of Summer and
The suddenness of Autumn...

Radiant Season

Crisp wind at dusk and chilling blast
Replacing warmth of season past
Is sharp reminder that you cleave
Sharp barbs of pain that swirl like leaves

Oh season – swift with magic wand
Transfixing things – your wondrous hands
Mixing, tinting, orange red with mellow
Shades of brown and green, gold-yellow

How fickle is your radiance
Unseemly this bright dalliance
Your tang is false, your garb's untrue
Smile of your beauty's full of rue

And yet this much I've learned from you
Though costly is my pastime new
That riches lie in store for those
Who gaze on changeling, transient pose

For your's the time that bids all things
Retire unto winter's wings
Your Autumn – known as radiant season
Is really knowledge come to reason.

To a Dear Friend
On Her Birthday[30]

When I consider life and all its care
I measure ties that are quite rare
And so it is on this – your day
I gladly want to have my say

About the treasures we have found
The thoughts, the plans in life we dare
To share – such as are bound to rise
As does the dew from flowers
Which blossoms into day

Then sets its sunlight
High above the mountain tops
To lay at rest – content until tomorrow
Again to share its new-found beauty or sorrow

Under a shroud of fog or rain
To remind us then that sometime pain
Is consequence of ties held all too close in
in heart-or-mind – or brain

So thus our friendship wends its way
Over a path that's here to stay
With all the sorrows and the joys
That Life store up – and strews like toys
We pick from.

It's hard to sum up the accrue
Or measure of this tie that binds our lives
It's all a way of wishing for you
All Happiness then – that is your due.

Written at the request of FSS

- 198 -

Storm At Sea[31]

Today I saw a storm at sea,
A choppy, fearful sight,
T'was if it were besides itself
And running from some fright.

Today I saw a storm at sea,
And oh – it gave delight,
It churned and foamed, it rolled and curled
As if from sheer delight

Today I saw a storm at sea,
Its bilious white and black
It spent its forces as if it knew
The power of its back.

Foaming and churning, happy and sad
Bubbling and beating, all silvery and glad.

Note: October 8, 1962, Yalta, Crimea "Rossia" Sanitorium

Paean To The Crimea

In what great century did your mountains rise,
To tower near level with your skies,
And in what age did stately trees,
Begin to sprout their roots and seize
The warm, moist earth to multiply
Their species in a thousand leaves,
That now lend beauty to the eye.

In which earth's crust were your depths, probed,
To fill your breasts with blue-green seas
That touch the shores of ancient lands
And is milieu for echoing chants,
Of paens of praise to you, Crimea.
And to your people's system-rare.

My heart will fill with thoughts of you
My brain and mind will fashion, too,
Memories, long to inspire me,
In climes and lands – so unlike thee!

October 11, 1962, Yalta, Crimea "Rossia" Sanitorium

Claudia visits China as guest of China Peace Committee where she meets
Chairman Mao and interviews Mme Soon Ching Ling, wife of Sun-Yat Sen,
on China's National Day, October 1, 1964.

YENAN
Cradle of the Revolution[32]
(Revised as Thoughts on Visiting Yenan)

No ivory towered dreamers these,
And yet they dared to dream
Bright thoughts – for mankind's future
Midst the rough, high tiaga
That is Yenan – site
Of self-wrought mountain caves and mist,
And crags that hid
From enemy eagles
The claws of war, and
Many thrusted invasions.

No idle dreamers these
Who fashioned from soil
Of centuries, crude weapons,
To lead in armed uprising
The vengeance of peoples who
Oppressed by feudal war-lords
Capitalist-bureaucrats and foreign invaders
Tore from vaunted arrogance
The vain hope that superior weapons
Wrought in overseas workshops,
Of the New world,
Would overcome and vanquish
Peasants, who for a thousand years,
Had groaned and fought
Risen and fallen
Before their superior might

What then turned the tide?
What organized the people
Simple in their aspiration
And desires, into a fighting fist
To crush forever their Chiangs
Their war-lords, backed
By the imperialist might of
US dollars and many-flagged guns?

It's true they also fashioned their own guns
with self-reliance, initiative and
Daring – to compel admiration to this day
True too, they captured the guns of the enemy –

But basic to their Victory
was the fruit of their understanding
Born of Mao's thinking
The teachings of the Chairman
Of the Chinese Communists
The tactic of unity, with all who
Loved this ancient land,
The service to the people's needs
The fight to win and
Change the mind of Man
Against the corruption of centuries,
Of feudal-bourgeois, capitalist ideas
The fusion of courage and clarity
Of polemics against misleaders
Who sought compromise with the enemy
These were the pre-requisites of Victory.

No idle dreamers these –
And yet they dared to dream
The dream – long-planned
Unfolds in Socialist China –

From Yenan - Cradle of the Revolution,
Of their dreams, their fight,
Their organisation, their heroism
Yenan – Proud monument to Man's will
To transform Nature, and, so doing
Transform Society and Man himself!

Note: Written on the 'plane, returning from a two-day visit to Yenan. August 28, 1964

IV
Afterword

When Socialist Values Harmonize with Human Desire for Liberation: Assessing Claudia Jones' Politics[1]

Alrick X. Cambridge

In memory of Gertrude Elias, Peter Blackman, Lionel Jeffrey, John La Rose, Emile Burns, Gerry Cohen and Arthur Evans, and Gilian Noel, and in gratitude to various members of The Black Liberator editorial board: Colin Prescod, Cecil Gutzmore, St. Elmo Hughes, EG Howarth, Neville Fearron, Gerlin Bean, Hazel Savage; and to Malcolm Budd, Janey Fisher, Richard Hart, Cleston Taylor, Stephan Feuchtwang, Caroline Knowles, Carole Boyce Davies, John McClendon, Len Folkes, Anthony Neunie, Peter Sadler, Harry Goulbourne, David and Hazel Selbourne, Ranjana and Bill Ash, and Sonia Townsend, all of whom gave or has given a lot to the movement for human liberation.

The overall attempt here is to assess the political activity of Claudia Jones as arising from her ideological positions. The fulcrum of that political activity we claim was organized around her imaginative Leninist understanding[2] of the national and colonial question.[3] That assertion, so to speak, is our central thesis. Our subordinate thesis is the supporting claim that the Leninist influence was threaded through all the several political locations, or sites, or movements that were combined into the core organizational structure of Jones' political activity. Accordingly these two theses, central and subordinate, mention political activities which we argue are inseparable from Jones' personality as a communist. We begin by setting out the salient sites that in our view constituted the core organizational structure of Jones political activity.

The political force of internationalism. Jones' internationalism was direct. She firmly held the belief that only the political movement, mutual struggles, and active solidarity of labouring people on a world scale organized around the Marxist communist perspective would be decisive in helping to change the world for the communist good. This in fine was Jones' understanding of the political force of internationalism.

The conventional Marxist theory of history. Like most communists of her time Jones held that class struggle was the engine of historical change, namely the motor of revolution.

The Leninist theory of imperialism. Jones' conventional communist understanding of imperialism as the highest stage of capitalism in terminal decline entailed that the socialist revolutions in conjunction with the national liberation movements would hasten its final collapse.

The national question. As asserted already, the imaginative Leninist perspective on the national and colonial question was in our view the primary influence on, and the chief source of, Jones' political activity and the dominant dispositional force that was threaded through all the other salient sites that were combined into the core organizational structure of Jones' political activity.

The role of black workers as autonomous catalysts in the labour movement. Jones' position was this: Within the capitalist production system, black and white workers participate on equal juridical terms as workers in capitalist production. The policy of divide-and-rule on *racial* and *cultural* lines enters ideologically to the benefit of the capitalist class and the disbenefit of the working class, as a class. Black workers are then forced to organize autonomously around extra-class lines to resist extra-class exploitation more often than not in opposition to both white workers and capitalists in order to resist super-exploitation (in particular of black workers) and safeguard the overall interests of workers as workers.

As already mentioned these were the sites that made up the core organizational structure of Jones' political activity; and we now add a supporting rationale; namely that the sites were threaded through by certain Marxist and Leninist ideological thoughts that Jones discovered and came to understand more cogently in the struggle that forged her political personality. In the struggle Jones becomes aware that she was a communist whose principles comported with the desire for human liberation, the deliverance of which she came to fully comprehend that only labouring people in all their glorious self-ascriptions could realize through political struggle around the sites.

We turn now to a brief description of Jones' imaginative Leninist understanding of the national question. The core of the Leninist national and colonial question is the principle of the right of oppressed nations to self-determination, that is, the right of a national group; or nationality; or nation to secede from an imperial nation; or great nation; or national group oppressing it. To secede is to breakaway. Thus the three principles implicated here are those of (1) the will or right to breakaway (to secede) from an oppressor nation; an oppressor group; or an oppressor nationality; (2) the principle of self-autonomy; and (3) the principle of self-determination.

There was a contested political background within the European communist movement to the stated principles about which we are unable to go into more fully here. Suffice it to say that Lenin argued for his principles amidst the contestation in order to justify the politics of national and socialist revolutions against imperialism in the period of its deepening economic and political crises between 1914 and 1924. Lenin saw that World War I had brought on the terminal decline of moribund European imperialism and his prognosis was that the anti-colonial liberation movements in conjunction with the European socialist revolutions would make the capitalist system collapse. It is not to our purpose to offer any judgment on Lenin's theory of revolution here. What is to the point is to understand what Jones had made of the three principles implicated by the Leninist platform and the refraction or threading of them through the sites that organized the core structure of Jones' political activity.

Now given the contested political background of the principles within the European communist movement it is by no means an unreasonable assumption that Jones must have always been acutely aware – as a leading member of the CPUSA – that the principles' application to the Black American situation would also be misunderstood and controversial. But Jones was always deeply confident of the national character of the historic struggles of black America and to her way of thinking the national character of these historic struggles was the primary justification needed for the imaginative application of the principles of the national question to them. Thus the starting point of Jones' understanding for the strategic challenge to the special type of extreme Jim Crow terror immanent to anti-Black racism and segregation that affected Black America as a subject population was the assimilation of two overarching lessons: the historic lessons of Black America, as summed up in their historic movements, campaigns, and conceptions from the struggles around abolition; around reconstruction, democracy and liberty; around the subsequent struggles for civil rights and human dignity; and the refraction of all these historic lessons primarily through the lessons of the anti-colonial national liberation movements as Jones the partisan communist had imagined them through Leninist principles, as a current in the world liberation movement and catalyst in the American class struggle.

Before we go further we should make it clear that the claims – hence the two theses – set forth at the start of this discussion are a reconstruction of Jones' politics, and are based upon the observations and study of her political activity. The results are arrived at by a process of reflection upon Jones' action and what we recall of her theoretical conceptions rather than interpretation of her written word. In the process of reconstructing her politics, certain features of her political personality are brought out in order to show the reader what is intended in speaking of her forging. The idea is this: that in actually participating in and organizing the movements of the kinds and range that she did – they all together, in a complex unity of forces and ideas, contributed in great measure to forming Jones as a communist.

Now since a larger rationale supports the unity of the sites and concerns Jones' final political values we say something about these. We approach this by considering whether Jones would ever have detached herself from her deeply held communist principles after the fall of the Soviet real socialist system? Our reply is no. Before Jones died she was already hyper-critical of that system as lived in the Soviet bloc. She leaned towards China instead. We know more of the repression and terror of both systems now than before. But had Jones known she might still not have wished the Soviet system to fall. One crucial reason is this. Jones held the view that the Soviet system could still be a counterweight to the rampant character of the US-controlled world system of corporate imperialism and military adventures. Was she mistaken? It obviously depends on one's point of view. But in hindsight even from a communist point of view we should now say that up to a certain point Jones was mistaken about the Soviet system as a counterweight to US imperialism and neo-colonialism because of the cost in human lives. To judge the issue correctly we do have to weigh in the balance what good was achieved against the cost of individual lives. We do not have to agree with the right libertarian moral claim of Robert Nozick that no human life must ever be sacrificed for the greater good to see that our qualified negative reply to Jones' stance could still be challenged. Providing a knockdown answer to the question is not easy, one way or the other.

At any rate, unable to find reasonable justification for the repressive misde-meanours of Soviet totalitarianism, it is not hard to see why some have become communist apostates. So why are we confident that Jones would never have rejected the communist commitments of revolutionizing human society? Our reply is this: that because the essence of Jones' politics was human liberation it is hard to imagine that she could ever have rejected that essence. For she would have reasoned – if to realize communism was my sole aim in life, my guiding light, then that would necessitate that I would need to struggle for a world in which the human essence could be realized. But for that to be realized requires that progressive individuals like myself consciously work for the universal – namely the common good of all humankind. As we reconstruct Jones' final ends here it is a political position, which, out of loyalty and commitment, she would never have failed to struggle for continually since these final ends are communist principles that sustained her life and forged her individuality; and these communist values would have continued to sustain Jones in our view no matter how disagreeable were the opposing repressive systems and supporting values of Soviet and corporate capitalist injustices in the world. Thus in our view it was Jones' loyalty and commitment to communist principles that were her deep ethical compass, and the source of her moral authority.

Now recall that at the start of this reflection we set forth the sites within which Jones worked. Given the way in which we have constructed the core organiza-tional structure of sites and described them, it may not seem so strange that we here propose to argue that the site which influenced Jones' politics most was not the contested corpus of Marxist-Leninist theory but rather precisely the Leninist theory of the national question in the era of worldwide national challenges to imperialism and colonization. The implication is that we must now admit that in

Jones' politics all the other sites are more or less refracted through one site: the imaginative application of the national question to one degree or other. Characterizing the national question as the site which actively influenced Jones' actions most satisfies our need for specificity. But the characterization also satisfies another requirement, to provide the reason why Jones' passion for human liberation was so intensely directed. We argue that the reason was because the national question, as she imaginatively understood it, bore directly upon the millions of dispossessed humanity in the colonized world, including the colonized African American masses in the US whose strategic struggle Jones viewed as making an essential contribution to the realization of human liberation. The national question directly addressed them hence, it being central to Jones' political perspective and the reason she lived her practice within its two fronts, the colonized world and the imperial centre.

Jones held firmly to that view, namely that forging struggle and solidarity on two fronts, both in the colonized world and the imperial centres among the labouring majority, would massively explode the contradictions within imperialism, destabilize and weaken the ruling classes, and make the conquest of workers power progressively more feasible. These crucial axes of the Leninist theory of world revolution as refracted through her imaginative application of the national question are central to Jones' politics: the injunction to work from the foregoing perspective for the utter destruction of the world power of imperialism and to liberate the wretched dispossessed masses from their thrall.

Jones might never have publicly stated this platform as her end and aim in such bold terms as reconstructed here; but she knew her Lenin and hence knew that the force of political practice was to transform amorphous spontaneity into organized end-results having a specific form and content – a directed objective. She also knew that it was an implication of the Leninist theory of world revolution that internationally communist directed organized struggle and solidarity among the world's masses – African, Asian, Latin American and European – would contribute to deepening the political and economic crises of moribund imperialism in terminal decline; that it would generate further instability among the ruling classes; that it would induce their political disorganization; that if it were sufficiently massive it would cripple the machinery of imperialist world power; that it would galvanize the ranks of international labour; that it would create the optimum political circumstances for the conquest of power and that the socialist reorganization of human societies could then be placed on the political agenda. But what is interesting is the manner in which Jones practiced her politics – or at any rate the way in which we have reconstructed her as imaginatively doing so – and how all the sites that constituted the core structure of her political activity were drawn together within it. So we might notice the call upon the force of internationalism; upon the theory of class struggle as the motor of revolution and historical change; upon the Leninist theory of dying imperialism in its final stages and the revolutionary role of the Third World liberation movements in hastening its collapse; upon the role of black workers as autonomous *catalyst* in the labour movement; and upon the national and colonial question. Jones' significance today resides in just this: *that the political agenda she organized her struggles around are still alive today in one form or another.*

And now we must go further and say we are aware that if we assert a thesis about Jones' politics to the effect that the fulcrum of her activity was influenced by her imaginative understanding of the national question, then it will need direct empirical support. This discussion cannot meet a strong version of that test. Instead we do the second best thing – namely to provide certain redolent examples from the US and British arenas, which indicate a general disposition on Jones' part to be mostly influenced by that site and which we argue nevertheless does support our central thesis. In this regard we offer five suggestive examples below, which accordingly capture the evidential support for our subordinate thesis and hence support our two theses set forth at the start.

The view of Black America as an oppressed nation

From the late 1930s and for several decades, strategic role as a current in the international liberation afterwards, the special type of extreme Jim Crow terror intrinsic to white racist discrimination against and segregation of, the American black population were conceived by the CPUSA as a form of national oppression. To the Party's thinking accordingly black people as a racial group was an oppressed nation; and because of its own special features and characteristics as a national minority, its central autonomous movement and in the continental US class struggle flowed. Black autonomy here not only implied real organizational self-determination. Self-determination was also to be actualized through the call for secession from the US Union for certain Southern Black States where the black population were the majority – if secession (the right to breakaway) was the true political desire of blacks as a nation. The policy in fine was the result of the Party understanding of the national question as applied to the 'Negro Problem'. We do not here judge the policy one way or another. The point we make instead is this: that as a national Party leader and organizer with responsibility for the creative execution of policies around issues of black autonomy and national self-determination, Jones would have been *naturalized* in the Party's ethos about the strategic significance of the national question to the extent that it became an inherent quality of her political practice not only in the American arena, but also in the British arena of exile and anti-colonial movements involving African, Asian and Caribbean constituencies.

Let us now ask: Did Jones have a contrasting conception of the character of anti-Black racism independently of the conventional communist one? And if so what was it? The short answer to both questions is no: she had a conventional communist perspective. But to get clarity on that negative reply a digression is necessary.

Anti-Black racism and the practices to which it gives rise are harmful and inhumane attitudes towards blacks on the part of whites. Directed at blacks as objects, anti-Black racist effects produce immense destructive results on their victims. By contrast to those whose ascriptions are black or brown, those whose ascriptions are white are in many undeserving ways privileged by their racial status (colour) and moreover benefit (advantaged) in many equally undeserving ways by virtue of their racial status, which are then enforced more often than not by juridical, cultural and sanctioned political violence, repression and terror.

But notice our negative assumption here, namely that the racial (colour) ascriptions of populations as black and white are not given laws of biology: these are categorical ascriptions acquired historically overtime through definite political and cultural subjections; subjections enforced by political violence and sanctioned repression and terror.

Instructively, the privileging and benefiting, as well as their racial categorical and ascriptive determinations, whether violently, culturally, or otherwise sanctioned, are explanatory mechanisms of anti-Black racist discriminations. The categorical and ascriptive determinations in fact explain aspects of the anti-Black racist mechanisms, but they do not entirely explain anti-Black racism's intensity until they are further connected to and supported by institutional mechanisms of subjection, oppression, economic exploitation, and sanctioned political violence **and terror.** We maintain then that all of these institutional mechanisms, subjection, oppression, exploitation and sanctioned political violence and terror working in combination bear upon and contribute to the production of the unjust generation of anti-Black racist inequalities. In this regard racist ascriptions and categorizations in their effects function in order to create racial (and ethnic) divisions and oppositional relations among and between the differentiated population categories and groups that they give rise to; and moreover these same effects also function as mechanisms to generate hierarchies of social privileges and economic values. Thus as mechanisms these racist effects are productive of status divisions and wealth and accordingly they distribute power relations over the populations subject to their force.

The lesson to draw from the foregoing is this: that in order to go further and understand anti-Black racism's causal emergence requires that we investigate the rise of racist categorizations and ascriptions themselves. My approach to that problem, accordingly, is to view the politics of anti-Black racism in historical terms, namely as consequential existences that arose out of the emergence of, and opposition to, European racist ascriptions and categorical descriptions of colonized populations different from their own, in the era of European maritime exploration and primitive capitalist accumulation.

As digressions go it could be said that ours as it stands is too programmatic to be of any comparative political use; but we would argue that such a response is an overstatement; conventional communists and others should find nothing disagreeable in the above; for it is a help rather than a hindrance to the further understanding of anti-Black racism in the following contrasting way.

Communist parties and activists in the last century were apt to understand the phenomenon of racial ascriptions and racist injustices rather differently from the forgoing conception of them: they would not have understood either in terms of the rise of racial ascriptive categories enforced in the manner we described but rather in material economic terms. Accordingly party communists in that era might have replied to the explanatory claims asserted above about anti-Black racism that, whether the rise of anti-Black racist practices are best explained causally in racist categorical terms or not, capitalists use techniques of racist methods as cultural tools, as social mechanisms, to divide-and-rule the working class, black and white, in order to sanction super-exploitation and extreme oppression of both (but notably of black workers) to the optimal advantage of capitalists. Accordingly the party communist's conventional account of anti-Black racist discrimination was explained essentially by recourse to material determinations alone. In this account therefore the phenomenon of race was conceived as false consciousness about human difference and introduced into the class struggle through multiple ideological mechanisms of capitalist domination with the function to obscure the reality of class domination. Thus on this view the phenomenon of race was *secondary* to material class differentiations. We disagree with this theory but acknowledge it as still having powerful political resonances.

Let us end the digression by concluding that whatever else these two contrasting positions disagree about (whether explanation of racism by racial categorical or material terms) they both agree that anti-Black racist mechanisms play a key role in differentiating black and white workers both in the labour market and production and therefore in explaining super-exploitation within these two material structures. Thus what the racial categorical perspective objects to is the claim that anti-Black racist exclusions can be explained *solely* by reference to material determinations alone.

At any rate the two contrasting perspectives presented here give rise to better and worse policy options the relative merits of which we cannot pursue further here.[4] We must take it for granted that Jones was an implacable anti-racist even though her perspective on racist injustices was more or less the conventional communist one. And even if they were unfamiliar with the details, no one could reasonably doubt Jones' credentials as a steadfast anti-racist, given her formidable accumulation of heroic anti-racist struggles in America and Britain whether on the imperial or colonial fronts.

Imperial and colonial fronts: political interventions in the British and West Indian national situations

Now had it occurred to Jones a question which might have intrigued her is the counterfactual thought that although for centuries the British were a major slaving nation they never established slave communities in the colonial fringes of the United Kingdom or on the mainland on the model of the white American colonies in the Southern States. Counterfactually of course had they done so, then issues of national self-determination would have arisen for Jones to make appeal to and intervene politically in, in the 1950s and 1960s. The retort will be: British slavers need not have contemplated doing what the counterfactual proposes because they had hundreds of colonial plantations in the tropics on which they could grow tobacco, sugar cane, cotton and coffee from which they derived massive profits. None of these outcomes were probable in inclement UK. Yes, but is that the complete answer to the question the counterfactual implies? For consider: if the British had established slave communities in the UK producing commodities (other than the tropical ones) they could then have freed them a century earlier than they in fact did and then used the free black labour force to develop and expand the industrial revolution still more and still further.

At any rate there have been no national black populations claiming national self-determination from the British going back to this era to which Jones might have applied her imaginative understanding of the national question. What there were, were several settlements of hundreds of free blacks, former slaves, in London, Bristol and Liverpool who for various historical reasons could not have constituted a cohesive political force as a national group against national oppression of the special form of extreme Jim Crow terror inherent to American anti-Black racism and segregation on the scale practiced in the Southern States and to which the national question could apply. Some from these free black communities appear to have been assimilated into the white population; but those who have maintained strong connections with their black identities have left a flourishing cultural legacy which today's anti-racist black groups have laid claim to in their oppositional struggles against anti-Black racist discriminations. Many Black individuals from this latter constituency have formed a bridge between the communities of free Blacks and the exiled individuals of Pan-Africanists, Marxists and radical anti-colonialists, Asian, African and Caribbean, who arrived in Britain in the 1930s and turned to political agitation for their countries' right to national self-determination. These individuals, to our mind, constituted a constituency of anti-colonial partisans and we will refer to them as such hereafter. An issue that arises at this point is whether our thesis that Jones' politics was mostly influenced by an imaginatively applied Leninist national problem is compromised if the same analogy holds for any member/s of the constituency of anti-colonial partisans. It is not our view that our thesis would be so compromised; but it is certainly a debatable issue.

In many respects, by contrast, the Caribbean migrant communities and political constituencies generated by them that Jones encountered when she was exiled in Britain in the mid-1950s and 1960s were uniquely different from the previous 1930s constituencies of anti-colonial partisans and from the free slave communities before them. Admittedly the populations comprising the new West Indian migrant communities were the descendants of Caribbean plantation slaves; but they had a conception of themselves as black West Indians who were equal to whites and who would be resistant to any form of anti-Black racist discrimination that excluded them from civil society; or even from the private spheres. Some of these populations were highly skilled trades-people; agriculturalists; teachers; nurses; radical political activists; trade unionists; business people; lawyers; doctors; students; writers and intellectuals. Instructively a sizable cohort of these migrant populations since the late 1930s who had been introduced to nationalist politics and the parliamentary two-party system were active in these populations and in their migration they had left behind them movements in their Caribbean countries agitating for national independence. If you are from this migrant background as Jones was and you are exiled in Britain by the US immigration service because of your communist political affiliation; if you are a public intellectual and the publisher and editor of a newspaper, *The West Indian Gazette*, whose role according to Jones was to intervene into the British political situation and redress the balance of black injustices; to conceptualize and reflect the deep feelings of your communities, communities continually being demonized; persecuted; stereotyped; negatively categorized racially; and routinely brutalized; then you will use all your skill and talent to represent them politically.

It goes without saying that the kind of anti-Black racism that Jones encountered in Britain was vastly different from the American variety. British black West Indian migrants were still colonized subjects when they arrived in the mid 1950s. Independence was granted to the first West Indian nation in 1962. Jones arrived in 1955 and died in 1964 so she only experienced British anti-Black racism for just under a decade. But it was a crucial decade to be experiencing British anti-Black racism against the background of the decline of the British empire and the surge in national liberation movements and liberation wars 15 years after World War II; for in spite of the defeat of European Nazism, fascism, anti-Semitism[5] (and ostensibly anti-Black racism) in the war, both were still very much alive; and alive too was an active resurgent fascist movement. Anti-Black racist discrimination existed in Britain: it was vocal in employment; in work places; in public places; in the communities where black West Indians lived and even in parliament. Cases of segregation existed too although it was not the extreme segregated terror type practiced in the white Southern States of America or the extreme terror type practiced in apartheid South Africa. These cases embarrassed the British political classes concerned about their

Commonwealth image so much so that they were often denied or played down as the result of the prejudiced misunderstandings of certain un-British outcasts and misfits. Black and white racial conflicts erupted periodically; the most outrageous and publicized one being the black-white riot in Notting Hill following the murder of the black West Indian Kelso Cochrane in 1958. The police were racist and brutal; but there was no extreme Jim Crow terror lynching. Jones was aware of all these distinctions and features. She was well aware too that taken together the British forms of anti-Black racism did not comparatively speaking amount to the special type of extreme Jim Crow terror integral to the anti-Black racism of segregated America. In short: the special type of extreme Jim Crow terror integral to the anti-Black racism of segregated white America which oppressed black America as a national group and to which the national question applied because of the comparative distinctions and features mentioned here did not exist in Britain. Jones' strategy then was obviously to adapt her imaginative understanding of the national question to the new and different circumstances in Britain, both at the levels of her political and cultural interventions.

No one should be surprised to learn then that Jones saw her role as intervening politically in situations and executing objectives. The West Indian Gazette was an intervention into the British situation to expose racist and colonialist injustices. Thus independence from Britain of certain African countries was featured; similarly for certain English speaking West Indian countries and likewise, favourably publicized was the idea of West Indies Federation. All received due diligence; readers were assured of serious opinion and sound advice. We should therefore view The West Indian Gazette as a political organ of intervention, mobilization, orientation and direction. The West Indian Gazette was after all a political project and the ways in which it intervened and discharged its orientation to its readers about African and West Indian self-determination shows Jones' masterful imaginative application of the national question writ large. As an editor she would invest much energy and skill in certain issues of great concern to readers. For example the failed West Indies Federation; the break-up of which was a deep source of disappointment for Jones. She wanted there to be a larger Caribbean political community and was convinced that if national island leaders could suppress their petty island nationalisms and minor grievances, federation was feasible. Our conviction is that had Jones lived, it is quite probable that she would have used The West Indian Gazette to campaign for some other form of political and economic union of the English speaking Caribbean region which was not federal. It might also be of interest to mention here too that long before Jamaica's Prime Minister Michael Manley had defied America and established close and mutually advantageous ties between Jamaica and the Cuban people Jones had seen the virtue of doing so for all the English speaking Caribbean once each nation state had become independent of Britain.

Political Interventions on the International Front: Civil Rights for Black America, Afro-Asian Unity and Communist world strategy

It is worth repeating that in Jones' view all three situations mentioned in the heading were linked together through the core organizational structure of the sites and influenced by Jones' imaginative understanding of the national question viewed in relation to the movements for national liberation. It should come as no surprise then, as already developed at various points in this argument, that Jones' strategic mode of political interventions were always conceived of and imagined on two fronts, imperial and colonial, around the national question. The next group of suggestive examples continues our exemplification of these claims.

(i)   *Supporting Black America's civil rights march.* In this intervention we see Jones' role as principal organizer of the 1963 solidarity March on the US embassy in London to coincide with the great 1963 Civil Rights March on Washington of the same year. It was on that march that Martin Luther King Jr. delivered his resonating speech: 'I have a dream'. The event was obviously significant because of that occasion; but in our view the event was no less significant because Jones as chief organizer managed to bring together groups of people from many different walks of life, Asians, Africans, West Indians and British; from different political persuasions; and even from different faiths. It cannot be far fetched to hold that in organizing this political action Jones was here extending her internationalist understanding to a struggle against the national oppression of black America which her imagination had never left behind.

(ii) *Supporting Afro-Asian Unity.* Or again consider how Jones applied that same imagination to forge what was then called Afro-Asian *unity* around the same period as the March on Washington. The groups involved here were Africans and Asians connected to their home countries' liberation movements; groups and individuals from the British left and from the West Indies, activists and students of a newer constituency of anti-colonial partisans. The interesting thing about this conception of Afro Asian unity at this time is that this international multiethnic constituency of partisans, Africans, Asians, West Indians and British white, were all being organized by an exiled West Indian communist deportee from the US around a conception of Afro Asian unity derived from the spirit of Bandung and from Duboisan ideas of Pan Africanism, all under the influence of the Leninist national question as Jones had conceived it.

All the political groups and constituencies mentioned here were all truly international antiracists then and committed to the politics of unification of all the anti-colonial forces as integral to the strategy of defeating US imperialism. As regards this strategy it cannot therefore be doubted that the glorious rise of the Black Power and Black is Beautiful movements – coming together as they did in the middle of the Vietnam and other liberation conflicts – constituted a powerful shock to the hegemonic political and cultural systems of British and American imperialism. Just imagine, revolutionary black groups, protesting daily and persistently, had found their voices (and their arms) and could then be counted among the central political forces in the global liberation challenges to the political and moral authority of British and American imperialism. The latter's responses were both to mobilize their respective repressive apparatuses against the black movements as they had been doing against the national liberation movements. It is not at all out of place to speculate that had Jones lived she would have embraced these movements; and in so far as Britain was concerned it should not be doubted that Jones might even have attempted to unify the various prominent black groups around a common strategic antiracist platform to make their impact more effective.

(iii) *Self-interest as a case of altruism: the communist's advantage is unselfish concern for the common good.* The final example arose in an early 1960s debate at the British Communist Party Headquarters and concerned charges raised by the Chinese communists against the Russian communists, namely that in ideological terms the Russians had underestimated the international strategic role of the national liberation movements in challenging the world hegemony of US imperialism and in consequence overestimated its power. US imperialism was after all, so the thought implied, 'a paper tiger', as Mao had quipped. The US military was busy dropping napalm on the North Vietnamese people at this time and the marines had overreached themselves by invading three other South East Asian countries, South Vietnam, Cambodia and Laos. The issue was how to defeat the Americans. Jones was a member of the British communist party at this time. As a colonial migrant exiled in Britain Jones had experienced national oppression in the US and knew a thing or two about the American military industrial complex and the power and terror it is designed to convey. So in her contribution Jones placed reiterated emphasis upon a certain political line – namely that it wasn't out of political expediency that communists express solidarity and support for national liberation movements; but rather out of principled revolutionary necessity to actualize the communist content of international solidarity with the dispossessed humanity in Third World theatres of war and moreover, to bring the realization of European communism closer to actuality. For these reasons Western communists were duty bound to bring to critical boiling point the optimum political conditions to frustrate US militarism; realize human liberation and safeguard World Peace. Jones was absolutely right. And in hindsight we might also notice something ethically powerful about the content of Jones' speech, namely that her reply raises the issue of self-interest as a case of altruism. In other words, that the communist's advantage is unselfish concern for the common good of the world's exploited and oppressed dispossessed masses. And again we see the national question imaginatively surfacing through her narrative.

Biography of Alrick X. Cambridge

Alrick Cambridge was born in Jamaica and received his early and secondary education there and graduate and post-graduate education at London and Oxford universities. He was Claudia Jones' loyal assistant for 18 months before she died in 1964. Subsequently he became an activist in The British Labour movement; and in the Black Power and anti-racist movements. His published books include *Antiracist Strategies* (1990) and *Where You Belong – Government and Black Culture* (with Stephan Feuchtwang) (1992), both published by Avebury Press, Aldershot, England and many other published papers and essays including, "C.L.R. James: Freedom Through History and Dialectics" in Alistair Hennesy, ed. (1992) *Intellectuals in the Twentieth Century Caribbean;* "C.L.R. James' Socialist Future and Human Happiness," in Boyce Davies et al (2003) *Decolonizing the Academy: African Diaspora Studies.* He was the founding editor of the *Black Liberator Magazine: A Theoretical and Discussion Journal for Black Liberation* which was published throughout the 1970s in London.

References to Introductory Essay

Boyce Davies, Carole. (2009) "Sisters Outside: Tracing the Caribbean/Black Radical Intellectual Tradition." *Small Axe.* 13 (1): 217–229.

Boyce Davies, Carole. (2008) *Left of Karl Marx. The Politics and Poetics of a Black Communist Woman.* Durham, North Carolina: Duke University Press.

Communist Manifesto. (Kerr edition, 1998: Chicago: Charles H. Kerr Publishing Company, 2003) New Introduction by Robin D. G. Kelley.

Davis, Angela. (2005) *Abolition and Democracy. Beyond Empire, Prisons, and Torture.* N.Y.: Seven Stories Press.

Gaines, Kevin. (2009) "Locating the Transnational in Postwar African American History." *Small Axe.*2009; 13: 193–202.

Drake, St. Clair. (1975) "The Black Diaspora in Pan-African Perspective." *Black Scholar,* 7:1 (Sept., 1975: 2–13)

Gibbons, Arnold. (1994) *Walter Rodney and his Times.* V.1. Identity and Ideology. Georgetown, Guyana. Guyana National Printers.

Gore, Dayo F., Jeanne Theoharis and Komozi Woodard, eds. (2009) *Want to Start a Revolution? Radical Women in the Black Freedom Struggle.* New York: NYU Press.

Gregg, Veronica, ed. (2005) Caribbean *Women: An Anthology of Non-Fiction Writing, 1890–1980* (African American Intellectual Heritage. University of Notre Dame Press).

Horne, Gerald. (1994) *Black Liberation/Red Scare. Ben Davis and the Communist Party.* Newark, New Jersey: University of Delaware Press.

James, Selma. (1994) *Marx and Feminism.* London: Crossroads Books.

James, Winston. (1998) *Holding Aloft the Banner of Ethiopia: Caribbean Radicalism in Early Twentieth-Century America.* London and New York: Verso.

Johnson, Buzz. (1985) *I Think of My Mother. Notes on The life and Times of Claudia Jones.* London, Karia Press.

Marx, Karl et al. (1951) *Woman Question: Selections from the Writings of Karl Marx, Frederick Engels. V/I. Lenin and Joseph Stalin.* New York: International Publishers.

Mullen, Bill and James Smethurst, eds. (2003) *Left of the Color Line. Race, Radicalism and Twentieth Century Literature of the United States.* Chapel Hill and London: University of North Carolina Press.

Mc Clendon, John. (2008) "Marxism in Ebony Contra Black Marxism." *Proud Flesh Journal.com*. Issue 6.

Perry, Jeffrey B. (2009) *Hubert Harrison. The Voice of Harlem Radicalism, 1883–1918*. New York: Columbia University Press.

Robinson, Cedric. (1983) *Black Marxism. The Making of a Black Radical Tradition*. London; Zed Books.

Rule, Ella, ed. (2000) *Marxism and the Emancipation of Women* Middlesex: Harpal Brar.

Rule, Ella. (2010) "Claudia Jones, Communist." *The Marxist-Leninist* (http://marxistleninist.wordpress.com/2010/03/01/claudia-jones-communist/) accessed 6/28/2010

Sherwood, Marika, Donald Hinds and Colin Prescod, eds. (1999) *Claudia Jones. A Life in Exile*. London: Lawrence and Wishart.

Turner, Joyce Moore. (2005) *Caribbean Crusaders and the Harlem Renaissance*. Urbana: University of Illinois Press.

Watkins-Owens, Irma. (1996) *Blood Relations. Caribbean Immigrants and the Harlem Community, 1900–1930*. Bloomington, Indiana: Indiana University Press.

Weigand, Kate. (2001) *Red Feminism. American Communism and the Making of Women's Liberation*. Baltimore and London: John Hopkins University Press.

Young, Cynthia A. (2006) *Soul Power: Culture, Radicalism, and the Making of a US Third World Left*. Durham and London: Duke University Press.

Notes

Introduction

1   There are two letters dated 23rd July, 1957 and 25th March, 1958. Available in the Claudia Jones Memorial Collection, Schomburg Centre for Research in Black Culture, New York. The Honourable Eric E. Williams was Prime Minister of Trinidad and Tobago who led the country to independence in 1962 and later to Republic Status. As an intellectual, he is known as the famous historian of, among others, the landmark text, *Capitalism and Slavery* (1944) which put forward what is now called the Williams Thesis on the logic of capitalism as the basis for the rise but also the end of transatlantic and new world slavery.

2   My unpublished essay, "Crossing Over Harold Cruse's Crisis," presented at the Callalloo Conference, 2009, addresses this aspect of Harold Cruse *The Crisis of the Negro Intellectual,* (1967) (New York: Quill, 1984). See also, Winston James, "Harold Cruse and the West Indians: Critical Remarks on The Crisis of the Negro Intellectual, in *Holding Aloft the Banner of Ethiopia, Caribbean Radicalism in Early Twentieth Century America,* (London: Verso, 1999): 262–291.

3   See Essays in *Left of the Color Line. Race, Radicalism and Twentieth Century Literature of the United States.* Ed. By Bill V. Mullen and James Smethurst (Chapel Hill and London: University of North Carolina Press, 2003). See also, Cynthia Young, *Soul Power: Culture, Radicalism, and the Making of a U.S. Third World Left,* (Duke University Press, 2006).

4   The term comes from Carole Boyce Davies and Babacar M'bow, "Towards African Diaspora Citizenship," in *Black Geographies and the Politics of Place,* ed. By Katherine McKittrick and Clyde Woods, Cambridge, MA: South End Press, 2007: 14–45.

5   Mary Helen Washington, "Alice Childress, Lorraine Hansberry, and Claudia Jones: Black Women Write the Popular Front," in *Left of the ColorColour Line:* 193–194.

6   Dayo F. Gore, "From Communist Politics to Black Power: The Visionary Politics and Transnational Solidarities of Victoria "Vicki' Ama Gavin" in *Want to Start a Revolution?: Radical Women in the Black Freedom Struggle,* New York: NYU Press, 2009): 72–94.

7   This information was provided by filmmaker Katie Sandler at the Black Venus conference at NYU, April 2010, who indicates that Rosa Guy told her this when she heard about the publication of my book, *Left of Karl Marx*.

8   Stuart Hall, "Cultural Identity and Cinematic Representation," in Mbye Cham, ed. *Ex-iles* (Trenton, New Jersey: Africa World Press, 1992): 220–236.

Notes to Autobiographical Essays

9   "The Scottsboro Boys" a play at the Lyceum Theatre on Broadway in New York, 2010 has generated new discussion in conjunction with the prison industrial complex but also the staging of black subjects.

10 This version is taken from the first published source: "13 Communists Speak to the Court," N.Y.: New Century Publishers, 1953.

11 This interview was first published in *Caribbean News*, (London, June, 1956).

12 This is reproduced from a handwritten document made available to me by Diane Langford. It was difficult to understand two words. These are the two italicized words in the text. However we have remained faithful to the turns of phrase, the meaning of the text and the writing pattern of the author.

Essays

Claudia Jones' starred notes

*   "The American Negro in the War," by Emmet J. Scott.
*   Joseph Stalin, Marxism and the National and Colonial Question, International Publishers, New York, p. 8.
*   Attorneys George W. Crockett, Michigan, Harry Sacher, New York, Abe Isserman, New Jersey, Louis McCabe, Philadelphia, Penna and Richard Gladstein of California, were all counsel for the eleven Communist leaders

13 *Jim Crow in Uniform* New York City, New Age Publishers, July, 1940. The pamphlet cost 2 cents. It included a short introduction by James W. Ford (1893–1957) who was a Vice Presidential candidate of the United States on the Communist Party ticket in 1932, 1936 and 1940 and was therefore the first African American to appear on a presidential ticket in the 20th century. He attended Communist Party gatherings in Moscow in 1928 and 1929 and was a delegate to the World Congress Against Imperialism. He was made head of the Harlem section of the CPUSA in 1933 so he would have been active in Harlem during the time when Claudia joined the Communist Part in 1936. He was knowledgeable therefore about the colonial world and would have been able to share the knowledge with people like Claudia.

14   *Lift Every Voice – For Victory* was published also as a pamphlet, being sold for
     2 cents and authored by Claudia Jones (New York, New Age Publishers,
     June, 1942). There is an ad for US Bonds and Stamps "For Victory." This
     piece was obviously written to promote the war effort, particularly since
     the Soviet Union's Red Army was also involved in the anti-Hitler effort.
     She is described as follows at the back of the pamphlet: "Claudia Jones,
     the author of this pamphlet, is a young Negro woman leader of the Young
     Communist League, Editor of the popular anti-fascist youth magazine, the
     WEEKLY REVIEW." On the cover is an armed and uniformed posed
     photograph of Joe Louis. And on the frontispiece is a photograph of a
     uniformed Joe Louis with boxing gloves, and in the company of excited
     "buddies at Camp Dix".
15   First published in *Political Affairs*, (June 1949); and in *Political Affairs*,
     53:(March, 1974): 29–42.
16   *The Daily Worker*, September 4, 1949.
17   "International Women's Day and the Struggle for Peace," *Political Affairs*
     (March 29, 1950) 32–45. This piece was published as "Women in the
     Struggle for Peace and Security," New York: National Women's
     Commission, Communist Party (April 1950): 3–16. This is the essay
     version of the speech delivered on International Women's Day, which was
     identified as the "overt act" in her trial.
18   Published in *Political Affairs*, 30 (February, 1951): 151–168.
19   National Committee to Defend Negro Leadership, 1660 Fulton Street,
     Brooklyn 13, New York, November, 1954.
20   Her first essay following her departure, in *Political* Affairs, 27(April, 1958):
     9–18. It provides an editorial note about her as follows:

> *Claudia Jones, a beloved leader of the communist Party of the United States, was jailed*
> *under the infamous Smith Act and upon release forced into exile; she is now living in*
> *England. The article which follows – one in our series relating the impact of American*
> *imperialism in various parts of the world – is especially timely. It was written, as Miss*
> *Jones comments, just before the March 25 elections to the Assembly of the West Indian*
> *Federation, whose formal appearance as a new member of the community of nations will*
> *occur this April-*the Editor.

21   A Souvenir of the Caribbean Carnival, 1959 at St. Pancras Town Hall,
     London, Friday 30th January, 1959, Organised by the *West Indian Gazette*.
     Carnival Cabaret Directed by Edric Connor. Televised by BBC Television.
22   *Freedomways*, (Summer, 1964): 340–357.

Notes to Poetry

23 Audre Lorde, "Poetry is Not a Luxury," *Sister Outsider. Essays and Speeches.* Freedom, CA: The Crossing Press.

24 Part of the letter to John Gates appears in *Left of Karl Marx* (pp. 105–106).

25 This poem is described as being written by Claudia for Elizabeth Gurley Flynn and memorized and given to her as she is about to leave prison in October, 1955 and then rewritten while she was on the train heading back to New York. Flynn would also give Claudia a poem dated October 24, 1955 and titled "Farewell to Claudia" which includes the line: "Sometimes I feel you've never been in Alderson," suggesting that she was beyond prison containment.

26 Puerto Rican activist, Blanca Canales Torresola, served a four-year term in Alderson around the same time as the communist women were incarcerated there. Elizabeth Gurley Flynn indicates in her autobiography in a chapter titled "The Politicals in Alderson" that she had seen a stout white-haired woman who spoke with a Spanish accent and who smiled whenever she saw her. When she mentioned it, Claudia responded: "That's Blanca, one of the Puerto Rican nationalists." Torresola was one of the women who headed the 1950 uprising in Puerto Rico in the struggle for independence. The poem mentions Jarama and Guernica. Guernica was a Basque town in Northern Spain that was destroyed by German bombs in 1937 during the Spanish Civil War and was the subject of the famous Picasso painting. Jarama was the site of the first aggressive act of World War II, also in 1937. See *Left of Karl Marx*, pp. 112–113.

27 According to Elizabeth Gurley Flynn, Claudia spent a great deal of time working in the craft shop and learned several crafts taught there – ceramics, pottery, metal jewelry, wood carving and leather work. She taught several girls to model clay and another to play the piano. This poem seems to use the experiential to come to some conclusions about creativity in the universe. See *Left of Karl Marx*, pp. 108–108 for further discussion.

28 Emmett Till born on July 25 1941 in Chicago was murdered by lynch mob on August 28 1955 in Money, Mississippi where he was visiting relatives, for allegedly whistling at a white woman and his body thrown in the Tallahatchie River, wrapped in barbed wire and weighed down by a cotton gin fan, where it was discovered three days later. His mother chose an open casket so that people could see her son's mutilated and disfigured body. His murder and his mother's courageous actions and the failure to convict the perpetrators in September 1955, led to this being also a major issue of the Civil Rights Movement. Several investigations and new examinations occurred in the 1990s up to 2007. Many plays, poems,

songs, documentaries, television shows, films would reference or use directly the Emmett Till incident as an iconic moment as the ultimate in the continuing history of the oppression of African Americans in the US. This poem was possibly written after the September trial as it mentions "white washed justice" referring to the way injustice was/is the norm when it dealt with/deals with black people in the US judicial system.

29   These two poems capture Jones in a reflective mood, perhaps written while contemplating the nature of life, its passing and the sense of human frailty. The references to autumn in both of them tell us that she was contemplating what it meant to enter mid-life, how it prompts the looking back on one's life with its dreams, difficulties and plans that were not able to be realized as one looks into the future. It seems to echo the autobiographical fragment which similarly spoke of life and its meaning.

30   A note indicates that this poem was written to FSS at her request, though there is no date on the poem but it is a mature poem written obviously to a friend of similar age as it references the sorrows and joys that Life has in store while friendship sustains.

31   These two poems were written during her time in the Soviet Union, the first one dealing with the rough beauty of nature and the second an anthem on the accomplishments of the Soviet Union at that time. Since Claudia was hospitalized during her time in the Soviet Union, there is a bit of a sad overtone to her at this time. There is also a letter available, written to Manchanda which details this period as well as the sense of difficulties that the *West Indian Gazette* faced consistently.

32   This poem was written as she returned from a two-day trip to Yenan, China and was republished in the Memorial issue of the *West Indian Gazette and Afro-Asian Caribbean News* surrounded by photographs of her trips to China and Japan. It shows her excitement at what was being achieved in China, where, during her visit she had had audience with Chairman Mao and Madame Soong Ching-Ling. There are also on the same page, condolences and statements of recognition from Cuba and Belgium, a cable from China – The China Peace Committee and the National Women's Federation, Japan and a large photograph of Claudia with other guests identified as at the Peking Airport. This poem is also titled "Thoughts on Visiting Yenan."

Notes to Afterword by Alrick X. Cambridge

1   In this paper the cognate terms 'politics', 'political activity', 'political practice' and 'politic thinking' are all used throughout as embodying communist beliefs, values and principles.
2   Whenever we speak of the Leninist 'understanding' and of the national question as the chief 'influence' on Jones' political activity the usage of the quoted terms are always to be taken as affecting the functioning of her imagination.
3   At various places the terms 'national and colonial question' or 'national and colonial problem' is shortened to 'national question'.
4   But see some of my prior work on this in Alrick Cambridge and Stephan Feuchtwang, eds. (1990) *Antiracist Strategies*. Aldershot, England: Avebury Press; Alrick Cambridge and Stephan Feuchtwang eds. (1992), *Where You Belong – Government and Black Culture*. Aldershot, England: Avebury Press.
5   Note that in this Afterword racism is constitutive of both anti-Semitism and anti-Black racism.

Index

Marshall Plan, 85, 91–92, 109
Marshall, Thurgood, 148
Martinez, Bill, 79
MCC – Marylebone Cricket Club,
  179
McCabem, Louis, 149
McCarthy, Joseph, 4, 16, 124,
  130–134, 136, 138, 148–149,
  152–153
McCleod Bethune, Mary, 130
McGee, William, 111, 129
McGowan, Rev. Edward. D, 134
Marxism-Leninism, 5,7, 9,18, 62, 65,
  68, 72–74, 85–88, 99–101,
  118–119, 120, 122, 133, 148, 162
Mason, Dolly, 150
Mason-Dixon line, 48
Miller, Dorie, 52, 54, 57
Mindszenty, Cardinal, 75
Mississippi, 63
Mongolia, 13
Morehouse College, 127, 140
Moore, Harriet, 129
Moore, Harry. T, 129, 144
Montserrat, 160
Morgan, Captn, 180
Moss, Annie. Lee,
Murphy, Al, 145
Myrdal, Gunnar, 132

N
Nabried, Thomas, 145
Nation of Islam, 24
National Association for the
  Advancement of Coloured People
  (NAACP), 14, 24, 33, 43, 105, 129,
  131–132, 144, 148,
    Resolution on McCarthyism, 131
National Association of Coloured
  Women, 84
National Association of Negro
  Women, 97

National Baptist Convention, 134,
National Bread and Butter
  Conference on Child Care, 93
National Baptist Voice, 138, 144
National Council of Negro Youth,
  14,
National Council of Negro Women,
  15, 71, 82, 112
National Convention (of CPUSA),
  61, 72, 106, 120,
National Committee of Communist
  Party (CP), 14–15
National Committee to Free the
  Ingram Family, 84
National Committee to Defend
  Negro Leadership, 131, 134, 151
National Emergency Decree, 104
National Federation of Negro Youth,
  51
National Fraternal Council of
  Churches, 134
National Grand Directoress of the
  Civil Liberties Committee of Elks,
  84
National Labour Conference for
  Peace, 108
National Maritime Union, 55
National Negro Congress, 14, 25, 40,
  42–43, 45–46, 48
National Negro Commission of
  CPUSA, 14, 61
National Peace Commission of
  Communist Party, 15
National Women's Convention, 147
National Women's Commission of
  CPUSA (Women's Commission),
  71–73, 88, 100, 102, 106–107,
  118
National Women's Party, 97
National Women's Rights
  Convention, 147
National Youth Administration

161, 167–168, 180
West Indian Independence Party (of Trinidad), 162
West Indian Federal Labour Party, 165
West Indies Commission, 157
West Indian Gazette & Afro-Asian Caribbean News, 4, 154–156, 166–167, 172, 179, 216–217
West Indian immigration, 4, 11, 17, 142, 154, 156, 165, 167–169, 171–172, 174–178, 181, 216
West Indian Regiment, 159
Western Front, 58–60
White, Walter, 43, 49, 132, 143
White, Trumbull, 35
Whitney, Anita, 87, 98, 119
Wiggins, Forrest. O, 130
Wilkins, Roy, 43, 49
Wilkerson, Doxey. A, 130–131, 133
Winston, Henry, 43, 125, 129, 131, 134, 136, 145, 148,
Winter, Carl, 125,
Williamson, John, 125
Williams, Eric, 155, 161
Williams, John, 38, 42
Wilkins, Roy, 43
Wilson, Pres. Woodrow, 27, 34
Woodson, Carter. G, 36
Woodward, Isaac, 129
Women's Bureau of US Department of Labour, 76, 94, 97
Women's Commission of the CPUSA, 71–73, 102, 107, 118
Women's Committee for Peace, 91
Women's International Democratic Federation (WIDF), 85, 91, 93, 109–110
Women's International League for Peace & Freedom, 90
Women in West Indies, 18–19
Women's Trade Union League, 97
World Peace Congress, 110
World War I, 25–26, 34, 37, 60, 153
World War II, 63, 104, 116
World Youth Congress, 44
Workers (white & black), 7–9, 16–17, 23, 28, 30–31, 37, 52, 55, 62, 64, 66–68, 73, 75–81, 83–87, 89, 93–98, 104–107, 109, 113–114, 124, 127, 130, 133, 135, 141,149, 159, 160, 163–164, 168–169, 171–179, 208, 211, 212, 214
Works Projects Administration (WPA), 14, 30, 42, 45
Women's House of Detention, 9
The Worker, 73, 118
Wright, Bishop. R. R. Jr, 130

Y
Yenan, 185, 202–203
Young, Charles. E, 36
Young, Coleman, 130
Young Communist League (YCL), 3, 9, 14–15, 23–24, 39–40, 50, 58
Youth Institute, 43–44,
Younglove, 7

Z
Zetkin, Clara, 98